Praise for *I Hear Her Words: An Introduction to Women in Buddhism*

I Hear Her Words: An Introduction to Women in Buddhism by Alice Collett is a thorough, comprehensive and well researched guide to the history and agency of women in Buddhism. We travel widely through time and space, discovering awakened and well-practised women of old to the present day. Collett brings to our attention inspiring quotes demonstrating the depth of insight that could have been missed were it not for their presence in this volume. – **Martine Batchelor** is the author of *Women on the Buddhist Path* and *Women in Korean Zen*.

In this wide-ranging and innovative introduction to women in Buddhism Alice Collett draws on sources from across the Buddhist world to interrogate the idea that Buddhism views women as inferior to men. Her argument is informed by her own considerable scholarship and introduces the general reader to the lives, works and teachings of an impressive range of, often lesser known, Buddhist women from East Asia, India and Tibet, and the West.

In the first part of the book Alice Collett challenges received ideas about the way women are portrayed in Buddhist texts, and by relating ideas about women to essential Buddhist doctrine develops a convincing argument that it is not Buddhism that sees women as inferior but individual (male) Buddhists.

In the second part the reader is introduced to the lives and achievements of a number of inspiring women who have, throughout history, played a crucial role in keeping Buddhism alive and relevant. Even readers familiar with the subject will encounter new evidence of the radical nature of women's spirituality within Buddhism and will welcome being introduced to so many diverse voices.

The author's blending of scholarly analysis and stories of women's lives makes this book a valuable addition to the growing body of work about women in Buddhism. – **Danasamudra**, co-founder of the Triratna Women Project and Librarian of the Sangharakshita Library.

D1086893

Alice Collett's book is a fascinating and engaging survey of recent research into women and Buddhism. Focusing on positive narratives of nuns and laywomen, this compelling work will be an inspiration to all. Citing a wealth of primary sources, including biographies, poems and inscriptions, the author highlights the pivotal roles that women have played both throughout Buddhist history and today, not least as highly respected teachers. This book gives these key figures a long-overdue voice and finally tells the '*her*-story' that they all deserve! – **Ann Heirman**, Professor of Chinese Language and Culture at Ghent University, author of *Rules for Nuns according to the* Dharmaguptakavinaya.

Written in a clear and accessible style, this book offers an excellent introduction into how women have shaped Buddhism from its beginning in India and over the course of its historical development throughout the Buddhist world. Drawing on her impressive long-term research on ancient Buddhist texts and a wide range of recent scholarship, Alice Collett's book inspires its readers to engage more deeply with this fascinating and important topic. By carefully listening to the often unheard voices of women who have enriched Buddhism through their spiritual practice and teachings, Collett provides new and refreshing perspectives on how Buddhists have implemented the Buddha's teachings to de-essentialise gender. – **Martin Seeger**, Professor of Thai Studies at the University of Leeds, author of *Gender and the Path to Awakening.*

A sweeping survey of Buddhist women in Asia from historical times to the present, showing their personal and societal struggles, their many contributions, and their unique wisdom. Impressive in its scope, this book serves our next generations with corrective insights and ushers in an era of greater gender equality in keeping with the Buddha's original vision. – **Judith Simmer-Brown**, Distinguished Professor of Naropa University and author of *Dakini's Warm Breath: The Feminine Principle in Tibetan Buddhism.*

I Hear Her Words

An Introduction to Women in Buddhism

Alice Collett

Ⓦ

Windhorse Publications
38 Newmarket Road,
Cambridge,
CB5 8DT
info@windhorsepublications.com
windhorsepublications.com

© Alice Collett, 2021

The right of Alice Collett to be identified as the author of this work has been
asserted by her in accordance with the Copyright, Designs and Patents Act 1988.

Cover design by Katarzyna Manecka

Typesetting and layout Tarajyoti
Printed by Bell & Bain Ltd, Glasgow

British Library Cataloguing in Publication Data:
A catalogue record for this book is available from the British Library.

ISBN: 978-1-911407-71-3

Hira Bansode's poem in *Poisoned Bread: Marathi Dalit Literature*, edited by Arjun
Dangle, Jayant Karve and Philip Engblom. Reproduced with permission of Orient
Blackswan Pvt Ltd. © Orient Blackswan Pvt Ltd 2009.

Thavory Huot, 'A Golden Ship', in *Sakyadhita Newsletter,* Winter: 17. Copyright ©
2017 by *Sakyadhita Newsletter*. Reprinted by permission of *Sakyadhita Newsletter*.

Robert A.F. Thurman, (tr.), *The Holy Teaching of Vimalakīrti: A
Mahāyāna Scripture*. Copyright © 1976 by Penn State University
Press. Reprinted by permission of Penn State University Press.

I heard her words, instruction by the one who gave me birth,
and I felt a profound urgency to reach the state of freedom.

Making an effort, intent, not relaxing day and night,
Urged on by my mother, I reached the highest peace.

Therīgāthā verses 211 and 212 (spoken by Vaḍḍha)[1]

CONTENTS

ABOUT THE AUTHOR

Alice Collett is an academic who specializes in women in Indian Buddhism. Her books include the edited volume *Women in Early Indian Buddhism: Comparative Textual Studies* (2013) and the monograph *Lives of Early Buddhist Nuns: Biographies as History* (2016). She is currently working on her fifth book, entitled *Women in Early Historic India: The Changing Political Landscape*. She has worked at several universities around the world – in North America, Europe, and Asia, and is currently Director of the South Asia History Project, United Kingdom.

ACKNOWLEDGEMENTS

This book would not have been possible without the kind and generous help of many people, to whom I am indebted. The first acknowledgement must go to Dhivan Thomas Jones, who had the initial idea that a book such as this might be of use. He and the team at Windhorse Publications approached me about it a few years before I said yes. Windhorse Publications is a branch of the Triratna Buddhist Community. In the nineties and noughties I was involved in this movement, but I left because there were a few things I was not happy with. For around fourteen years, I had no contact with the Order or movement, although I had not formally resigned. In 2019, I heard that things had changed, so I wondered if I might want to be involved again. I attended a few events for a few months, but ultimately decided against rejoining. It was during this brief period of being involved again, however, that I realized Dhivan was right, and a book such as this one would be of value.

The book is a broad introduction to the topic of women in Buddhism, and as such I have gone outside of my own field of expertise to create certain chapters. I have been fortunate enough to have received help from many quarters, from scholars helping me with inscriptions in languages I do not know, sending me photographs from their own research fieldwork, or agreeing to read and comment on draft chapters. Without their kind help this book would not be what it is today. I am indebted to Claudine Bautze-Picron, Marcus Bingenheimer, Cathy Cantwell, Matt Coward-Gibbs, Danasamudra, Elizabeth Harris, Christopher V. Jones, Hiroko Kawanami, Ye Myat Lwin, Lori Meeks, Elizabeth Moore, Martin Seeger, Sarah Shaw, and Ashley Thompson. All remaining errors are my own.

I would also like to thank the former Director at Windhorse, Priyananda, for his initial enthusiasm, and the current Director, Dhammamegha. Dhammamegha has been an encouraging and attentive editor. The book has benefited from her insightful comments. I would also like to thank all the team at Windhorse for their editing and other services.

PUBLISHER'S ACKNOWLEDGEMENTS

Windhorse Publications wishes to gratefully acknowledge a grant from the Future Dharma Fund and the Triratna European Chairs' Assembly Fund towards the production of this book.

We also wish to acknowledge and thank the individual donors who gave to the book's production via our 'Sponsor-a-book' campaign.

INTRODUCTION

I am not rejecting the world, but because of feeling a lonely sense of *mujō* [impermanence] I am rather seeking a way for my heart to take after pure water, which flows day and night.

Chiyo-ni, Japanese haiku master, on the day of her ordination[1]

Chiyo-ni was a renowned poet of her day, equal to Bashō, the best known of all Japanese masters of haiku poetry. Chiyo-ni does not garner the international fame accorded Bashō, because other male haiku masters of seventeenth- and eighteenth-century Japan failed to acknowledge her talent. In the modern era she was rediscovered and is now, again, a well-known figure in Japan, with a statue of her and a museum in her honour near her home town in north Japan. Chiyo-ni's potted history is a suitable preface for this book. Although she was a woman of accomplished talents, her life and works went unrecognized for centuries, due to bias and prejudice.[2]

As nuns and laywomen, women have been part of the Buddhist tradition since it began, in India, some 2,500 years ago. The place of women within the tradition is a subject that has occupied the minds of both practitioners and scholars of Buddhism for centuries. In this book, I provide an overview on the subject of women in Buddhism. Such questions as: Is there equality between the genders in Buddhist traditions? Do Buddhist texts say negative things about women? Do Buddhist ethics support prejudice against women? Are there any Buddhist doctrines that state, suggest, or imply that women are inferior to men? are addressed in the chapters of the book. Over the past twenty years, numerous books, book chapters, and articles have been written on the topic of women and Buddhism, and this current book is a survey of that research.

The book is aimed at anyone interested in the topic of women in Buddhism. It is intended for those seeking a compact account of the rich, often complex, and long neglected story of women's contribution to Buddhist tradition. Women have inputted to both the heritage of teachings and practices and the transformation of the Buddhist tradition up to the present day. Referencing and detailed scholarly information is kept to a minimum. For readers who wish to investigate further, there are references and endnotes that provide details on other sources to consult.

In the book, I argue one simple thing, that there is no justification to support the notion that women are inferior to men within Buddhist doctrine and ethical formulations. As Buddhism was born and developed within ancient and medieval societies that entertained traditional views of women, we do find, however, that social and cultural mores and norms that class women as inferior did find their way into Buddhist tradition and some Buddhist texts. Certain of these views then became ingrained as key elements of the tradition, such that members of Buddhist communities have, throughout history, attempted to subjugate women. The history of women within the tradition shows us that, often, the negativity did not prevail, instead many women did, frequently via the calmest and most compassionate means you could imagine; that is, simply by being themselves. In the pages of this book, you will meet with Buddhist women who were devoted disciples, became innovative leaders, instigated new teachings and traditions, were instrumental in bringing Buddhism to new shores, built monasteries and nunneries, created communities of nuns and were lauded as esteemed teachers. Like the life and works of Chiyo-ni, much of this history has remained hidden from view for centuries.

A New Historical Narrative

Buddhism begins with the life of the historical Buddha, who lived during the sixth or fifth centuries BCE.[3] Various accounts of the Buddha's life exist, but the basic story is that, as a young man, he had a realization about the true nature of the world and renounced his family life and social responsibilities in a quest for religious liberation. Most of the legendary accounts of his life (although not all) recount that he was royalty, and that one symbolic aspect of his renunciation involved leaving his wife, Yasodharā, and their newborn son.

Within his life story and the narratives that recount how Buddhism began, three women are important. They are Yasodharā, his mother Māyā, and his stepmother and aunt, Mahāpajāpatī Gotamī. According to the legendary accounts, when pregnant with the future Buddha, his mother, Māyā, had a dream of a white elephant, which symbolized that the being she would give birth to would be a great man. His mother died in childbirth, and he was raised by his stepmother and aunt. Mahāpajāpatī Gotamī becomes central in the most popular narrative concerning the beginning of the Order of nuns as she, along with her followers, is the woman who first makes a request from the Buddha to become a nun.

Whether in the legendary life story of the Buddha, or in popular recounted narratives about Buddhism, the portrayal of both Mahāpajāpatī Gotamī and Yasodharā is often largely unfavourable, or at least has significant negative undertones. The best-known detail about Yasodharā is that the Buddha-to-be left her when he renounced his worldly life in pursuit of religious truth. And he left her with a newborn infant. What is much less frequently commented upon, less widely circulated, is accounts of Yasodharā that portray her in a more positive light. Some of these are from Buddhist canons. As with other religions, Buddhism includes with its textual corpus both works that are considered canonical and other texts, commentaries, and subsidiary literature. One Pāli canonical narrative, written as an autobiography but composed centuries after the time of the Buddha, could even be said to have a 'feminist edge'.[4] In these verses Yasodharā describes how the Buddha, essentially, could not have achieved Awakening with her. In verse after verse, she describes the extent to which she put aside her own needs to provide what was required:

> I performed a lot of service,
> for the sake of you, O Great Sage;
> while you sought the Buddha's Teaching,
> I was [always] your attendant.[5]

She is also predicted to attain nirvana, as a result of helping the Buddha to attain his. This is foretold by a former Buddha who relates part of the narrative:

> She will be a like-minded [wife],
> with karma and conduct like [yours];
> through this karma she'll be loving
> for the sake of you, O Great Sage
>
> . . .
>
> Just as masters are protecting
> the goods that [they] accumulate,

so this one likewise will protect
[all] of the things that are wholesome.

Compassionate for [future] you,
she will fulfill the perfections.
Like a lion [freed] from a cage,
she will achieve Awakening.

. . .

The woman who's giving herself
for the merit of the Great Sage
attains companionship [with him],
[and] unconditioned nirvana.[6]

In lifetime after lifetime, as the dutiful and mindful wife, Yasodharā
protected the sphere of the Buddha-to-be, and enabled him to do what
he needed to in order to become who he became.

Similarly, with regard to the Buddha's stepmother and aunt,
Mahāpajāpatī Gotamī, the most popular narrative about her is one
within which the Buddha is portrayed as reluctant to begin an Order
for women and where special rules are put in place that nuns must
follow (more on these below). Much less often circulated, discussed,
and read are texts that portray Mahāpajāpatī Gotamī as the counterpart
to the Buddha; the founder and leader of the nuns' Order.[7]

In a canonical narrative about the life and death of Mahāpajāpatī
Gotamī, events that occur are reminiscent of those that are told as part
of the legend of the life and death of the Buddha. The account focuses
on Mahāpajāpatī Gotamī's wish to attain ultimate nirvana, to die, in
a death that mirrors that of the Buddha. When the nuns who were
her disciples realized that this was her wish, they decided that they
too wanted to go with her. So, at her death, five hundred other nuns
also attained nirvana. Her death was, indeed, an auspicious event:

Rising up, she reached nirvana,
like the flame of a fuel-less lamp.
There was an enormous earthquake;
bolts of lightning fell from the sky.

The thunder was rumbling loudly;
the deities [gathered there] wailed.
A flower-shower from the sky
was raining down upon the earth.

Even regal Mount Meru shook,
just like a dancer on the stage;
the [great] ocean was greatly grieved,
and he was weeping in distress.

The gods, snake-gods and titans too,
even Brahmā, awed at that time,
[said,] 'this one has now been dissolved;
in flux indeed is all that is.'

The [other nuns] surrounding her,
who practiced the Buddha's teachings,
they too attained nirvana [then,]
like the flames of lamps without fuel.

Then the Teacher told Ānanda
whose knowledge was [deep as] the sea,
'Go [now,] Ānanda, tell the monks,
[my] mother has reached nirvana.'[8]

It is typical that these two women – so significant in the legend of the historical Buddha – tend to be remembered more in a negative than a positive light. Within Buddhist texts, unconstructive views have long been expressed about women and their abilities. In Buddhist traditions, both formal and informal structures have been put in place within which women are relegated to an inferior status. But this is only half the story, only half the history. The other half – the more positive – is found within the lives of Buddhist women throughout history (and today). These women have overcome obstacles to gain ordination as Buddhist nuns, even in countries in which ordination for women had died out or never been introduced. They have battled family and social pressures to become esteemed teachers of others, often of both men and women. They have endured economic hardships to spread Buddhism across the globe. Many have become inspirational leaders pointing out the way to those in need. This book is about these women, it tells the other half of the story. In this book I draw on a wealth of recent scholarly material that provides us with insights into the lives of many women in Buddhist history the world over. Negative portrayals of women in Buddhism continue to be published, in spite of this accumulating research. It is now possible, however, to chronicle afresh, mapping Buddhist history and current practice with a new narrative.

As mentioned, Yasodharā and Mahāpajāpatī Gotamī both became nuns. While prominent, they are far from the only two women we know of from early Indian Buddhism. Numerous female disciples of the Buddha feature in the collections of early Buddhist texts. There are accounts of women who became famed teachers, like the nun Khemā, who taught a king. There is a book of poems of elder nuns, that might well be the words of some of these early disciples, as well as innumerable biographical accounts, in which women are held high as exemplars of tradition. There are even lists of pre-eminent women who model accomplished qualities, one of which runs to fifty-one names in its Chinese version.

Alongside the early texts, there are inscriptions made by women, often donor inscriptions at monument sites, many of whom identify themselves as Buddhist nuns. Some of these women also acknowledge their own teachers, who imparted Buddhist teachings to them, and were also often women. Certain of these women as well – counter to textual prescriptions of a gender-segregated community – align themselves within lineages of male monastic teachers.

The new Mahāyāna form of Buddhism began to emerge in India sometime between the first century BCE and the first century CE. Along with it came an abundance of new texts. These sources tell of many more exemplary women.[9] One is the laywoman Gaṅgottarā, who on meeting the Buddha puts to him one shrewd question after another, challenging central aspects of doctrine.[10] After conversing with Gaṅgottarā the text records that the Buddha smiled, which was a rare event and never done without just cause. Another Mahāyāna text is called the *Śrīmālādevīsiṃhanāda*, 'The Lion's Roar of Queen Śrīmālā'. The lion's roar is a metaphor for the Buddha giving a teaching. With the advent of Mahāyāna come bodhisattva figures, who can take female form. The best-known bodhisattvas are Avalokiteśvara and Tārā. Tārā is not the only female bodhisattva, Prajñāpāramitā is another, both have been called 'Mother of all Buddhas'. When Avalokiteśvara 'travelled' along the silk and trade routes to China, 'he' became a 'she' and manifested as the female Guanyin, a ubiquitous presence in East Asian Buddhism.

Also travelling along the silk and trade routes to China came, along with the whole edifice of tradition, the canonical accounts of female disciples of the Buddha. These were translated into Chinese along with other (particularly Mahāyāna) texts, as this was the form of Buddhism to take hold in China. Soon after the tradition was established there, a nuns' Order was begun. There were new challenges. Buddhist nuns had to take heed of rival female practitioners of other indigenous Chinese traditions, one of whom, on one occasion, poisoned their Buddhist counterpart. Inscriptions by and about women and other Chinese-authored texts, as well as, eventually, those penned by women themselves, detail and recount the lives and experiences of the many women of East Asian Buddhist traditions who gained followers, built nunneries, and taught with accomplished skill. A sixth-century record of Buddhist dwellings in the city of Luoyang says of one of the nunneries and its inhabitants:

> . . . with its many suites of spacious rooms, fitted with
> symmetrical windows and doors, red pillars and white
> walls, it was the height of elegance and beauty. The nuns
> here were among the most renowned and accomplished
> in the imperial city, skilful at preaching and discussing
> Buddhist principles.[11]

The next Buddhist tradition to emerge in India was tantra, adopting elements from its compatriot Hindu tantric tradition. The iconography of wrathful and fierce Hindu tantric goddesses was overwritten with Buddhist meaning and morphed into similarly fierce female tantric deities of Indian – later Tibetan – Buddhism. Historical women were equated with these commanding female forms, and a strength and confidence is evident in the biographies of female adherents of the

Tibetan tradition that resonates with these fierce icons. Tantra also galvanized women to write, and we have several Buddhist tantric texts composed by women dating from the tenth to the twelfth centuries.

In these same centuries, in the Theravāda countries of Southeast Asia, murals depicting early nuns were painted on the walls of temples of Pagan. Royal, affluent women were driving forward initiatives to educate young women and girls in Buddhist principles in the Angkorian Empire to the East. From Burma, inscriptions record that women were committed practitioners, eager to make donations that might accrue merit and lead to their attainment of nirvana. As the modern era dawned, women continued to practise Buddhism in different corners of the globe – South, Central, Southeast, and East Asia. They established new forms of Buddhist practice and teachings, composed poetry, built monasteries and temples, taught adults and children, initiated new formal institutional structures, created Buddhist Women's Associations, and took Buddhism to new countries.

Eventually, in the 1800s, Buddhism began to find its way to Western shores, and with this we have a surfeit of evidence of numerous women who played a significant role in making this possible. Female practitioners were involved in establishing women's hubs in migrant communities invited to work in the West. Female scholars began to translate Sanskrit and Pāli texts arriving from Asia. Western women travelled in Asia and authored sympathetic travelogues that influenced some of the best-known names in Western Buddhism. Others travelled to Asia more permanently to be ordained and live as nuns, becoming some of the first full Western converts to Buddhism. Today, there are many female practitioners in all Buddhist traditions practised in the West, and many prominent female Buddhist teachers. These include Pema Chödrön, a Western convert to Tibetan Buddhism, Zen teacher Jiyu Kennett Rōshi, an Englishwoman, and the German-born Theravāda nun Ayya Khema.

* * *

Whilst it is possible, as I have done above, to craft an historical outline of Buddhism that foregrounds the many women who have played a part, this is not usually how the history of women in Buddhist tradition is told. More often, the critical accounts of their role and presence are highlighted at the expense of the rest. The adverse part of the history has been much more in focus – both within Buddhist traditions themselves and in Buddhist studies scholarship – than the progressive. As a result, the lives and endeavours of the many women who have contributed to shaping the history and modern manifestations of Buddhism have been hidden from view.

A variety of beliefs and formal and informal institutional structures became part of Buddhist tradition as it became established. Many of these have been responsible for the poor treatment of women within each country in which it has existed. Focusing on what is negative in the texts and traditions of Buddhism in relation to women, four primary themes can be identified. These are

1. the belief that women are inferior to men,
2. that it is bad karma to be born a woman and that women need to be reborn as men in the next life to make progress on the path,
3. that women cannot be Buddhas, and
4. issues around the ordination of women.

Four Recurring Themes in Buddhist Texts and Tradition

The Inferiority of Women

Throughout the history of Buddhism many Buddhists – both men and women – have embraced the view that women are inferior to men, and should be treated as such. There appears to be textual support for such a view in, for instance, the example of a set of rules known as the eight special rules. The narrative that accompanies explanation of these rules describes how Mahāpajāpatī Gotamī decided she wanted to become a committed follower of the Buddha, and requested that he begin an Order of nuns. He eventually agreed, but on the proviso that all women ordained as nuns must adhere to eight rules. These rules have become part of sacrosanct Buddhist canons. They have been and continue to be used within Buddhist traditions both formally, in that they are followed to the letter, and socially, in that they ingrain a view that nuns should be considered inferior to monks, and women to men. Serious problems have, however, been identified with the formulation of these rules. The eight rules appear in the canons of different traditions, although not always in the same place and not always in the same order. In the Pāli *Vinaya* order, they are:

1. A nun who received higher ordination even a hundred years ago must bow to any monk who has received higher ordination even if it was that very day.
2. During the rainy season, a nun must not reside in a place where there are no monks.
3. Every fortnight, a nun must ask two things from the monks: the date of the observance day [an important ceremony] and when the nuns will receive instruction.
4. After the rainy season, a nun must invite feedback from both monks and nuns.
5. A nun who breaches a rule must be disciplined by both monks and nuns.
6. After having trained as a probationer for two years, a female novice should seek higher ordination from both monks and nuns.
7. A monk should not be abused or reviled in any way by a nun.
8. Nuns are not permitted to criticize monks. Monks are permitted to criticize nuns.[12]

These rules, especially the first one, appear to categorially formulate a hierarchy in which nuns are subordinate to monks. And this is how the rules have been interpreted and how they have been utilized: as a means to establish that nuns are inferior to monks.

One thing that the rules do demonstrate is the problem with overreliance on texts, both as a source for history and as a primer for tradition. Texts can be edited, they can be redacted, passages added, and sections removed. Such interventions took place in the history of the eight rules. In an important article published in 1999,

In Young Chung demonstrates that these eight rules could not have been formulated during the time of the Buddha.[13] One reason she gives is that two of the rules acknowledge the novice or probationary period – a period prior to full ordination (for both would-be monks and nuns). This was not part of the ordination process at the time of the Buddha. The arguments that In Young Chung makes in her article have now been widely accepted, at least amongst the scholarly community.

When Buddhism was revived in modern Taiwan, ordination became a popular choice for women. Eventually, nuns outnumbered monks. As this developed into a permanent ratio, it became an unwritten assumption that the eight special rules would not be adhered to. Given the respect nuns now garner in modern Taiwan, it seems inappropriate to request that a nun should bow to a monk.[14] In this modern period, numerous nuns have built and led their own monasteries, holding financial and management power over nuns and monks. Many of these are highly educated women, actively involved in teaching, education, charity, and cultural affairs.[15]

The silent, unwritten acceptance not to follow the eight rules continued for some time. This changed, however, during a series of events in the 1990s and 2000s that centred around one nun – *bhikkhunī* Zhaohui – who publicly denounced the eight special rules. At a conference in 2001, leading a group of monks, nuns, laymen, and laywomen, she publicly initiated the tearing up of posters that had the eight special rules written on them. This created a media storm in Taiwan, and prompted a renewed debate on the relevance of the rules, with a variety of views being expressed.[16]

Karma and Rebirth as a Woman

Even amongst those with a basic knowledge of Buddhism, it is widely known that Buddhism espouses a doctrine of karma. It is often misunderstood as an 'eye for an eye' dogma; that if a person acts badly, they will be met with equivalent retribution for their actions. This is a superficial understanding of karma. The word karma means 'action' and the karma doctrine means that actions have consequences;

good actions have good consequences and bad have bad. The doctrine is linked to morality, such that actions and intentions that are ethically positive will have a positive outcome and vice versa.

In a recent book, James Egge explored the karma doctrine in Buddhism and traces the development of it.[17] He has established that there were phases in its development in early Buddhist tradition. The idea evolved over time. One aspect of what comes to be the principal exhortations of the doctrine is that it is bad karma to be born a woman. This is not stated in any Buddhist canonical works, but comes to be expressed in commentaries and other subsidiary literature, as well as in inscriptions. It was, there appears, a 'shift in attitude' between the time of canonical accounts and the later commentarial and other literature. The compliers, collators, authors, and editors of the canons did not consider rebirth as a woman problematic. Instead, there are instances in Buddhist canonical texts in which female rebirth is presented in a positive light.[18]

Doctrinally, as well, the idea that female rebirth is bad karma is questionable. If it is always bad karma to be reborn as a woman, this presupposes that life as a woman is always and invariably worse than life as a man. So, for instance, high-status Indian queens of antiquity, who lived lives of relative luxury, were waited upon hand and foot and wielded significant power, in this context have to be understood as having lives that entailed greater misery than the life of a beggar with leprosy.[19] Whilst arguably, and in general terms, women do live and have historically led lives that entailed greater suffering than men, karma is a natural law and does not operate on the basis of generalizations.

Despite it being the case that to say birth as a woman is bad karma does not accord with the doctrine, and is not stated in Buddhist canonical sources, this also became a mainstay of tradition. Like the eight special rules, it has not, however, remained unchallenged. In 2001–2, Wei-Yi Cheng conducted fieldwork interviewing and surveying opinions of Sri Lankan and Taiwanese nuns. Asking a question about karma, she found 'more respondents who do not accept the idea of women's inferior karma than those who do'.[20] Cheng reports that many viewed the idea as an oversimplification of Buddhist doctrine, although a variety of opinions were expressed. One Taiwanese nun made the comment that:

> . . . the sex ratio in the world is approximately half male and half female. If [sexes are determined] by the inferiority and superiority of karma, how is it possible to be half and half of the population?[21]

Women Becoming Buddhas

Buddhism began with the life of the historical Buddha, who was male. Initially, in the earliest schools of thought in Buddhism, it was believed that practitioners could not themselves become Buddhas, although they could attain what the Buddha had attained – the experience of Awakening or state of nirvana. The early schools of thought, however, do not hold that the historical Buddha was the sole Buddha, but that others had existed before him, and would arise afterwards. They maintain that none of these were nor could be women.

One text of the Pāli canon categorically states that it is not possible for women to become Buddhas, nor take on any other similar leadership roles:

> It is impossible, it cannot happen that a woman could become an Accomplished One, a Fully Enlightened One – there is no possibility. . . It is possible that a man might be an Accomplished One, a Fully Enlightened One – there is such a possibility.[22]

Writing on this topic, Bhikkhu Anālayo notes that this section is missing in the Chinese version of this discourse. The most likely reason for this, he concludes, is that 'the theme of women's inability is a later addition to the exposition'.[23] The understanding of the possible goals for the practitioner changed with the advent of Mahāyāna Buddhism. The belief developed that a practitioner may eventually become a Buddha. Here again, certain texts state that women cannot become Buddhas. For example, the *Bodhisattvabhūmi* states:

Completely perfected Buddha-s are not women. And why? Precisely because a bodhisattva, from the time he has passed beyond the first incalculable age (of his career) had completely abandoned the women's estate. Ascending (thereafter) to the most excellent throne of enlightenment, he is never again reborn as a woman.[24]

As you can see from this passage, there is often no answer as to *why* this might be the case. Here the argument is circuitous; women are not Buddhas because Buddhas are not women. It appears that this proposition was never fully accepted, as there exist other texts that do predict certain women will attain Buddhahood. There are also others that record that the historical Buddha was female in past lives and others that portray women with qualities similar to a Buddha, such as we have seen with Mahāpajāpatī Gotamī.[25] The Tibetan tantric tradition fully acknowledges that there can be female Buddhas. In her survey of opinions of modern Sri Lankan and Taiwanese nuns, Wei-Yi Cheng asked the question, 'Do you agree that one can become a Buddha in a woman's body?' Of the 492 Taiwanese nuns she questioned, 74.4% answered yes. Only 9.7% disagreed.[26]

The Ordination of Women

As we have seen with the narrative accounts of Mahāpajāpatī Gotamī and Yasodharā, and the issue of the eight special rules, along with the establishment of the Buddhist religion in ancient India an Order of nuns came into being. Although the narrative about the eight rules implies that nuns were not on an equal footing to monks (an implication that is challenged in chapter 1), other parts of Buddhist canonical literature indicate that the community of monks and nuns were equal. For instance, in one passage from the Pāli canon, the Buddha recounts how he wants his community to be when he dies or attains final nirvana. In a passage that is repeated four times, once with monks as the subjects, then nuns, then laymen, and finally laywomen, he is reported to say:

> I will not attain final Nibbāna . . . until I have nun disciples
> who are wise, disciplined, confident, secure from bondage,
> learned, upholders of the Dhamma, practising in accord
> with the Dhamma, practising the proper way, conducting
> themselves accordingly; who have learned their own
> teacher's doctrine and can explain it, teach it, proclaim
> it, establish it, disclose it, analyse it and elucidate it; who
> can refute thoroughly with reasons the prevalent tenets of
> others and can teach the efficacious Dhamma.[27]

Although the Buddha instigated a following with a fourfold community of monks, nuns, laymen, and laywomen, the Order of nuns has not continued to be operational in all Buddhist countries, and in some is believed to have never been established when Buddhism first arrived there. In such countries, namely those of South and Southeast Asia and Tibet, women could not take full ordination as nuns. Instead, other possible routes to a renunciate lifestyle were developed. In these cases, women will often don the garb of nuns, wear robes, and shave their heads. Rather than following the monastic code that a nun commits to doing at ordination they will instead commit to following a set of ethical precepts, either eight or ten.

Although there was no formal Order of nuns in some countries in which Buddhism was the major or state-sponsored religion, investigations over the past two decades have unearthed evidence of women practising that seems to indicate women being ordained as nuns or living as nuns. This history is explored within the pages of this book.

Initiatives to re-establish the Order of nuns in Buddhist countries within the last century have come to fruition in the last few decades. As we will see, a nuns' Order has been re-established in some of these countries. The absence of the option of full ordination for women, which has often resulted in women who choose renunciate lifestyles being seen as inferior to monks, has created some odd cases. In Thailand, women who are accomplished scholars teach monks but nonetheless consider themselves lower status than those they teach. One such example is Mae Chi Bunchuai Sriprem, a Pāli scholar who has received an esteemed title and is a well-respected teacher at the elite Mahamukut Monastic University in Bangkok. When questioned about the fact that she was a teacher to monks, she replied, 'well, sure, I teach monks, but they are not "my students", they are above me.'[28] Despite this view, Mae Chi Bunchuai did consider herself something of an expert in the Pāli language.

* * *

This book presents an overview of women in Buddhist traditions from the lifetime of Siddhattha Gotama, the historical Buddha, up to the present, and across the globe. To my knowledge, it is the first such introductory survey of the subject. I have charted most of the main countries and regions within which Buddhism has been adopted. While researching and writing, I was presented with an overwhelming amount of data on women from Buddhist history, past and present. It has not been possible for me to include and acknowledge all women in Buddhism's past, nor all women still living today. Many have made significant contributions to the spread of Buddhism. They have left in their wake popular teachings, having overcome obstacles in order to practise. They have received ordination and become nuns, even when it was forbidden for them to do so, or when they were faced with prison time, or admonished, criticized, reviled, even abused. Women have, in each tradition, each county, each region, made a space for themselves.

I begin the book with assessments of Buddhist ethical formulations, Buddhist texts and some basic doctrine. These comprise Part I of the book. In Part II, I turn more fully to the lives of Buddhist women. In chapter 1 I pose the question: Does Buddhism support gender equality? I look at this both from the point of view of Buddhist ethics and with recourse to feminist input and feminism's often uncomfortable relationship with Buddhism and Buddhists. In chapter 2 I focus on Buddhist texts. I highlight the range of attitudes to women expressed in the texts, including the worst comments made about women. Any alleged faults of women articulated in chapter 2 I assess in relation to Buddhist doctrine in Chapter 3. In chapter 4, the first chapter of Part II, I offer some portraits of Buddhist women. I begin with some of the better-known Indian nuns who are considered to have been direct disciples of the Buddha. Also included in this chapter are portraits of Chinese, Japanese, and Thai Buddhist women, who lived at various points in the history of Buddhism. Chapter 5 is concerned with the history of women in South and Southeast Asian countries. In this chapter I concentrate on Sri Lanka, Burma, Cambodia, and Thailand. Next, in chapter 6, the history of women in Central and East Asian traditions is related; primarily China, Korea, Taiwan, and Tibet. Finally, in chapter 7, I turn to Buddhism in the West, and survey and discuss the various women who were instrumental in Buddhism's journey to the West, as well as others who have worked to establish Buddhism in various Western countries.

When I began this project I intended to bring together, in an accessible way, the main themes in the flourishing scholarship on women in Buddhism through the past two decades. My first working title was *Women in Buddhism: The Basics*. The publishers, however, insisted on a less prosaic title. They asked me if it was possible to include in the title an extract from a Buddhist text. I flicked through the *Therīgāthā*, and happened upon the verses from which the title comes, spoken by the monk Vaḍḍha about his mother. When the title of the book became *I Hear Her Words: An Introduction to Women in Buddhism*, a bit of magic happened. The project began to form itself into a book focused on the lives, works, and teachings of Buddhist women, more so than I had anticipated when I began. It is, then, something that feminists might term a '*her*-story' (rather than *his*-story), which, as I say, was not my intention, but in order to do justice to the inordinate amount of women who have contributed to Buddhism over the centuries, I didn't feel like I had much of a choice! And, in this short book, I certainly have not done full justice to this history of women in Buddhism. I remain aware that, as I write this introduction after finishing the rest, there are not only individual women but lives, stories, and practitioners in certain countries that do not get a mention, such as, for instance, Buddhist women in Mongolia and Nepal. Many women who have devoted their lives to spreading Buddhism – past and present – receive but a brief mention, if any mention at all.

What I hope to illustrate in this volume is that women have – both literally and metaphorically – ripped up the rule book. They have challenged the eight rules, demanded to be fully ordained alongside men, proved that they are not inferior by becoming teachers of both women and men and leaders who have inspired others, and they have engaged in the pragmatic and theoretical work of establishing Buddhism in various countries. Buddhist traditions have been reconfigured to include female Buddhas, and the bodhisattva path reimagined to revitalize the more usually low-status 'feminine' qualities of nurture and care, making these centre stage in the path to Awakening and attributes to which both men and women should aspire. And rebirth narratives have been composed in which illustrious women were men in former lives, thereby demonstrating that it is not necessary to be reborn a man to succeed on the Buddhist path. Such narratives are few and far between but every one of these should be amplified, as women's history is often hidden.[29]

Many women are part of the history of Buddhism, therefore to say 'Buddhism is negative about women' negates them on numerous levels, and as such is a form of sexism in itself. It negates their existence and their contribution. If influential women who overcame obstacles to be ordained, set up nunneries, and taught others are part of Buddhist history – which this book categorially demonstrates is the case – we cannot say Buddhism is negative about women. If we do, in so doing we are disaffirming their contribution. The contributions of these women must be woven into the acknowledged history of what Buddhism was in the past, what it is now, and what it is capable of becoming in the future. The modern manifestations of it are shaped by its past, and these women are part of Buddhism's past, as well as its present and future.

Returning to the female haiku master whose words began this chapter, Chiyo-ni composed poetry about being a woman, and the struggles involved. Chiyo-ni was an ordained Buddhist nun. If we say 'Buddhism is negative about women' we disavow her voice and her contribution – we continue the historical lack of recognition of her life and work.

what the butterfly
wants to say – only this
movement of its wings[30]

Part I

Asking Questions About Buddhism

CHAPTER 1

BUDDHISM AND GENDER EQUALITY

How easy it is to repeat the precepts, how simple they seem. . .
But how many reflect on the significance of these five abstentions:
from evil and foolish living; from those ordinary ways of life
which create suffering for ourselves and others (individuals,
nations, animals, all forms of sentient life).

In fact modern life, consciously or unconsciously, violates these
precepts continuously. It is difficult indeed to live a harmless life;
to do so it is necessary to have acquired a certain amount of *Sammā
diṭṭhi* (right views), views that are not steeped in ignorance. . .

Grace Constant Lounsbery[1]

In this chapter I ask the question: Does Buddhism support gender equality? In the first part of the chapter I look at Buddhist ethics, and in the second part I explore the relationship between Buddhism and feminism. I begin the chapter with the words of Grace Constant Lounsbery, the founder of the first Buddhist organization in France, La société des amis du Bouddhisme (The Society of Buddhist Friends). This organization was set up in 1929 and ran for several years. It started the first French journal specifically on Buddhism. Each of these achievements is quite a feat for a woman living in Europe in the early 1900s (women were not granted equal voting rights in France until 1944). Lounsbery also wrote a book on Buddhism, and contributed an article to the *Wheel Publication* of collected essays on ethics from which the opening quote for this chapter is taken.[2] As well as her Buddhist compositions, Lounsbery also authored other works including books of poetry. Certain of her poems illuminate the compassion that underlies Buddhist ethics, which she reveals herself to feel, despite her own aristocratic, privileged circumstances. In her poem, 'The Beggars', published in 1911, she writes:

> Sordid stroller of the street,
> Eyes of hunger, shuffling feet,
> What have I to do with thee
> And thy trailing misery —?
>
> Take this pittance, turn away
> Go thy aimless, angry way,
> Dull resentment in thy mind
> Smouldering against mankind.
>
> Why, within my secret room,
> Through the softly-scented gloom,
> By the fireside's glint and glow,
> Steals the vision of thy woe?[3]

The little that is known about the life of Grace Constant Lounsbery makes visible the intersection of Buddhism, Buddhist ethics, feminism, colonialism, and privilege, all issues that are examined in this chapter. Although the American-born Lounsbery lived in France, which at the time was a colonial power, she was critical of the ruling political ideologies. The book in which this poem was published is entitled *Poems of Revolt*, and includes other poems that challenge the political superstructures of the day. We can see from the poem about the beggar that she was at least aware to some extent of her privileged position, but the parameters of such awareness are less clear. In a verse in another poem from the collection, she does allude to an awareness of the pertinent issues of colonialism, race, and power:

> For the head shall not war with the hand
> Nor the woman do battle with the man
> Each for all be our cry, each for all be our call
> Without class, without caste, without clan.[4]

Grace Constant Lounsbery was not alone in her views. Other Western women who travelled to and within Asia at the time of colonialism, as wives of Christian missionaries or colonial administrators or independently, held views that were considered 'troublesome' or 'embarrassing' to the white men enforcing colonial rule.[5] Western feminism was developing at the time when the West was colonizing parts of Asia. As Buddhism is in origin a religion of Asia, colonialism led to increased interest in and engagement with Buddhism in the West. The interplay of these factors during the colonial period foreshadows what was to come.

Buddhist Ethics

Like Grace Lounsbery, we all have stories to tell about ethics and our own moral code. We can recall times when we acted especially morally, times we might remember with pride, or times at which we fell short of our own moral standards. As adults, we teach our children about morality, but also scold unnecessarily. We are compelled to help if we see an opportunity one day, but walk away the next. We bear the harm of another's ruthlessness stoically, then tread on someone else's toes ourselves. We are angry that the pain of others impacts us, and simultaneously saddened by their trouble. The idea that human beings each have a moral compass, with which we navigate life, and that we can each act with ethical integrity or choose to flout moral codes are universal concerns found both within the vestiges of societies that existed in history and in communities around the world today.

As with other religions, ethics are an important part of Buddhism. This is the case with all Buddhist traditions, as ethics are fundamental to what it means to be a Buddhist. Whilst it is the case that formulations of ethical codes and ideas about ethical agency change, ethics remain the backbone of the tradition. Ethical principles can be found detailed in the earliest Buddhist canons, reformulated in later literature, and are the foundation of Buddhist monastic codes. These ethical principles, do not, at first glance, appear to be concerned with gender equality. This impression occurs if we conceive of gender equality from a rights-based point of view, that is, that it is the right of any individual woman to be treated fairly. To the contrary, Buddhist ethics are guiding principles for the practitioner. They are articulated to encourage appropriate treatment of others and oneself. At their base, both systems are concerned with non-harm, but they use different language and are engaged in for different ends – one religious, the other social and political.

The fundamental ethic of Buddhism is ahimsa, or non-harm. Each of the other ethical precepts comes out of this primary one. In Theravāda Buddhism, there are three popular and well-used lists of ethical precepts, one of which is shared with Mahāyāna. The first precept on each list is concerned with causing injury or harm. This is because respect for life (non-harm) is the fundamental moral imperative. This first list of five precepts is to be observed by the Buddhist laity:

- abstention from injury to living beings
- abstention from taking the not given
- abstention from sexual misconduct
- abstention from false speech
- abstention from taking intoxicants which cloud the mind

The first four of these five accord with universal ethical principles concerning the sanctity of life and fundamental comprehensions of right and wrong. The last one of the five, however, is particular to Buddhism. This final precept is specifically concerned with abstention from substances that will harm the practitioner's ability to meditate, perform Buddhist observances, and gain self-mastery over the mind. The next longer list of eight includes other precepts which are concerned to deter frivolous habits that may affect one's ability to practice. These include eating too much or at the wrong time or indulging in other luxuries such as attending entertainment shows.

Another set of ethical precepts, popular in both Theravāda and Mahāyāna circles, is a list entitled the Ten Good Paths of Action. This list of ten divides into three precepts relating to bodily action, four relating to speech, and three concerned with the mind. This list has also proved popular with Western audiences, as the elements of it coincide more effortlessly with Western moral codes. The ten precepts are:

- abstention from injury to living beings
- abstention from taking the not given
- abstention from sexual misconduct
- abstention from false speech
- abstention from slanderous speech
- abstention from harsh speech
- abstention from frivolous speech
- abstention from covetousness
- abstention from hatred
- abstention from false views[6]

These three lists of common formulations of ethical precepts in Buddhism are not the only ones. Another list, found in some Mahāyāna texts, for example, includes a precept not found here but that relates to ensuing discussions in this book – not to praise oneself and disparage others.[7] There is one other simple, important point on Buddhist ethics to note before turning more to the topic of women. Buddhist ethics has been termed an 'ethics of intention', and indeed, it is the intention behind the action, rather than the action itself, that is deemed to be ethical or not. Each day we are alive, we cannot help but do harm; we may tread on an ant whilst walking, or accidentally drop a glass vase that shatters into fragments that scratch another. This harm caused is not intentional, so it is not unethical, in Buddhist terms. If, however, we set out to find a trail of ants and take pleasure in stamping on them, or we deliberately throw a vase at someone with intent to injure, these actions are unethical, because of the intention behind them.

The Principle of Non-Harm

The exact nature of what constitutes harm, and who decides, are at the heart of questions about Buddhist ethics and gender equality. The issue is not whether it is right to enact harm upon another human being or not. Rather the concerns are with what exactly is harmful and why. The primary question, therefore, when attempting to address these issues – both within Buddhist texts and Buddhist traditions and more broadly – is this: Is discrimination ever justifiable? Or does it always and invariably cause harm? That is to say, is it ever acceptable to treat one group of people differently to another because – due to some facet or characteristic – they deserve special treatment? If that is the case then the discrimination that results in the differential treatment is justifiable, and helpful rather than harmful.

The verb 'to discriminate' has a much broader application than its more usual modern uses suggest. It simply means to recognize a distinction between two things, with 'to differentiate' being a synonym. We are able to discriminate between a red circle and a blue circle because we can see they are different colours. Few, however, are likely to treat a red circle less well than a blue one (or vice versa) simply because they are different colours. This simple example is a good way to highlight how discrimination that causes harm can come about.

Few people, I imagine, would deny that there exist biological differences between men and women, so that on some occasions (however rare they may be) men and women require differential treatment. Men cannot conceive and give birth, therefore when a pregnant woman needs some help related to the fact of her pregnancy, in such an instance treatment of her will be different to treatment of any man.[8] That there is at least some limited amount of divergence is undeniable. Many proffer other potential differences between men and women, some biological and others resulting from social conditioning. This can give rise to discrimination that causes harm.

Discrimination that causes harm can manifest when *acknowledgement* of difference becomes *judgement*. Exaggeration of potential small differences can bring about harm, whether intended or not. Discrimination then, the noticing of difference, can be the tipping point, where awareness morphs into judgement and harm ensues for that judgement. This process, when awareness of difference and need for adjusted treatment turns into judgement and discrimination that causes harm, can be exemplified by the treatment of women within the history of Buddhism. This can be seen using the example of the eight special rules.

The eight rules have shaped Buddhist tradition, and acted to favour those who wish to cast women as inferior, by apparently propagating the view that women are indeed lower than men, and need to act accordingly. But this may not be why the rules came into existence. The contrary is also possible, if we examine historical context. It is quite possible the rules came into being in order to protect nuns from harm. As the rules appear to so categorically ascribe an inferior position to women vis-à-vis men, that might seem instinctively unlikely. But within the historical situation out of which the rules came, it is possible to imagine a scenario in which the rules were set in place to safeguard nuns.

In the early phase of the tradition, Buddhist nuns were an oddity on the Indian landscape. These women renounced family ties and social responsibilities, chose not to marry, shaved their heads, and wore plain robes. For women to make such choices was difficult for ancient Indian society to comprehend. Normative roles for women at the time were largely domestic; they were expected to marry and raise children. Any other sort of independence for women was generally frowned upon. Early sacred Hindu texts even prescribe that women should not, and by implication cannot, be independent.[9] An often-repeated quote from one important such text is:

Men must make their women dependant day and night, and keep under their control those who are attached to sensory objects. Her father guards her in childhood, her husband guards her in youth and her sons guard her in old age. A woman is not fit for independence.[10]

From a modern perspective, it may be difficult to comprehend how people could be puzzled by woman's motivation for religious practice. But in this ancient Indian context, the evidence indicates that this was the case. A woman alone, or acting independently, was unconventional. It was even the case that such women were viewed as sexually available. An unguarded woman was considered available for any man who might decide to act on his desire to have sex with her, regardless of whether she was willing or not. Again, early Hindu texts – that provide us with a context for the ancient Indian setting out of which Buddhism grew – advocate such acts as appropriate behaviour, acts that would be illegal and classified as rape or sexual assault in most modern countries. Some rules in the monastic code of conduct for nuns, therefore, are in place as a means to protect nuns from this type of harm; a type of potential harm that they were in danger of because of their unconventional status, as unmarried women. Certain of the rules governing monastic behaviour refer specifically to this. Monastic codes differ amongst the different Buddhist traditions, and the rule I relate here is one example of that. In some monastic codes it is presented as one rule with four parts, in others it is arranged as four separate rules. I will relate the version of the rule from the Pāli canon, in which it is one rule with four parts.

Each of the parts has its own narrative alongside it: a story that recounts the (apparent) initial reason why that part of the rule was made. In the first part, a nun is said to quarrel with other nuns, and therefore decides to go to visit her family. She leaves the nuns' dwelling and travels alone along the road to her village. When the other nuns who have been sent to find her do so, they ask 'Were you violated when you were travelling alone?' She replies that she was not. Nonetheless a rule is made that nuns should not travel alone. Next, two nuns are travelling together and desire to cross a river. The boatman tells them he cannot take them together, they must go in his boat one at a time. This they do, but each of them is violated by the man. His insistence they go separately was a connivance to get each one of them alone. A rule is then made that nuns should not cross rivers alone. Third, a man conspires to get a certain nun alone who is part of a group staying overnight at his village. A rule is made that nuns must not be away from the group at night. Lastly, a nun stays behind from a group to defecate. This brief separation from the group is enough for her to be accosted and violated, so a rule is made that nuns must not stay behind a group.

It is quite possible that, initially, the eight rules were put in place to protect nuns. As noted above, there was little understanding of why women might choose to become nuns in ancient India, and no respect for their celibate status. Women were expected to be under the guardianship of men. If they were not they were viewed as sexually available. Therefore, in order to make clear that nuns were not sexually available to any man who sought to gratify himself, the community needed to make clear to villagers, townsfolk, city dwellers, and all inhabitants of north India that the nuns who followed the Buddha were under the guardianship of the monks. If monks are seen to be overseeing the activities of the nuns, the status of monks as the guardians of the nuns is established. Then the nuns are considered to 'belong' to the monks and thereby unavailable to other men. If this is the case there was no malfeasance; the rules were not originally put in place to cast nuns in a lower status to monks, but to safeguard them from sexual assault.

With regard to questions of ethics, intention, and harm, we can see then that gender issues are far from straightforward. As in this case, we can view history by highlighting factors that reshape perspectives on a problem. But such reassessments are not always possible. The question of gender equality and Buddhist ethics also highlights that ethical engagement on a mundane level is connected with political viewpoints. For anyone who considers themselves a liberal, who believes that women are equal to men, anything – like the eight special rules – that casts women as inferior causes harm, because such things denigrate women, and deny their capability and agency.

I Hear Her Words

Such a position, however, presupposes a viewpoint that women and men are equal. If one does not hold such a view, then unequal treatment is not unethical, as it is not harmful but appropriate. Take this example of a Thai monk, who speaks openly about his views on women in front of women, as if he has no comprehension that his words may cause harm. This is an episode recounted by Sid Brown of an experience during fieldwork in the mid-1990s that formed the basis of her book on women in Thai Buddhism. She comments on how these women, known as *mae chis*, are not always respected and valued:

> . . . most Thais I met through channels not related to māechī were surprised to learn that I would be interested in māechī – clearly because they did not consider them worthy of study. Understanding that my project involved learning about Buddhism, they recommended that I turn to monks, the agreed-upon experts. . . Sometimes they explained that in Thailand women's duties in relation to Buddhism are to sustain the monks, the true practitioners. One particularly exasperating conversation began when I asked one monk about the relation of women to Buddhism and he replied, identifying Buddhism with monks and monks with the recognised sangha, 'Women are very helpful to the sangha. They can help the sangha very much because they can do things that monks cannot do, like cook.' Neither of the two māechī who were with the monk and me at the time of this conversation – sitting right there with us – lived amongst monks. Neither cooked for monks. One lived in a samnak [monastery] made up of women only; the other lived alone in an apartment . . . when I indicated these two māechī beside us and asked how women such as these serve Buddhism he said, 'It is the same, they can cook for monks too.' He laughed and continued, 'You know what we call monks, yes? The belly of Buddhism.' He did not see any discrepancy between his words and the reality sitting right there in front of him.[11]

The ethical question here then must be: Does the monk intend to cause harm? It is only if he intended to cause harm that his speech and behaviour can be deemed unethical. At first glance, it would seem that no harm is intended, as he appears to have no awareness of the possibility that others might perceive his words and his views as harmful to women. If one believes that women are indeed inferior to men, and are only good for domestic activities such as cooking, then to say so is simply a statement of fact, and not a statement based on prejudice. It is not unfair or unjust. In which case, can it be called unethical? For those who do believe that women are men's equals, and that women are as able as men, such beliefs and statements are indeed harmful. It is here that Buddhism and feminism are counterposed; as here, from a modern, liberal standpoint, there is a need to raise awareness such that women's true character and abilities can be perceived correctly.

The last of the three mind precepts on the second list of ten is concerned with ignorance, which is also referenced in the quote that begins this chapter. Ignorance as an aspect of Buddhist doctrine is discussed in chapter 3. But, with regard to this precept, can we claim that the Thai monk who spoke with Sid Brown was wilfully ignorant? If we can, would this then be a confirmed breach of the ethical precepts? Can we claim this of him, even if he was raised and schooled within a society that maintains traditional values and roles for women? Can we accuse him of wilful ignorance if he has been taught to hold such views as this his entire life? We return to these questions in chapter 3 where I highlight the interconnectedness of Buddhist ethical systems with doctrine and philosophy.

Buddhism and Feminism

Just as it is possible to accuse this monk of a type of ignorance, it is equally possible to make such accusations against many types of people we meet, whatever their religious or political stance. With regard to feminism, feminists have certainly attracted more than their fair share of criticism. This has come from many quarters, some of which can be and has been called 'backlash'. Other criticism, however, reveals the limitations of liberal political agendas.

The modern scholarly debate on women in Buddhism began in the late 1800s with the work of British female scholars Caroline Rhys Davids (née Foley), Mabel Bode, and Isaline Blow (I. B.) Horner. It was not until much later, however, in the 1970s, 1980s, and 1990s, that the questions of feminism's relationship to Buddhism, and what might constitute a Buddhist feminism, were asked. The lives and thought of these early scholars did prefigure the later debate, which can be seen especially in the life and work of Caroline Rhys Davids. Caroline was the wife of the well-known Pāli scholar Thomas Rhys Davids, and between them they had a significant impact on how Buddhism was initially received in the Western world.

Exploring the life of Caroline Rhys Davids through her diaries and letters, it seems her own values and aspirations reached beyond limitations placed on women by Victorian society. These values and aspirations resonated with those of the early Buddhist nuns she studied. As her diaries and letters make clear, Caroline Rhys Davids was an intelligent, independent, and adventurous woman. She enjoyed travel, in particular mountaineering expeditions in the Alps, which is not an activity we might usually associate with Victorian ladies. Prior to her marriage, Caroline Rhys Davids struggled with the very idea of marriage, aware of the loss of freedom often suffered by women upon marriage. In a letter to her future husband, written a few weeks after his proposal, she wrote of a conversation she had had with his mother:

> She thinks I ought to go down on my knees and thank heaven . . . for a good man's Love. . . And she looked quite severe when I suggested it was rather premature to hazard any such statements and thought me . . . without judgment when I maintained that married life would not easily form a compensation for what I was giving up.[12]

In another letter Caroline Rhys Davids made clear what she believed she was giving up. Writing about her own mother, she said:

But married life, both in her own life and that of all her sisters but one, has [not] resolved itself into something most worthy of the name, but rather into reckless, perpetual childbearing with of course much domestic management and the odious nothings called social duties thrown in.[13]

Although Caroline Rhys Davids did marry, it was obviously with some reticence. This personal struggle of hers, to not be bound down and curtailed by a life of domesticity, she found reflected in the struggles of Buddhist nuns, who were the subject of her first article, published in 1893. Reading stories of Buddhist women who renounce domesticity and their lives as wives and mothers, she imagined them accepted into the male world of religious renunciation and accepted as men's intellectual equals. She assumed that, in the ancient dispensation of the Buddha, a figure she greatly admired, women became – as she wished to be – considered on a par with their male counterparts. Of the female Buddhist renouncer, she wrote:

. . . she . . . laid down all social prestige, all domestic success, as a mother, wife, daughter, queen, or housekeeper, and gained the austerer joys of an asexual rational being, walking with wise men in recognized intellectual equality on higher levels of thought. . .[14]

Whilst it is true that some of the women described in early Buddhist literature do engage their intellect in their religious endeavours, this is not always the case. But the nuns do often speak of their release from domesticity as a freedom, and their expressions can be conflated with feminist concerns. This apparent emphasis on intellect, along with the relinquishing of domesticity, obviously resonated with Caroline Rhys Davids' personal struggles. In this period of her life, she was reluctant to give up her status as an independent woman with no need for a man to support her, with little desire to be married and swallowed up by the duties incumbent in the role of wife and mother.

Confining women to the domestic sphere has been a broad concern of many feminist movements. Feminism and feminist thought takes many different forms. But it is the type known as modern Western second-wave feminism, of the 1970s, 1980s, and 1990s, that has come to form the basis of everyday awareness of feminism. A common understanding is, typically, that feminists see history as a history of patriarchal oppression of women by men. But this is an oversimplification. The use of the term 'feminism' to apply to a system of thought and lobbying groups does begin in premodern Europe, but the principles behind feminist thought can be seen present in most societies in human history, operating in a variety of ways.

During the period of second-wave feminism, some of the first scholars to be writing about women in Buddhism were Indian. Uma Chakravarti and Kumkum Roy have both enjoyed careers as prominent scholars of ancient Indian history and have written about women in Buddhism. At the age of 15, Uma Chakravarti had an experience that was to have a deep impact on her life. She witnessed the mass conversion to Buddhism headed up by Dr B.R. Ambedkar, that began the Ambedkarite Buddhist movement in India, which we return to in chapter 7.[15] Chakravarti became a scholar, joining Miranda House, the women's college at the University of Delhi in 1966.[16] She published her first paper on women in Buddhism in 1981 which was followed, a few years later, by a coauthored paper with Kumkum Roy (1988). Both papers set early Buddhism within the broader context of early Hindu tradition.

In the introduction to a book of collected papers (published in 2010), Kumkum Roy reflects on this earlier period. She notes that economic and social changes in India impacted academia in the 1970s and 1980s, and this drove female scholars to begin to ask questions about gender. She writes:

> Soon enough we realised that focusing on women was
> only one of several strategies that were required of us.
> Women (claims to sisterhood to the contrary) were not
> a homogenous, unified, naturally given category. It was
> therefore necessary to come to terms with heterogeneity,
> to ensure we did not suppress differences in trying to
> retrieve our own versions of the past. We also grappled

with the concept of gender relations – of locating women within frameworks of gender difference, and/or gender hierarchies and stratification. . . And, inevitably, we became aware that upper case patriarchy was a gross oversimplification – we needed to come to terms with varieties of patriarchies, which could be more or less oppressive, and within which some women could exercise (and be seen to exercise) a semblance of power.[17]

In moving away from the notion of one coherent patriarchal system that seeks to undermine women, it remains important not to veer too far in the opposite direction. It is important not to deny the problem altogether, but to recognize what has been or might have been lost. This book is largely concerned with a history that has, until recent decades, been lost. It is not a history of feminism because to apply the word 'feminism' to this lost past would be anachronistic. Reading this lost past we must stand outside of the simplistic model of patriarchy / oppression / resistance and understand multiple ways in which power dynamics interweave in all aspects of life. In the history of women in Buddhism a variety of factors are at play, interpersonal, political, social, religious, economic.

There is no doubt that second-wave feminism played an influential part in shaping both the modern Western and global world. Without it, the relatively positive conditions enjoyed by many Western women today would not be what they are. With regard to Buddhism, though, second-wave feminism took two missteps. Firstly, in their engagement with Buddhist texts, these scholars tended to focus on highlighting what is negative. This resulted in certain passages of Buddhist texts being cited often, and other parts being ignored. The consequence of this was a distorted picture. The second issue was with race.

Rita Gross's influential work *Buddhism After Patriarchy: A Feminist History, Analysis, and Reconstruction of Buddhism* (1993) can be seen as a landmark in the writings of feminist scholars on Buddhism. As a graduate student at the University of Chicago in the 1960s, Gross was the first to write a PhD thesis on feminism and religion in the USA.[18] As well as *Buddhism After Patriarchy* she authored many other works both on Buddhism and feminism and religion and feminism more generally. Other scholars, alongside Gross, began writing about the history of women in Buddhism and feminism during the same period. Certain of these scholars highlighted the negative representations of women in Buddhist texts. They did this whilst at the same time seeking to reconstruct or extract from Buddhism something that could be, in Gross's terms, 'usable' for contemporary women. *Buddhism After Patriarchy* has been lauded as a magnum opus, and was the first book-length feminist critique of Buddhism. Of her objectives in the book, Gross writes:

> My primary task in this book is a feminist revalorization of Buddhism. In feminist theology in general, the task of revalorization involves working with the categories and concepts of a traditional religion in the light of feminist values. This task is double-edged, for, on the one hand, feminist analysis of any major world religion reveals massive undercurrents of sexism and prejudice against women, especially in realms of religious praxis. On the other hand, the very term 'revalorization' contains an implicit judgement. To revalorize is to have determined that, however sexist a religious tradition may be, it is not irreparably so. Revalorizing is, in fact, doing that work of repairing the tradition, often bringing it much more into line with its own fundamental values and vision than its patriarchal form.[19]

Gross's contribution to the debate certainly needs to be fully acknowledged, as without her input the debate would not be as advanced it is today. There are, however, many problems with her contribution. A year after *Buddhism After Patriarchy* was first published, Noriko Kawahashi composed a review that highlights crucial issues. She writes:

> I wish to question Gross's view of Asian women. Gross makes several statements implying that the carriers of patriarchal Buddhism are Western Buddhists, and that Western Buddhism is the single most promising ground

in which feminist Buddhist theology might blossom. This is because, according to Gross, Western Buddhism is 'the only form of Buddhism subject to significant feminist influence'.[20]

It is clear that Gross did not always understand racial dynamics with sufficient sensitivity. Whilst she paints in broad brushstrokes an ideology that envisions no prejudice or discrimination based on other factors, in other parts of the work she seems less aware. In *Buddhism After Patriarchy* she even goes so far as to claim that any advances on the question of Buddhism and gender are not likely to be made by Asian women:

> . . . I am writing as a Western Buddhist and am convinced that many of the most significant and necessary developments in Buddhism regarding gender issues will first be articulated by Western Buddhists.[21]

Analogous criticisms of other of Rita Gross's work were made by other scholars. In Kwok Pui-lan's assessment of Gross's *Feminism and Religion: An Introduction*, published in 1996, she identifies similar issues:

> Gross's discussion completely overlooks the feminist movements that are developing in many parts of Asia and does not envisage that Asian Buddhist women can be change agents within Buddhism.[22]

In her professional career, Rita Gross only ever had one graduate student, and this student, Hsiao-Lan Hu, has recently written a critique of Gross and her contribution. This book chapter includes discussion of Gross's latent racism, which Hu describes experiencing at first hand, as well as witnessing it within Gross's writings.[23] Hu writes of Gross:

> It is through refusing to see the reality of her whiteness, the reality of how her identity as a white American woman allowed her to presume her experience as a woman to be universal . . . that she participated in systems that diminish people of color. . .[24]

It is not only Gross but the broader modern liberal feminist approach that has been criticized. Some of the primary themes defined by this approach on gender in Buddhism are not borne out. Nirmala Salgado, a Sri Lankan born scholar, began her conversations with nuns in 1983, which culminated in her book of 2007. In her book, on modern female renunciates in Sri Lanka, she argues that many 'abnormalities' that have been recognized in modern scholarship are unrecognized by modern Buddhist women. She writes:

> For example, nuns do not always acknowledge – or they simply reject – the perceived need for *upasampadā* [full ordination]. I argue that frameworks that have been used in discussing female renunciation tend to centre on binary opposites that are grounded in liberal feminism. I suggest that avoiding the repetition of the colonial events . . . can help us better think about lives of female (religious) figures without turning them into subjects who must speak differently from the way they do.[25]

Salgado goes on to demonstrate that concerns relating to women in Buddhism highlighted in modern scholarship do not always map onto the lives and concerns of Buddhist women today. Similarly, in the Introduction I include evidence from the work of Wei-Yi Cheng, from her book entitled *Buddhist Nuns in Taiwan and Sri Lanka: A Critique of the Feminist Perspective*. Cheng relates the incident of a copy of the eight rules being publicly torn up in order to highlight how a rights-based feminism is not always the most fitting and appropriate response to a problem. She writes:

> After 'the storm' this 'silent conspiracy' was broken, and a monk must now ponder whether he should ask a nun to pay homage to him or run the risk of being accused of not observing the precepts. If this indeed was a common reaction among Taiwanese monks, then it is sad that a feminist action may have caused such anti-feminist consequences.[26]

With regard to the question of gender equality, feminism might not always be the answer. Whilst in this chapter I have attempted to dissect what we mean by gender equality, there is a separate layer to the question that I have not brought to light. Specifically, when we ask the question, Does Buddhism support gender equality?, what do we mean by 'Buddhism'? That is, are we asking what do Buddhist texts say on this, or are we asking, as has been the focus here, about Buddhist ethics? Or – importantly – are we asking, as with our Thai monk, what do members of the Buddhist communities say on this? With regard to this last aspect of the question, here again we need to ensure we incorporate women and women's views as part of the question, as well as the answer.

In other words, as I noted in the Introduction, if our definition of 'Buddhism' does not fully include all members of Buddhist communities past and present, why not? Many of the women whose lives are told in this book are women who lived on various continents around the globe and are from diverse cultural backgrounds. If we ensure that women and their lives, efforts, and contributions are fully acknowledged as part of Buddhism and its history, then when we ask a question about 'Buddhism' we are asking about all women, and not just about men and their views. If we mean by 'Buddhism' all the women whose lives are told in this book, is the question still relevant? And if we mean by 'Buddhism' all the Buddhist women of today, for whom gender issues are not always central to their day-to-day lives, what of the question then?

* * *

Sometimes, it seems, harm can be caused, even by those who are committed to a liberal agenda, and who both privately and publicly state their intention to do good, to promote fairness, justice, and equality.

Buddhism is not based on nor does it serve the same appeals for social justice as feminism. But with the principle of non-harm as its ethical basis, it can appear to parallel feminist concerns. With women in Buddhist history overcoming obstacles to become nuns who renounce lives of domesticity, it can appear as a tradition that has more in common with feminist ideals than is in reality the case. Buddhism is a religion, and the aim of engagement with ethics is realizing the religious goal.

The question does need to be raised, however, as to whether ideas about Buddhist communities and Buddhist teachings in history fully acknowledge the many women who have been part of them. Have the contributions of these women to Buddhism been fully appreciated? If they are, then the answer to the question, Does Buddhism support gender equality?, must be that, although certain Buddhist texts and members of some Buddhist communities assert that women are inferior to men, Buddhism would not be what it is today without the contributions of women.

CHAPTER 2

WOMEN IN BUDDHIST TEXTS

Lustful thoughts do not arise in me
You should conceive no lust for women who are without lust
This Lord of Sages before me is my witness
That what I say is true and never false.

Spoken by the female bodhisattva Candrottarā[1]

The verse that begins this chapter was spoken by the female bodhisattva Candrottarā. It is taken from a text that focuses on this young girl. Her story is that she is so incomparably beautiful that men are not able to control themselves when they are around her. Some potential suitors even make threats to her parents, if they will not grant her hand in marriage. Feeling a need to calm the situation, Candrottarā decides to act. In the episode of the text from which the verse is taken, she decides to face her suitors. When she appears before them, they begin to run towards her. Consumed by their passion for her, they are unable to control themselves. At this, Candrottarā, enabled by her abilities as an advanced bodhisattva, rises up into the air, to the height of a palm tree. She offers a teaching to the crowd below, on the dangers of sexual desire and attraction.

The story of Candrottarā captures the best and worst within Buddhist texts on women. As we have already seen, Buddhist texts are multilayered. There are competing 'voices' that express conflicting and contradictory ideas about women. We have seen that there are positive portrayals and accounts of women, as well as negativity. In this chapter, I offer fuller examples of a range of Buddhist texts that talk about women. An assortment of views are expressed, across a spectrum. This extends from honorific and respectful to vilifying and derogatory. The juxtaposition can be unsettling.

I will focus on the theme of sexual desire, central in the Candrottarā story as elsewhere. In narratives, episodes, and passages of text on this topic, we find examples that can be placed along all parts of the spectrum. At one end are exemplary women who demonstrate they have abandoned desire, like Candrottarā. Such women, of whom there are many, expound profound teachings on Buddhist doctrine, often to an audience that includes both men and women. At the other end are texts that blame women for being attractive to men. Women are branded as poisonous, detestable, and manipulative. The final section of the chapter focuses on such examples, the worst expressions of contempt for women found in Buddhist literature.

For Buddhism, desire is a problem. Broadly speaking, any type of sensual desire, or pleasure, should be avoided. For any that seek to make progress on the path, both the desire for pleasure and the experience of it are obstacles. Desire for pleasure should not be acted upon. If desire for pleasure is acted upon, and pleasure experienced, this will inevitably lead to the arising of more desire. The renunciate who follows the path set out by the Buddha should take steps to ensure they relinquish desire. Of all desires sexual desire is one of the most challenging, as it is amongst the most powerful. A monastic must work to overcome this. Hence, the texts that situate male desire for women as a product of the mind and mental events that needs to be overcome are doctrinally endorsed, as they accord with fundamental Buddhist principles. Those that position women as the problem are not.[2]

In this chapter, I focus on Indian Buddhist texts. Many Buddhist texts are difficult to date. Some include teachings and practices that likely date from the time of the Buddha. To the extent that a timeline can be adjudged, it does appear that the earliest Buddhist canons do not include the most negative comments about women. The farther in time we move away from the historical Buddha, the more likely we are to find texts that are increasingly negative about women. If we acknowledge this trajectory, that the worst passages about women come later, it does then appear that the Buddha himself had a positive view of women. The Indian texts that are the focus of this chapter date potentially from the time of the Buddha to the seventh century CE.

Nuns Overcoming Desire

Only a limited number of the many narratives on the lives of women in Buddhist literature focus on female desire or female sexuality. When female desire is discussed, it is more commonly in narratives in which men are the main characters and the women peripheral to the story. In one canonical example, however, there are short stories of nuns who demonstrate that they are no longer enticed by worldly pleasures. The actions of these nuns reflect those of the Buddha.

In legendary accounts of the life of the Buddha, when he came close to achieving Awakening there were attempts to stop him. These are made by a character called Māra. Māra appears as a person, an entity, in Buddhist texts. He is most often depicted as a force that hinders. He is the personification of all that holds the practitioner back from making progress. In accounts of the Buddha's life, the Buddha-to-be sat under a tree and decided to remain there until he has realized the truth. Māra made efforts to ensure this would not happen. In Māra's first attempt, he sent his daughters, who danced provocatively in front of the meditating Buddha-to-be, in the hope of seducing him, which they failed to do.

In the short stories of nuns who have overcome desire, the nuns also decided to find a secluded spot to meditate. In each case, Māra saw them, and approached them. This time, he disguised himself as a handsome young man and attempted to distract the nuns from their practice. Māra either directly propositioned the nuns or, as in these verses to the nun Āḷavikā, appealed to them to take advantage of life's pleasures:

> There is no escape from the world,
> so what will you do with your solitude?
> You should enjoy the delights of sensual pleasure,
> do not be remorseful later.

Āḷavikā is, however, like the Buddha, unyielding. Her reply is:

> Sensual pleasures are like sword stakes,
> [mind and body] the executioner's block.
> What you call delight in sensual pleasure
> has become non-delight for me.[3]

In another story, Māra attempts to seduce the nun Vijayā. He says to her:

> You are young and beautiful,
> and I a young man.
> Come, noble woman, let us rejoice
> with the music of a fivefold ensemble.

Vijayā is not tempted even for a moment. She replies:

Forms, sounds, tastes, scents, and tactile objects
that are pleasing to the mind,
I give them back to you, Māra,
I am not in need of them.[4]

Māra wholly fails in his attempts to stop these nuns meditating, just as he failed in his attempts to stop the Buddha. The nuns, instead, demonstrate their meditative prowess. They are not, even for an instant, attracted by the invitation of the young man, who they recognize as Māra. They recognize that there is no real worth in the pursuit of worldly pleasures. They show themselves to be praiseworthy disciples of the Buddha, following closely in his footsteps.

The Problem of Desire

Many Buddhist texts contain passages or sections that demonstrate a parity between men and women. Men and women are talked about as equals. Their pursuit of the goal of Buddhism, the practices they need to enact, the doctrines and ethical principles they should follow, are the same. The reason for the equal treatment is that the path can be practised by both men and women. It is a path for all human beings to pursue if they seek to attain nirvana. Both men and women need to overcome sexual desire and broader desires for the sensual pleasures the world can offer. There are distractions, and any who focus on these and become preoccupied with them will not progress on the path nor, ultimately, attain the goal. There are many examples in which this problem is related concerning both men and women. The following example gives two identical passages, one about women, the other men:

> Monks and all present, a woman attends inwardly to her
> feminine faculties; her feminine charms, manners, ways,
> desires, her female voice and feminine adornments.
> She is excited by that, takes pleasure in that. Being ex-
> cited and pleased she attends outwardly to masculine
> faculties; masculine charms, manners, ways, desires, the
> male voice and male adornments. She is excited by that,
> takes pleasure in that. Being excited and pleased, she

longs to be bonded with what is outside her, longs for
whatever happiness and joy arises based on the bond.
A woman taking pleasure in her femininity goes into
bondage in relation to men. In this way, Monks and all
present, a woman does not overcome her femininity.

Monks and all present, a man attends inwardly to his
masculine faculties; his male charms, manners, ways,
desires, his masculine voice and male adornments. He
is excited by that, takes pleasure in that. Being excited
and pleased he attends outwardly to feminine faculties;
female charms, manners, ways, desires, the female voice
and feminine adornments. He is excited by that, takes
pleasure in that. Being excited and pleased, he longs
to be bonded with what is outside himself, longs for
whatever happiness and joy arises based on the bond.
A man taking pleasure in his masculinity goes into
bondage in relation to women. In this way, Monks and
all present, a man does not overcome his masculinity.[5]

A similar section to this can be found in a Mahāyāna text. Again,
desire is equally a problem for both men and women:

. . . there are times when a woman internally thinks, 'I
am a woman'. After thinking internally, 'I am a woman',
she thinks about an external man, 'A man!'. After
thinking about an external man, 'A man!', she becomes
passionate and longs for sexual union with an external
man. A man also thinks internally, 'I am a man', [the
rest] as before. Because of their mutual desire for sexual
union, they have sex.[6]

These above examples demonstrate an evenhandedness. Other
passages that focus on desire highlight a drift away from equity to
a focus on male experience. This is well illustrated by two examples
of essentially the same passage. The following passage appears
twice in the Pāli canon. In the first instance, the problem is uniform,
men and women have the same experience. Two separate passages

discuss first male desire for women, then female desire for men. In the second occurrence of the passage, the teaching on female desire is missing:

> Monks and all present, I do not see even one other form that so obsesses the mind of a man than the form of a woman. The form of a woman obsesses the mind of a man. I do not see even one other sound that so obsesses the mind of a man than the sound of a woman. The sound of a woman obsesses the mind of a man. I do not see even one other odour that so obsesses the mind of a man than the odour of a woman. The odour of a woman obsesses the mind of a man. I do not see even one other taste that so obsesses the mind of a man than the taste of a woman. The taste of a woman obsesses the mind of a man. I do not see even one other touch that so obsesses the mind of a man than the touch of a woman. The touch of a woman obsesses the mind of a man.

> Monks and all present, I do not see even one other form that so obsesses the mind of a woman than the form of a man. The form of a man obsesses the mind of a woman. I do not see even one other sound that so obsesses the mind of a woman than the sound of a man. The sound of a man obsesses the mind of a woman. I do not see even one other odour that so obsesses the mind of a women than the odour of a man. The odour of a man obsesses the mind of a woman. I do not see even one other taste that so obsesses the mind of a woman than the taste of a man. The taste of a man obsesses the mind of a woman. I do not see even one other touch that so obsesses the mind of a woman than the touch of a man. The touch of a man obsesses the mind of a woman.[7]

The second appearance of the passage is as follows. It is not identical to the first example, but the same sentiments are expressed, albeit with different wording:

Monks and all present, I do not see even one other form so enticing, so desirable, so intoxicating, so binding, so infatuating, such a hindrance to winning the supreme peace from bondage than the form of a woman. Monks and all present, those who cling to a woman's form – impassioned, greedy, enslaved, infatuated, attached – they grieve for a long time, besotted by the female form. . .[8]

The same shift towards a focus on male experience is in evidence elsewhere. In a much-cited exchange, women become the object of attention for the practitioner (who is male). This example, highlighting the need for monks to stay away from women, comes in a dialogue between the Buddha and one of his chief disciples, Ānanda. Ānanda asks the Buddha:

'Sir, how should we behave towards women?'
[the Buddha replies] 'Do not see them, Ānanda.'
'But if we do see them, Blessed One, how should
     we behave?'
'Do not speak to them, Ānanda.'
'But if they speak to us, Sir, how should we behave?'
'Practice mindfulness, Ānanda.'[9]

When women are sidelined rather than included they are recast as a problem. Instead of being proactive practitioners on the path, they are an obstacle that impedes spiritual progress. Once this die is cast, a rationale begins to develop as to exactly why it is women are such trouble.

Women Are the Problem, Not Desire

The majority of passages in Buddhist texts on desire focus on male attraction to women. When feminists began to study Buddhism it was these passages that formed the axis of their studies. Certainly, it is here we find the most misogynist excerpts amongst the wealth of Buddhist literature. The misogyny has, therefore, received a good deal of attention. It is my view, however, that the cited passages on misogyny do not deserve the level of attention they have received, for three reasons. First, while there are a significant number of Buddhist texts that centre on male experience, the misogynist passages are not the majority. The attention they have received is disproportionate to the amount of passages there are. Second, we do not know how representative they were. These could have been the views of a handful of monks who happened to be those who composed or collated texts. Third, much of the attention devoted to these passages has focused on the negative portrayal of women. But men do not come off well in the narratives either.

The *Saundarananda,* 'Handsome Nanda'

Aśvaghoṣa, who lived sometime in the first and second centuries CE, was a convert to Buddhism. Schooled in Brahmanical tradition, he become an accomplished poet, and composed two major works of Buddhist poetry. His best-known work is the *Buddhacarita*, or 'Acts of the Buddha'. This is an account of the life of the Buddha. The account contains a few sections that depict women in a negative way. But it is his lesser known work, entitled 'Handsome Nanda', that includes a full-blown condemnation of women. It includes the chapter 'The Attack on Women'.[10] In both these works, Aśvaghoṣa takes narratives well known within the Buddhist tradition and transforms them into epic poems.

The story of Nanda, who was a half-brother to the Buddha, is told in various Buddhist sources. Nanda is depicted as a man who is reluctant to give up his worldly life, addicted as he is to the pleasure the world can bring: most especially, the pleasure of being with women. Two accounts of Nanda that likely predate Aśvaghoṣa's version, a narrative and a verse text, do not include the vilification of women found in Aśvaghoṣa's poems.

In both earlier accounts, women are not blamed for sexually manipulating men, but rather Nanda's problem is apportioned as his own. It is Nanda's mental affliction that he must conquer. One early version depicts Nanda lamenting that he is not fit for the life of celibacy, because of his yearning for women and sensual pleasures. When the other monks learn about his obsession with sensual pleasures, they tease him. The other indicates the same, with Nanda admitting his mental turmoil:

> Distracted by my addiction to ornamentation,
> I was conceited, vain and afflicted
> by desire for pleasures.[11]

Changing tack, in his version of the story Aśvaghoṣa squarely puts the blame on women. This ceases to be a hindrance that Nanda needs to overcome. Instead, like all men, Nanda is simply at the mercy of poisonous women:

> Like creepers poisonous to the touch, like scoured caves
> still harboring snakes, like unsheathed swords held in
> the hand, women are ruinous in the end. When women
> want sex they arouse lust; when women don't want sex
> they bring danger. . . Women behave ignobly, maliciously
> spying out the weakness of others. . . When nobly-born
> men become destitute . . . it is because of women.[12]

Aśvaghoṣa goes on:

> Women have no regard for handsome looks, wealth,
> intelligence, lineage or valor; like hordes of crocodiles
> in a river, they attack without discrimination. A woman
> never remembers sweet words, caresses or affection.
> Even when coaxed, a woman is flighty, so depend on her
> no more than you would on your enemies.[13]

Later in the narrative, another character comments on Nanda's predicament. In this section, we begin to see how this vilification of women might arise:

> How pitiful that the wayward deer has escaped from the
> great danger posed by the hunter, but now in his longing
> for the herd is about to leap into the net, fooled by the
> sound of singing! Here is a bird that was enmeshed in
> a net, freed by a well-wisher to glide through the forest
> of fruit and flowers, now voluntarily trying to get into

a cage! Here is a young elephant pulled out of the thick mud at a treacherous riverbank by another elephant, that wants to once more descend into the crocodile infested river, impelled by its thirst for water! Here is a lad sleeping in a shelter with a snake, who, when woken by a mindful elder, is filled with confusion and tries to grab the fierce snake himself! Here is a bird flown away from a forest tree ablaze with a raging fire, that wishes to fly back there, its qualms forgotten in its longing for its nest! Here is a pheasant in a helpless swoon of lust when separated from its mate through fear of a hawk, living in wretchedness and attaining neither resolution nor modesty! Here is a wretched, undisciplined dog, full of greed but lacking decency and wisdom, who wants to feed once more on the food he has vomited![14]

In this passage, the man is represented as the deer trying to escape a deadly hunter. He is a bird trapped in a net, or a young elephant at the mercy of dangerous crocodiles, who are ready to pounce. The man is a young lad, in fear of a snake. He is a bird escaping potentially lethal fire, a pheasant who is no match for a hawk, and a greedy dog, unable to control itself. Most of these similes cast the man as a vulnerable creature, in fear of and at the mercy of a more powerful entity than he is himself. This is far from a depiction of robust masculinity. Men are frail creatures, easily frightened and easy prey. The evenhandedness seen earlier is gone. Desire is no longer the human experience that needs to be overcome by those treading the path. The danger is women, not desire.[15]

The *Mahāratnakūṭa*, 'The Collection of Great Jewels'

Women who are identified as the problem are rarely grandmothers, mothers, or sisters. Such contempt is usually reserved for women with whom a man might have sexual relations, that is wives or other sexual partners. The writers of such texts assume that because of their sexual power, and men's tendency for infatuation, wives can easily manipulate. The verses that follow are from 'The Collection of Great Jewels', an anthology of over forty texts, some of which include otherwise unknown stories of wise and insightful women.[16] The narrative within which these verses below can be found is the well-known story of King Udaya. There are various versions of this story, found within the texts of different Buddhist traditions, from several countries. The story, however, remains essentially the same.[17]

The king has two wives, one who followed the Buddha and another who was jealous of the first. In this version of the narrative, the king was initially deceived by the jealous wife, who came to court maligning the Buddha and his teachings. As a result, the king was angry that the other wife, Śyāmāvatī, was following the teachings of the Buddha. He became so angry, in fact, that he shot an arrow at Śyāmāvatī. She forgave him, and in so doing demonstrated a faithful patience. Due to Śyāmāvatī's virtue, the king was converted to Buddhism. He was, however, repentant that the other wife – the jealous one – made him act inappropriately towards Śyāmāvatī. He requested that the Buddha explain to him why women are so unscrupulous. The reply that the Buddha gave fluctuates between situating male desire as the problem and pathologizing women – depicting them like a disease.[18] The worst part of the long reply is:

> Just as a fire in a deep pit
> Can cause fire damage without smoking.
> A woman also can be
> Cruel without pity.
>
> As the filth and decay
> Of a dead dog or snake
> Are burned away,
> So all men should burn filth
> And detest evil.
>
> The dead snake and dog
> Are detestable,
> But women are even more
> Detestable than they are.[19]

The contempt for women is a generalization and one that should not naturally arise from the context. The king was converted to Buddhism by the moral behaviour of one of his wives. Prior to this vilification of all women, one woman had shown herself to be morally commendable. Hence, to conclude that all women are more detestable than dead dogs does seem – to put it mildly – unfair. In the story, the king was significantly (and unduly) influenced by first one woman, then another. He told the Buddha:

> Lord, because of woman's deception, I am perplexed and ignorant. For this reason I have intense hate. Lord, because you bring peace and benefits to all beings, I want you to explain, out of compassion, the flattery and deceit of women. Do not let me have close relationships with women. Then, after a long time, I will be able to avoid all suffering.[20]

The king expressed that he had been fooled by the deception of women. He was confused and unsure what to do. He asked the Buddha for help. Once again, the man was helpless when faced with a calculating woman. Again, it seems that this fear is the source of the hatred.

The *Śikṣāsamuccaya*, 'The Compendium of Training'

The same pattern is repeated in another Mahāyāna text, 'The Compendium of Training'. This text was composed and collated by the seventh-century Indian monk Śāntideva. Another of Śāntideva's works is his most notable, his guide to the bodhisattva path. 'The Compendium of Training' is an anthology. Śāntideva makes each of his points by quoting liberally from a variety of other Mahāyāna works. The manual is a training in the Mahāyāna path. Śāntideva focuses on renunciation of what can hinder and development of factors that enable progress on the path.

The most misogynist parts of the work are found in chapter 4, a chapter concerned with what is harmful.[21] The following extract is from a text called the 'Discourse on the Application of Mindfulness to the Holy Teachings', a text that outlines the hellish consequences in store for whosoever breaches the ethical precepts. The denigration of women is found in a section on breach of the precept on sexual misconduct. The section appears to be cited to show the consequences for those who breach the precept in any way. Yet the language and imagery are entirely centred on a male subject. As a result of sexual misconduct, the man is reborn into a hell-world.[22] But his insatiable desire for women does not stop, regardless of the consequences:[23]

> When he sees [women], the fire of attraction that has
> been habituated in him since beginningless time flares
> up, and he runs towards these women. But they are
> made of iron, created that way by karma. They seize
> him, and starting with the lips, they devour him, leaving
> nothing behind, not even [a remnant] the size of a
> mustard seed. He is born again, and again he is eaten.
> He experiences harsh, unbearable sensations, because
> of them, the fire of attraction does not cease; instead, he
> runs towards those women even more, and the pain he
> suffers does not interfere with attraction. Those women
> of iron and adamant, their bodies burdened with blazing
> garlands, crush that hell-being like a handful of sand. He
> is born again, and so on as before. . .
>
> Women are the root of the lower realms:
> They destroy your wealth in every way.
> Men who are subject to women
> How could they possibly be happy? . . .
> A woman is the greatest of all disasters
> In this world and the next.
> Therefore, if a man wants to be happy, he should give
>   up women.[24]

The female denizens acted violently towards the man who was, nonetheless, unable to abandon desire. In these passages, women destroy men, both literally and figuratively. The female denizens chewed him up and spat him out. Incapable of self-control, he returned for more.

Śāntideva also quotes from another version of the story of King Udaya. The same contempt for women is on display in this version. Because 'ignorant' men are so obsessed with sexual desire, and thereby women, they are unable, again, to resist temptation:

When he sees a wound, he runs to it, like a fly.
When he sees impurity, he runs to it, like a donkey.
Just as a dog runs to a slaughterhouse for the sake of
     meat—
That is what they are like, ignorant men who take
     delight in women.
Those fools are obscured by ignorance,
Completely covered by the mass of darkness.
Attached to women they are infatuated
Like crows draw to filth. . .[25]

The temptation, the woman's body, is likened to all things foul and revolting. A monk who does not adhere to his monastic vows of celibacy, who yields to temptation and seeks out women for sex, is compared to a fly that feeds from a fleshy wound, a hungry dog that runs into a bloody abattoir. A woman's body is a foul-smelling vessel of filth:

These fools, who spend their time on filth,
Who eat mucus and saliva.
As was said before, don't know
That the place they're attracted to is reviled by everyone.
Like flies who see a wound,
They are attracted to what is contemptible. . .

The Buddha criticized women
For being foul-smelling, like dung.
Therefore only lowly men
Have intercourse with women, who are lowly.
Like some fool who goes into the house
While carrying a bag of filth,
Whatever kind of actions you do,
You get results of the same kind.[26]

Immediately following these verses, Śāntideva cites this prose passage from the very same text, the same version of the story of King Udaya:

> Out of the wealth they earned with painful effort
> for their own livelihood, they cannot give gifts to
> religious wanderers and Brahmins, or to the destitute,
> the wretched, the poor, and beggars, because they are
> subjugated by women, conquered by women, controlled
> by women, slaves to women. Because of their love for
> women, they have to nourish them, and so they cannot
> give generously or undertake moral discipline. A
> man who is full of attraction puts up with a women's
> scolding; he puts up with their ridicule, stares, and
> criticisms. When he is mocked by a woman, that man is
> discouraged and depressed, but he still looks to her for
> happiness.[27]

The prose section continues to be negative about women. They are painted, once more, as a force of nature that pulls men away from doing good. In this passage, however, we can identify a fear of women and their assumed ability to control men who might fall under their spell. If a man slavishly obeys a woman, a wife, he is not able to do his own bidding. He must do as she says. If he desires to act generously, to offer some material help to others less fortunate to him, he will not be able to do that, subjugated, as he is, by the domineering woman. He seems, in this passage, to be completely at the mercy of a force of nature that controls him: women. He puts up with being admonished, and with criticism, unable to say no to such treatment. Once more, anxiety about the potent power women can wield over men suggests itself to be the true source of the vilification.

It has been argued that Śāntideva was not, in his exposition of these passages, attempting to denigrate women, but rather to help monks in their attempts to overcome desire.[28] Even if this was one of the reasons behind such compositions, the consequences have been that women have been more broadly reviled. Like Māra's daughters, women can be stereotyped as seductresses in Buddhist literature. Blame of women manifested into an imagined reality of an army of women with voracious sexual appetites, ready to sexually (and psychologically) devour men at any opportunity. So conceived, such imagined women will do everything in their power to pull men away from practising the Buddhist path.

The sexuality of women is not the only aspect of their character that has come under attack within Buddhist texts. The attacks dovetail into condemnation of women more broadly. Women are characterized as low, vile, debased, wicked, manipulating, and calculating. Women can also be said to possess only limited intellect. And the female body, as above, can be described as incomparably foul. This occurs not only in Indian Buddhist texts but in texts of other Buddhist countries, regions, and traditions as well. Again, these are not the majority, but what appears can be equally vociferous.

Beyond India

Depicting women in this way can appear, at times, to be positioning women as subhuman. Although this is implied, I do not know of any Indian text that says this explicitly. I have found only one example of this being expressed somewhat explicitly. The following brief extract is from a long chapter in *Women in Tibet: Past and Present*. In his chapter in this volume, Dan Martin's contribution is about Tibetan women who lived in the eleventh and twelfth centuries who were recognized from their 'accomplishments in the area of Buddhist religion'.[29] Whilst I am focusing on this brief expression of misogyny, I am at pains to stress that the remainder of Dan Martin's chapter – which stretches to over thirty pages – is concerned with the opposite.[30] Martin begins his chapter with some brief comments about some of the best known women from the period, including Machig Labdrön, the founder of the *Chöd* tradition. Martin then goes on to discuss women disciples, nuns, teachers, leaders, and lineage transmitters. He then turns his attention to a prominent male teacher of the time, Phadampa Sangye, with whom many of these women had contact and who 'was surely an advocate of a kind of women's liberation'.[31] The same, however, cannot be said of one of the commentators on Phadampa's teachings. Following what could be constructed as a less favourable depiction of women than other of Phadampa's teachings are, the commentator, in his commentary, launches into an attack on women:

> The likes of woman are bad receptacles [for the teachings]: they clearly place their trust in the causes of suffering. Having little sorrow for their own lot in saṃsāra, since they view suffering as an ornament, they do not escape from household works and get no chance to work on Dharma . . . it is because they have no escape (*bud*) from household chores that they are called 'women' (*bud-myed*). . .

> 'Because they have not accumulated the accumulations, they take low rebirth.' This means firstly that because their bodily receptacles are inferior, the minds that rely [on those bodies] are also inferior. Their minds being of limited scope, their thoughts are incapable of anything more than minor objectives.[32]

This commentator then takes a step further:

> The receptacle for finding one's way to heaven and liberation is the precious human body. Even those who do not find human rebirth, if they are simply born as women, they turn into the unadulterated [nature] of animals, so their nose ropes are lost to others [i.e. their independence]. While the attainment of independence is rare [for anyone, for women] it is more rare, and they are extremely few.[33]

This is the only example I have seen in which women's nature is explicitly construed as subhuman. That is, those who do not 'find human rebirth' might be born as women. If they are born as women they have the nature of an animal. All forms of Buddhism, throughout history and from around the world, are based upon the fundamental principles that Buddhism exists and Awakening is possible only because it is possible for human nature to transform. In all examples bar that of this unnamed Tibetan commentator, however much women are reviled for their nature, it is never implied that their nature is anything other than human.

* * *

Some monks and male practitioners have, through the centuries, had issues with women. As a consequence, women have been reviled in Buddhist texts. When feminists began in earnest to write about Buddhism, harsh comments such as those highlighted garnered most attention. It is not clear, though, the extent to which such views were endorsed by the majority of practitioners at the time of composition or subsequently. All that they illuminate is that there was at least a handful of Buddhist authors, probably monks, who held such views. In identifying what these passages tell us about men it is not my objective to defame men as a group. My objective is to offer a critique of these passages. The way men are depicted is as unrealistic as the portrayals of women. My aim is to show that it is not only women who come off badly in such passages of text.

There has been a tendency to see these misogynist passages as a reason to doubt Buddhism and Buddhist tradition. This can happen if the passages are taken as indicative of Buddhism as a whole. But there is another way to assess them. The nuns and female bodhisattva, Candrottarā, who began this chapter are exemplars of Buddhist tradition. The short stories of the nuns portray them as impervious to Māra's actions, reflecting the attributes of the Buddha. Like the Buddha, the nuns easily recognized the dangers of sexual pleasures, and were not tempted by them, not even for a moment. The men, the monks who berate them, these men are not operating in concord with the teachings of the Buddha. They are not, as the nuns did, simply saying no to sexual desire. They do not, with unerring resilience, imitate the founder and leader of their tradition. Rather than acknowledge powerful feelings of desire, they blame women. Instead of focusing on their own mental afflictions, preoccupations, and obsessions, they cast aspersions on women. In so doing, their actions do not reflect those of the Buddha, who was unmoved by Māra's daughters.

I Hear Her Words

CHAPTER 3

GENDER AND BUDDHIST DOCTRINE

It is said that water is able to wash away impurities,
But how do you know the water is not dirty?
Even if you erase the distinction between water and dirt,
When you come in here, you must still be sure to bathe!

Chinese nun Zhitong (d. 1124)
Inscribed over the entrance to the bathhouse at Baoning Monastery[1]

The question of the nun Zhitong is deceptively simple. Water, of course, can easily be dirty. But in advocating the obliteration of a cognitive distinction between the water and the dirt, for all those who come along to the bathhouse with a desire for ablution, she strikes at the heart of the Buddhist worldview.

In this chapter, I examine three key Buddhist doctrines and discuss how each relates to the issues of gender and to Zhitong's probing question. The three doctrines are dependent arising, the doctrine of no-self, and the Mahāyāna notion of emptiness. These are central teachings amongst many others. Doctrinal schema in Buddhist traditions interlace to produce a comprehensive system. Therefore, at times, I also refer to other aspects of Buddhist doctrine and practice.

As we have seen, both Buddhist texts and Buddhist traditions can claim that women are inferior to men. When this is asserted, the most common reason given is an appeal to the limitations of women's nature, characteristics, and abilities. They are good for nothing but domestic chores. Women's minds are of limited scope, they are flighty, overly emotional, irrational. Women are manipulative, controlling, mean-spirited. They practise deception at every opportunity. They are detestable, they mock, and they prey on the weaknesses of others. Each of these criticisms are directed to all women. Women as a group are the same. This is just how they are. It is their nature. They cannot change. No amount of 'sweet words' will help.

But to say that women are inferior to men because of their nature contradicts basic Buddhist doctrines. At its heart Buddhism, as a religion, is concerned with human transformation. The attainment of Awakening and realization of nirvana are possible only because the transformation of human nature into something other – and better (from a Buddhist point of view) – is possible. This transformation can only be conceived of and achieved because of the nature of sentient beings and the nature of the world. Both of these are malleable and adaptable, constantly in flux and ever changing. Hence, an allegation that women's (deleterious) nature is fixed, static, and unchanging flies in the face of everything that Buddhism teaches. If human nature is fixed and unchanging Buddhism could not exist, because the quintessential goal of Buddhism – Awakening – would not be possible.

A range of Buddhist texts illuminates these points. The following discussion draws on Buddhist canons and their commentaries, as well as other literature. I also make use of the long tradition of Mahāyāna philosophy, including excerpts from the work of key thinkers. Buddhist traditions and forms of Buddhism in various countries emphasize and focus on different aspects of doctrine and practice. The doctrines I focus on here, whilst not consistently and continuously central in every Buddhist tradition, certainly underpin many basic facets of what constitutes a Buddhist worldview.

Dependent Arising

In Buddhism, the attainment of Awakening and realization of nirvana are possible because, ultimately, change is possible. The way in which change occurs is presented in Buddhist texts in a number of ways. One of the key principles relating to this is the doctrine of dependent arising. This doctrine is important in early Indian Buddhism and the Theravāda tradition and is modified in Mahāyāna; it tends to be known as the doctrine of *paṭicca-samuppāda*. In Pāli, *'paṭicca'* means 'cause' or 'condition' and *'samuppāda'* 'arising together'. The doctrine is based on the principle that nothing comes into being in the world without a cause. All phenomena arise in dependence on something else. Nothing comes into being independently. The principle can be described as:

> When this exists, that comes to be; from the arising of
> this, that arises. When this does not exist, that does not
> come to be; with the cessation of this, that ceases.[2]

According to the doctrine of dependent arising, all things come into being and pass away. All phenomena are in a constant state of motion, part of the flux and flow. And the doctrine relates to the entire phenomenal world we experience – and, importantly, to ourselves. To illustrate this doctrine by way of a concrete and easy example, here are reflections of a modern Buddhist practitioner on the causes and conditions of one particular plant flowering outside his kitchen window on a particular day:

Despite its seeming delicacy, the Lavatera outside my kitchen window would probably sustain on soil far poorer than that in my garden. It would probably thrive in a climate much drier than the last few damp English summers have been and it is reasonably resistant to pests and encroaching weeds. What it really would not survive, outside my kitchen window, is my not liking it. Plants that I don't like get no space in this small patch of London garden. If I didn't like it, it would not be there now. An absolutely crucial condition for the continued existence of this shrub is my desire to have it where it is. My taste in flowers is a significant condition for the existence of that particular plant, and my taste in flowers, of course, is itself conditioned. It depends, in part, on the way I was brought up, so my mother and father and their ideas of good and bad taste are important conditions for the existence of my Lavatera. If they had taught me differently, it would not be there. Indeed, if my mother and father had not met, at a tennis party, in Johannesburg in 1948 it would not be there, as I would not have been around to have planted it. If my mother had been too ill to attend a tennis party on that day, no Lavatera. Her good health on that day is an important condition in its life. And it follows that if my parents didn't exist in the first place, neither would our plant, so another important set of conditions for its flourishing is the history of my entire ancestry.[3]

The same doctrine is specifically applied to the coming into being and passing away of the human being. This is expressed as the circle of twelve causal links. Each aspect of a person comes into being dependent upon something else.[4] Although this is presented as a cycle (of existence) it does have a starting point, which is ignorance (in Sanskrit *avidyā* and in Pāli *avijjā*). The word *avidyā* is the Sanskrit word *vidyā*, meaning 'knowledge', with the negative prefix -*a*. This negative prefix does not only mean the exact opposite, like English prefixes non- or un-. It can also imply something that appears like the thing negated, but is not exactly it. This ignorance can appear as something other, it can appear as understanding, but is not. Each causally conditioned by the other, the twelve links are:

> . . . dependant on ignorance, volitions arise, dependant on volitions, consciousness arises, dependant on consciousness, name-and-form arise, dependant on name-and-form, the six senses arise, dependant on the six senses, contact arises, dependant on contact, feeling arises, dependant on feelings, craving arises, dependant on craving, clinging arises, dependant on clinging, existence arises, dependant on existence birth arises, dependant on birth old age and death arise. . .[5]

The twelve links describe how a human being comes into existence. The process starts with ignorance. From this a human being comes to be formed, piece by piece. Consciousness arises, then the human body. The human form gains senses, and these interact with the world. From this contact, desires arise. These desires are both everyday mundane desires and existential ones, including the desire to continue to exist. The human body wears out eventually, but the impulses, mental habits, and desire to continue to exist mean the entity begins the cycle again. The twelve links are taught as a cycle, a cycle of existences, as the human being in constant motion, coming into being, experiencing the world, feeling desire. Every aspect of this process, the process of life and death, comes about dependent on something else. Consciousness, as an aspect of this process, like all of human nature, comes into being dependent on certain other conditions, and it ceases to be accordingly as well. Thus, human nature is not static and unchanging, quite the contrary. And the possibility of the transformation of human nature into something that may be beyond our current level of comprehension, is a fundamental part of the foundations of the Buddhist tradition. Without it Buddhism itself would not be possible.

To judge a woman as inferior to a man because of her 'female nature' is undoctrinal, according to dependent arising. Negative characteristics of women identified in chapter 2 – that women are wicked, vile, debased, cruel without pity, detestable, devious, weak, lacking intelligence – are each aspects of human nature. Human nature is, according to the teaching of dependent arising, causally conditioned. It is subject to constant change. Therefore, if a person is cruel or devious, their cruelty or deviousness is causally conditioned. Their cruelty or deviousness has arisen, come into being, as a result of a certain set of circumstances or conditions. There will always be reasons why a person exhibits cruelty towards others, and those reasons, like all things, are subject to change. Once those reasons change, once the conditions that have caused the cruelty to arise cease to exist, then the cruelty will cease to exist.

Take as an example a woman who is a wife and mother, whose husband treats her badly, and whose extended family make constant unwanted demands on her time. They frequently request that she also take care of the other children in the family, as well as her own, never taking her needs into account. They expect her to do more than her fair share of the domestic chores, and criticize her if she does not. They don't value her opinion, nor her contribution to the upkeep of the family. Such a woman might, when under duress, be unkind to her own children, without wanting to be, but because of the stress caused by the treatment she herself receives. But if she were to leave the marriage and find better circumstances for herself that made her happier, the cause of her unkindness would cease. Once the cause of the unkindness is taken away, the behaviour ceases. It is even possible to say, in relation to this, that if all of the women around you are cruel and devious, as Aśvaghoṣa relates, or King Udaya complains, maybe that is because of something *you* are doing. Maybe *you* are the cause? Maybe if you treated them better, they would treat you better. If the conditions that made them act negatively (i.e. you) changed, the negative behaviour would change.

On the question of low or weak intelligence, Buddhist texts acknowledge that there are some who are less able than others, but also that this aspect, again, is subject to change. In a well-known episode from the legendary account of the Buddha's life, when he is deciding whether to teach the truth he has discovered, it is said he surveys all beings in the world and sees some able to comprehend his teachings, and others less so:

> . . . the Blessed One saw beings with little dust in their eyes and those with much dust in their eyes, with keen faculties and with dull faculties, with good qualities and with bad qualities, easy to teach and difficult to teach, and a few who dwelt seeing blame and fear in the other world. Just as in a pond of blue or red or white lotuses, some lotuses might be born in the water, grow up in the water, and thrive while submerged in the water, without rising up from the water; some lotuses might be born in the water, grow up in the water and stand at an even level with the water; some lotuses might be born in the water, grow up in the water but would rise up from the water and stand without being soiled by the water – so too, surveying the world with the eye of a Buddha, the Blessed One saw beings with little dust in their eyes and with much dust in their eyes, with keen faculties and with dull faculties, with good qualities and with bad qualities, easy to teach and difficult to teach, and a few who dwelt seeing blame and fear in the other world.[6]

This is, as you can see, not a gendered example. There is no suggestion that women are the beings blinded by the dust in their eyes. And for those for whom growth is difficult, all is not lost. Buddhist texts advocate activities and exercises that enable a person to overcome their lack of intelligence, such as, for instance, keeping the company of wise friends or learning to ask better questions. On keeping the right company, the *Dhammapada* says, in a chapter on the wise:

> If you see a wise man who
> Sees your faults, tells what is blameworthy,
> You should keep company with such a one
> As a pointer-out of treasures:
> If you keep company with such a one,
> It becomes better, not worse, for you.[7]

According to the doctrine of dependent arising, all things arise in dependence on conditions, and change when those conditions change. This is the case for human beings as well as for all of the phenomenal world. Women are bound by this law to exactly the same extent as men. All aspects of a woman's character, personality, and nature are subject to dependent arising. The only possible argument that could challenge this would be that women are not human, and thereby their nature is not human nature. As noted in chapter 2, I have only ever found one instance of this in the Buddhist writings with which I am familiar. And, certainly, this one assertion of a single, unnamed Tibetan commentator cannot be taken as 'the Buddhist view'. I have advocated elsewhere that in instances such as these, rather than taking the words of one author, or sometimes perhaps several, as 'the Buddhist view' it is better to understand these as the words of one monk (in this case), who happened to have authored a commentary on the teachings of a Buddhist teacher.[8] As we will see in Part II of this volume, there are myriad historical examples of eminent women who did practise, made good progress on the path and became teachers, demonstrating – if it needs to be demonstrated – that women, like men, can progress on the path to Awakening and thereby must be human and have human nature.

The doctrine of dependent arising offers a way to look backwards at what caused an event to come about in the first place. The same causal nexus, however, applied to a forward projecting model, can account for Buddhist ethics and the Buddhist notion of no-self. The graphic on the next page demonstrates this.

The solid lines represent all of the possible causal conditions that caused an event to happen. The dotted lines represent the possible outcomes of an event that happened today. To demonstrate, let's say that, today, you told a lie. You told the lie to two people. Your lie affected the behaviour of those two people, and each one of them told other people. Your lie had multiple impacts. Because of your lie, you were not able to sleep, worrying that the lie might be discovered. The next day you were very tired. Your fatigue impacted on your actions. The changes to your actions affected several people, and caused them to behave differently, which in turn had an impact on

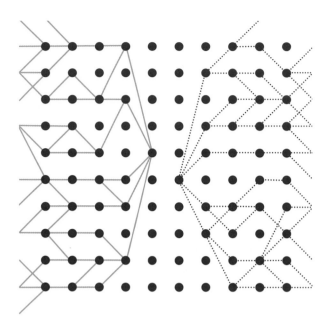

Dependent Arising and Ethics

other people, people you do not come into contact with. In this micro graph that represents just a few outcomes of a single moment, we see that one lie can produce many possible consequences. If we now imagine ourselves within each of these trajectories, that is, the person we are the day we tell the lie, and the person we become as a result of the consequences of the lie, we can also see multiple possibilities with regard to our self – who we are and who we can become. This is all possible whether we are male or female. And whilst some of the choices we make day-to-day might be influenced by our gender to some extent, because we are all human we have the opportunity to make these choices.[9]

The Doctrine of No-Self

The Buddhist doctrine of no-self has often been misunderstood. The doctrine does not posit that there is no existent self (which would be counterintuitive), but rather that there is no fixed and permanent essence to the self. The term used for the doctrine in Sanskrit is

I Hear Her Words

anātman, in Pāli *anattā*. From the use of this word we can see how some of the Buddha's ideas were formed via his response to the world around him. The Buddhist doctrine of no-self was a response to the Brahmanical worldview prevalent in the historical milieu from which Buddhism arose.

A key aspect of Brahmanical worldview is that of *ātman*, the self or soul that transmigrates. The Buddhist doctrine of *anātman* essentially says, no, not that.[10] There is no eternal soul that has an essence that continually transmigrates through lifetimes. The Buddhist doctrine of no-self is linked to the notion of dependent arising; the self, who we are, is subject to change. Who we are is causally conditioned. This is easy to see if we think about our parents, and the physical similarity that most of us share with our parents or other family members. Our physical self, then, we can understand as causally conditioned. With regard to our personality and character traits, some of these we can also easily understand as causally conditioned.

Early Buddhist teaching on the nature of the self focuses on the constituent parts that comprise human life. Each person is made up of five component parts, usually called aggregates. They are material form, feeling, perception, volition, and consciousness. Men are not composed of different aggregate parts than women. Men and women are made of the same parts. Each of these aggregate parts are impermanent, they arise on the basis of conditions, and pass away when the conditions cease to exist. The body begins to form at conception and, following death, begins the process of decomposition.

The English word 'aggregate' is used here to emphasize that each of these parts of which a person is comprised are each themselves made up of many other parts. The material body is made up of flesh, bones, tissue, and so forth, which are themselves a combination of the elements, earth, water, fire, air. Feeling is produced from a combination of factors. If we touch something that is hot, our nervous system sends messages to the brain to remove our hand, because of the unpleasant feeling. We become angry with ourselves for being careless, or scared of the physical pain and any potential risk of further pain. Exactly how we respond to each experience we have is causally conditioned.

Applying these ideas to the negative statements about women, it is easy to see they do not accord with this theory. The corporeal bodies of men and women are made of the same stuff. The bones of a man are made of the same material as the bones of a woman. Their skin is the same. The components that comprise the human eye the same. A male ear is not formed differently to a female ear. Limbs, joints, internal organs, are all constituted the same. Therefore, for the Buddha to say women are foul, or any comment in the texts explicitly stating that the female body is vile, filthy, or base, can only be true if all human bodies (including male ones) are foul.

Similarly, deceit, villainous will, manipulation, being mean-spirited: these are all component parts of the spectrum of human behaviour and experience. Each is born from feelings, perception, volition, consciousness. All are impermanent and subject to change. Each person feels, thinks, wills, or enacts such things at certain times. Such feelings, thoughts, and volitions come and go in any human psyche. There are good feelings and bad feelings that come and go. Perceptions alter, moments of consciousness arise and pass away. To say that one woman's feeling of greed, at one moment, should define her is antithetical to this teaching. To say that a woman has a consciousness filled with deceit at all moments, and for that she should be maligned, denies the reality that change is not only possible but necessary.

As with dependent arising, so with the doctrine of no-self. Both are doctrines central to Buddhism – both are part of a system that advocates that human nature is malleable and subject to change. Human nature is shaped by circumstance and can change in different circumstances. Throughout the history of the tradition, many Buddhist thinkers have commented on the false view of a separate, permanent self. The best-known earliest example of a doctrinal exposition on the nature of the self is in a text in which a monk, Nāgasena, is in conversation with a king.[11] In attempting to teach the king about the idea that there is no fixed, permanent essence to the self, Nāgasena espouses that, in reality, there is no Nāgasena. He tells the king that Nāgasena is merely a word, a name, and if we look and try to find who or what Nāgasena is, we cannot find anything that constitutes this person we see in front of us. Nāgasena asks, are any of the component parts that make up his body the real Nāgasena? Is it his hair, his teeth, nails, skin, bones, kidney, liver, heart, intestines? None of these are Nāgasena, and neither are any of the other aggregates. Applying this to statements about women, there is, in reality, nothing there that constitutes a 'woman'. 'Woman' is an empty word, just as the name Nāgasena is only a name, and if we look we see no entity can be apprehended.

For Mahāyāna Buddhism it is the same. Featuring the laywoman Gaṅgottarā, one Mahāyāna text relates a conversation between her and the Buddha, a dialogue in which she demonstrates complete and full comprehension of his teachings. The nature of the self comes up several times. When the Buddha greets her, as she approaches, he asks her 'Where do you come from?' Gaṅgottarā answers that, if the self is illusory (that is, nonexistent), how can she have come from anywhere? There is no self to have done the coming, no self to have been, initially, somewhere else. There is no self within the 'you' pronoun in the sentence. She then takes up all the component parts that comprise the human person, and questions the Buddha as to why, when the self is illusory, he persists in even talking about its constituent parts:

> 'If all things are empty space, why does [the Buddha]
> speak of form, feeling, perception, volition, and
> consciousness. . .'
>
> The Buddha told Gaṅgottarā: 'When I speak of a
> "self", for example, although I express the concept of a
> word, actually the nature of a "self" is inapprehensible.
> I speak of form, but in reality the nature of form is also
> inapprehensive, and so it is with the other[s]. . . Just as
> we cannot find water in mirages, so we cannot find a
> nature in form, and so it is with the others. . .' [12]

According to this answer, no aspect of our form, nature, or being is graspable or comprehensible – by implication this includes female nature.

Other Mahāyāna philosophers made similar evaluations on the nature of the self and the world in which we live. The phenomena we experience do not have true substance, are empty perceptions:

Change and no change, suffering and ease, the self and
   not-self,
the lovely and repulsive – just one suchness is the
   emptiness they are.

Perceptions – mere words, so the leaders tell us,
Perceptions forsaken and gone, and the door is open to
   the beyond
Those who succeed in ridding themselves of perception
They have reached the beyond, fulfil the teacher's
   commandments.[13]

Nāgārjuna, the most influential of all Mahāyāna Buddhist
philosophers, also writes about emptiness, and the nonexistence of
entities we conceive of as existent:

Those who see essence and essential difference
And entities and nonentities,
They do not see
The truth taught by the Buddha.[14]

Another influential Mahāyāna philosopher, Vasubandhu, even
goes so far as to indicate that when a person walks from A to B, the
person who arrives at B is not the same as the person who left A. Only
fools, he says, see an entity and a thing called 'walking'.[15] Liberation,
or Awakening, can only be achieved, according to Vasubandhu, by
completely eradicating all forms of belief in a self. In response to a
question about why an individual might have the experience, 'I am
happy, I am not happy', part of Vasubandhu's reply is:

People of ordinary intellect come to believe 'I am white; I
am dark; I am fat; I am thin; I am old: I am young.' They
identify themselves with these things.[16]

Utilizing these categories of existence and experience – 'I am a woman,
you are a man, I am honest, you are deceitful' – needs to be abandoned
for any who seek liberation.

References to other key aspects of doctrine and practice are often
conjoined with these philosophical evaluations of the nature of the

self. The need for compassion towards all beings is often particularly linked with Mahāyāna Buddhism, although it is present in the majority of Buddhist systems of thought. Any practitioner who seeks to distil perceptions as 'mere words', who aims to understand the perceptions of self and no-self as ultimately empty, should, as well, according to this text, have 'an even mind towards the whole world'. They should cultivate 'the notion of father and mother' towards all others. They should have 'benevolence and a friendly mind' towards others, be 'amenable' and 'soft in speech'.[17]

Another teaching that relates to the doctrine of no-self is ignorance, or *avidyā*, as noted above. To perceive things that are impermanent as permanent is ignorance. Schools of Mahāyāna do not all concur on the exact nature of ignorance, nor how it manifests in relation to perception of self. But for certain philosophers and proponents of the various schools of Mahāyāna Buddhism, *avidyā* results in seeing unity where there is plurality, permanence where there is transience, and universality in place of what is unique and particular.

Universality is a characteristic of condemnations of women and their traits, which typically paint all women the same stripe. In reality, of course, each woman, as with each man, is unique. The human condition is transitory, not permanent. As all things are subject to change, and ultimately empty, to say women's nature is not, and to decry it as static and unchanging, is a form of this type of ignorance, *avidyā*.

For Dharmakīrti, another important Mahāyāna philosopher, who lived during the sixth or seventh centuries, ignorance is responsible for a deluded person seeing momentary things to be lasting, unchanging, permanent. For Dharmakīrti, the false view of a self is the foundation for other aspects of ignorance:

> Once [the notion of] self exists, the notion of other [arises
> and] from this distinction between self and other [is
> born] grasping and aversion: bound by these two, all the
> moral faults arise.[18]

It is only once we have created a perception of another person or being, separate to us, that we can begin to experience aversion to them.

Śāntideva, encountered in chapter 2, is another influential Mahāyāna thinker who writes on the nature of the self. Śāntideva's best-known work is the *Bodhicaryāvatāra*. The focus in this work is compassion, which is a key tenet of Mahāyāna Buddhism. Advocating compassion towards all beings and at all times, Śāntideva reflects on the nature of anger and hostility towards other beings:

> I feel no anger towards bile and the like, even though they cause intense suffering. Why am I angry with the sentient? They too have reasons for their anger.

> . . . Beings are by nature pleasant. So anger towards them is as inappropriate as it would be towards the sky if full of acrid smoke.[19]

Śāntideva's *Compendium of Training* cites many examples that disparage women. To say that all women are foul, detestable, villainous, wicked, ungrateful, deceitful, morally inept, manipulative, does not strike the same chord that Śāntideva aims for here. Arguably the comments on women are not meant as statements of fact, but rather as a means to disable men's desire for them.[20] That is to say, Śāntideva does not truly believe that women are foul and deceitful, but rather that it is useful for a monk to think about them this way. If a monk develops a dislike of women, and seeks to avoid them, this will help him in his pursuit of the goal. Looked at in this way, assertions that women are foul are teachings aimed at monks and other male practitioners. They are not intended as statements of fact. The truth is the relentless need for compassion, and to develop the perception that in reality there is no self, and no 'male' or 'female'.

In a different chapter of the *Bodhicaryāvatāra*, Śāntideva offers another teaching that is, again, not a comment on the nature of the world as we experience it, but a way of seeing and perceiving the world that is useful for the adept, or skilled practitioner, to develop. In this chapter, Śāntideva teaches that the religious adept should practise exchange of self and other. He teaches that we are all connected, and connected to such an extent that any suffering experienced by one entity is suffering for all. Suffering is not 'owned' by the person experiencing it, therefore if others suffer we all suffer. In Śāntideva's words:

> I should dispel the suffering of others because it is suffering like my own suffering. I should help others too because of their nature as beings, which is like my own being. . .

> One should acknowledge oneself as having faults and others as oceans of virtues. Then one should meditate on renouncing one's own self-identity and accepting other people.

> In the same way that the hands and other limbs are loved because they from part of the body, why are embodied creatures not likewise loved because they form part of the universe? . . .

> Therefore, in the same way that one desires to protect oneself from affliction, grief, and the like, so an attitude of protectiveness and of compassion should be practiced towards the world.[21]

According to this view, which is reminiscent of the Mahāyāna ethic mentioned in chapter 1 – not to disparage others and praise oneself – even if another person is cruel, devious, ungrateful, immoral, or indeed of low intelligence, the correct response to them is one of compassion. Vilification of others is not appropriate for several reasons:

1. Disparagement or unjust criticism of others causes harm.
2. To only acknowledge faults in others and not in oneself is egotistical and antithetical to the aim of realizing selflessness.
3. One should experience concern for others, and seek to protect them from harm.

Compassion is the most fitting response because, essentially, any faults of others are causally conditioned. Also, because of the interconnected nexus of conditions that underlies human social life – because we are not as separate as we think we are – any suffering of one is related to, connected to, and can be shared by others. Any harm that we enact can bring bad consequences for us, as well as for the person to whom we do the harm.

Emptiness and Sexual Transformation

As we have seen, when a woman is perceived as trouble for men this is primarily because of two issues, her body or her traits and characteristics. Another way in which the body and biological sex enter the picture in Buddhism is in narrative episodes on sexual transformation. The idea of spontaneous sexual transformation is not an exclusively South Asian phenomenon, however, it does appear in both Brahmanical and Indian Buddhist texts, and seems to be a literary device that rather captured the imagination of early and early medieval South Asian storytellers and writers. Within the Indian Buddhist tradition, its presentation in – mainly – Indian Mahāyāna texts has received a great deal of scholarly attention. Scholars express a range of views. These concern the extent to which the theme of sexual transformation is intended to illustrate that Buddhist doctrine advocates for gender equality. The key debates in Buddhist studies have been fashioned around questions such as, 'Is it or is it not an assertion that sex and gender are unimportant?' and 'Does a woman need to change into a man to make progress on the path?'

The Mahāyāna notion of emptiness can be seen as a development of the doctrine of dependent arising. As all things arise in dependence on others, and cease to be when those conditions cease, they can be said to be empty of inherent existence. Things do not exist independently, are not self-originated, are ultimately interwoven into the flux and flow of conditions. A table is created by raw materials such as wood and metal, and a carpenter is necessary to construct it. The table ceases to exist if it is taken apart or breaks. Therefore, it has no inherent existence and our conceptual category of 'table' is empty. In episodes of sexual transformation, our categories of sex and gender, male and female, are demonstrated to be empty, to have no inherent existence in and of themselves. Especially since the 1980s, a great deal of scholarly debate has centred on how, exactly, such examples relate to views about – and treatment of – women in the history of Buddhism. The same examples have been described as the preconditions for the idea that women need to be reborn as men to make progress on the path.

A passage in the *Vimalakīrtinirdeśa* is the best-known example of a story of sexual transformation. The *Vimalakīrtinirdeśa* is a Mahāyāna text, in which a layman, Vimalakīrti, proves himself to be more able than non-Mahāyāna monks. Śāriputra, one of the Buddha's direct disciples in early texts, is cast as the 'fall guy' in the *Vimalakīrtinirdeśa*; paling in wisdom and understanding compared to the great Vimalakīrti. In this following passage, one of the goddesses present teaches him a lesson on emptiness:

Śāriputra: Goddess, what prevents you from transforming yourself out of your female state?

Goddess: Although I have sought my 'female state' for these twelve years, I have not yet found it. Reverend Śāriputra, if a magician were to incarnate a woman by magic, would you ask her, 'What prevents you from transforming yourself out of your female state?'

Śāriputra: No! Such a woman would not really exist, so what would there be to transform?

Goddess: Just so, reverend Śāriputra, all things do not really exist. Now, would you think, 'What prevents one whose nature is that of a magical incarnation from transforming herself out of her female state?'

Thereupon, the goddess employed her magical power to cause the elder Śāriputra to appear in her form and to cause herself to appear in his form. Then the goddess, transformed into Śāriputra, said to Śāriputra, transformed into a goddess, "Reverend Śāriputra, what prevents you from transforming yourself out of your female state?" And Śāriputra, transformed into the goddess, replied, 'I no longer appear in the form of a male! My body has changed into the body of a woman! I do not know what to transform!'

The goddess continued, 'If the elder could again change out of the female state, then all women could also change out of their female states. All women appear in the form of women in just the same way as the elder appears in the form of a woman. While they are not women in reality, they appear in the form of women. With this in mind, the Buddha said, "In all things, there is neither male nor female."' Then, the goddess released her magical power and each returned to his ordinary form. She then said to him, 'Reverend Śāriputra, what have you done with your female form?'

Śāriputra: I neither made it nor did I change it.

Goddess: Just so, all things are neither made nor changed, and that they are not made and not changed, that is the teaching of the Buddha.[22]

In the debate on the question of such episodes of sexual transformation, two polarized views have been expressed. In one of the earliest publications on this, Nancy Schuster argues that the phenomenon of sexual transformation appears to be illustrating something of what could perhaps be called a feminist agenda, in that it demonstrates that the conceptual categories of sex and gender are, ultimately, empty – used as it is in these episodes to illuminate the key Mahāyāna concept of *śūnyatā* (emptiness). She concludes her discussion of the topic by stating that:

'Changing the female body' is a narrative theme which was probably developed by Mahayanist writers in order to confront traditional Buddhist views of the spiritual limitations of women. . . [In Mahāyāna texts] . . . this notion is criticized and put in its proper place according to the perspective of the *śūnyavāda* [doctrine of emptiness]. In these texts, the supposition that maleness and femaleness are ultimately real is negated by the realization of the universal emptiness and sameness of all dharmas.[23]

In a publication that appeared a few years later, Diana Paul devotes about 30% of her book on women in Mahāyāna to the topic of sexual transformation. Paul attempts a survey of attitudes to sexuality and the body across a range of Buddhist texts, both Mahāyāna and non-Mahāyāna, and then provides translations of key scenes from Mahāyāna texts during which one type of sexual transformation or another occurs. Having studied some of the same texts as Schuster, Paul's view is quite different. She says:

> The Buddhist considered the body itself as imperfect and degenerate, whether in ascetic or erotic engagement. The body indicated imperfection and immorality. . . Since the feminine represented the deceptive and destructive temptress or 'daughter of evil', the feminine body represented imperfection, weakness, ugliness and impurity. Transformation of sex represented a transition from the imperfection and immorality of human beings (the female body) to the mental perfection of Bodhisattvas and Buddhas (the male body).[24]

Quite aside from the two opposing views exemplified by Nancy Schuster and Diana Paul's respective arguments, a third interpretation is possible. Perhaps these episodes are not intended as a comment on gender at all. Schooled as we are, in the modern world, in the scientific paradigm, it can be difficult for us to imagine worldviews outside of science. We understand biological sex as nontransmutable. Our sex organs grow as part of us, when we come into being in the womb. They are fixed and cannot be changed, unless we undergo surgery. This is a scientific view of sex, and one so ingrained it is almost impossible to imagine conceiving of biological sex in any other way. But, without science to guide us, how would we understand sex and different sex organs? It is not necessary to transpose a scientific or European

Enlightenment worldview onto ancient Indian ideas. And so it is unnecessary to wonder why key Buddhist texts use stories and images of sexual transformation to demonstrate the emptiness of existence and experience as conceptual categories. Perhaps there existed an understanding that transformation of sex was eminently possible, and, as such, represented an excellent example of emptiness.[25]

Another, related aspect of sexual transformation to consider is whether it is only sex that changes or gender as well. If merely biological sex transforms, and not one's gender, then the negative assessment of the narratives – that they are proposing a woman needs to change into a man – become unworkable. In Mahāyāna examples, as with Śāriputra and the goddess, bodies change but minds do not. Śāriputra maintains his own mind, as does the goddess. Śāriputra has the mind of the man in a female body, and the goddess vice versa. This can be compared with many Hindu narratives in which the transformation is more complete; a person who transforms has no memory that they were previously another sex.

Other Mahāyāna examples are similar, such as the example of Candrottarā discussed in chapter 2. The text about Candrottarā implies that she was an advanced bodhisattva when she was born, because as soon as she was born she grew to the size of an eight-year-old, and began reciting dharma. She gives profound teachings, which impact the audience such that they have 'no thought of desire, no hatred, no hostility, no greed, no delusion, no anger, no jealousy, no envy, no defilement of any kind, or other anguish'.[26] Other texts depict female teachers in Mahāyāna with analogous attributes. So those of female gender have qualities similar to an advanced bodhisattva.[27]

One question put to Candrottarā is, 'One cannot become a Buddha while being female. Why don't you change your sex now?' Candrottarā replies, 'the nature of emptiness cannot be changed or altered. This is true of all phenomena. [Consequently] how can I change my woman's body?' [that is, when it is already empty]. She then does change from a girl into a boy; she changes sex, and then continues to teach and help others in the same way she (or now he) had when female. So no change of gender is proffered. S/he still maintains her same mind, the mind of an advanced bodhisattva, who can teach in a profound

I Hear Her Words

way, no loss of memory of having been another gender is indicated, no taking on of male characteristics or qualities, she is the same, except that she is now biologically male.

In the well-known story in the *Saddharmapuṇḍarīkasūtra*, the *nāga* princess character changes sex. Like Candrottarā, the character and qualities of the person she is do not change after her change of biological sex. Therefore, I would argue that, in both cases, following the change of biological sex both remain gendered female. Their mental qualities, character, and attributes (to offer profound teachings or to act as an example to others) do not change once their sex changes. Whether the episodes and narratives are interpreted as misogynist, sexist, androcentric, or none of these depends on the extent to which one sees it through a lens that understands biological sex as a (generally) incontrovertible category of existence and experience. If it is not, if gender is the reality and biological sex the appearance, then we need to be discussing the question in different terms.[28]

These are the three possible ways to read the episodes on sexual transformation: that they are positive about women, negative about women, or not intended as a comment on sex and gender at all. Historically, the view sponsored by most Buddhist traditions tends towards the second; that the passages demonstrate women's bodies as 'wrong', and women need to transform into men so they might make progress on the path.

* * *

As we have seen, Buddhist doctrine does not support any claims for any inviolable aspects of human nature, nor harsh speech towards others. Compassion underpins every aspect of teaching and practice. Thereby, with regard to any human being we meet or come across, compassion should fortify all responses. The contempt for women in the texts highlighted in chapter 2 has no place in Buddhism. As demonstrated, it seems that some of the contempt may be due to male fear and anxiety about women. Other negative accounts may have been included in the literature for teaching purposes and not to support a divisive worldview. When male anxiety is the issue, the right response is one of compassion. By this I mean that if I were to come across a man who expressed contempt for women born from anxiety, I would not be a good Buddhist practising the precepts if I (psychologically) beat him with a stick for it. The right response is compassion, always and unreservedly.[29]

In the inscription that begins this chapter, the twelfth-century Chinese nun Zhitong talks about developing awareness of the nondifferentiation of phenomena. When entering a bathhouse to take advantage of what it offers, one might muse on the nature of water. Whilst usually considered something that cleans, in reality water might contain dirt. When reflecting on the vital questions discussed in the last two chapters, whether we understand the 'dirt' to be women themselves or views about women, as Zhitong points out, the ultimate aim is not to sift the dirt from the water and then try to scrub ourselves clean with that, but to realize the nondifferentiation between water and dirt; not to collect the dirt into an impenetrable ball to use in an attack, but to take a bath anyway, regardless of any imperfections the water might carry. This stands as a good metaphor for the topics we turn to next. As we will see in Part II of this volume, countless Buddhist women through the centuries have done just that.

Part II

Voices Through the Centuries

CHAPTER 4

PORTRAITS OF
BUDDHIST WOMEN

Her springs and autumns were seventy-eight . . . she died at
Guangtian temple. The disciples lament that the sun of wisdom
has sunk its rays, grieve that the lamp of compassion is forever
extinguished. [We] held her funeral according to the scriptures,
and collected the relics.

Excerpt from an inscription at Bao Shan entitled 'Reliquary for the
great nun Dharma Master Puxiang of Guangtian temple'[1]

The disciples of the Chinese nun Puxiang lamented her passing. In their collective sorrow that the 'sun of wisdom has sunk its rays' they have, as well as grieving, done something important; they have created a record, carved into the rock, of the life of an important female Buddhist teacher from seventh-century China. And these disciples are not alone in their efforts. In fact, we have an extraordinary amount of material on the lives of Buddhist women down the ages; more than one might imagine, given the prejudice Buddhist women have suffered and continue to endure.

In this chapter, I offer portrayals of Buddhist women within the tradition. I begin with ancient India and the first Buddhist nuns. There is a huge amount of material available about the lives of many early Buddhist nuns who, the texts tell us, were direct disciples of the Buddha. In this chapter, I retell the biographies of three of the best known of these: Dhammadinnā, Bhaddā Kuṇḍalakesā, and Paṭācārā. One source we have for understanding something of their lives is a collection of poetry apparently composed by the nuns themselves, in their own words: the *Therīgāthā*.[2] I have chosen these three biographies because they illustrate gender-related issues present in many of the biographies and stories of early Indian Buddhist women. Whilst we cannot know for sure that nuns with these names really existed, or if their biographies are historically accurate, similar biographies can be found again and again of Buddhist women throughout the history of the tradition.

Following the accounts of Dhammadinnā, Bhaddā Kuṇḍalakesā, and Paṭācārā, I turn to early medieval China. We are lucky to have a good source, composed in the sixth century, that relates the lives of forty-six of the first Buddhist nuns who lived between the fourth and sixth centuries. It appears to have been composed some centuries after they lived. I present the biographies of three nuns: Zhu Jingjian, the first Buddhist nun in China, An Lingshou, who became a nun despite pressure from her family to marry, and Daoxing, whose life was deeply impacted by a rival nun from another Chinese religious tradition, Daoism.

Next, I move on to the modern period and discuss some other women from East Asian Buddhist traditions. From this period as well, we have some material that was authored by Buddhist women themselves. First, I relate the life of a seventeenth-century Chinese woman, Qiyuan Xinggang, quoting from some of her own writings. I then give an account of Chiyo-ni, who we have already encountered as the best known of all female haiku masters in Japan, and sometimes called the greatest female haiku master that ever lived. This chapter concludes with a biography of a Buddhist woman from twentieth-century Thailand, Kaew Sianglam (1901–1991). Her biography is part of a collection recently brought to light by scholar of Thai Buddhism Martin Seeger. In all these life stories, we see and hear of the struggles of Buddhist nuns and Buddhist women throughout the history of the tradition. Such struggles continue to reverberate today.

What is striking about the biographies and writings by and about women is how similar their struggles are across place and time. An array of archaeological and textual evidence reveals that, down the centuries, and in countries the world over, Buddhist women have struggled to be accepted as accomplished practitioners and as the teachers and leaders that many were. Despite this, notwithstanding the challenges and ongoing disapproval they experienced, they thrived anyway. And they did so with such resilience, aptitude, and grace that their stories were passed down to us, and so can be told again today.

Early Buddhist Nuns in India

In the early Indian setting, we find a rich and diverse biographical tradition of both monks and nuns. The *Therīgāthā*, verses of elder nuns, and its male counterpart, the *Theragāthā*, verses of elder monks, are the primary source for many of these. The stories are told for a number of reasons. The earliest biographies date to (at least) a few hundred years after the death of the Buddha. At this time, Buddhism was flourishing in north India and the biographies appear to be, in part, used to attract religious converts. They served to inspire and, specifically for women, to communicate that whatever circumstances you might find yourself in – with a father, for instance, who refuses to allow you to become a nun – and however limited your opportunity may be, advancement on the path is always possible.

The texts I have used as a basis for these three accounts are the words of the nuns themselves in the *Therīgāthā*, as well as biographies and discourses from the Pāli canon, a list of pre-eminent nuns from the canon and also later Pāli commentaries.[3] Here I focus on the Pāli accounts from the Theravāda tradition to demonstrate how biographies can vary even within one Buddhist tradition. Similar variation also occurs between traditions and when biographies are translated into different languages. The Pāli canon and commentaries were composed in two separate historical periods and different places and hence present, at times, incompatible attitudes to and portrayals of women. As I will show, these texts and the other evidence we have about the lives of Buddhist women are not completely reliable as historical evidence.

Biographical accounts of Dhammadinnā alter over the centuries. She changes from being portrayed as an esteemed teacher, with a profound comprehension of the teachings that she deftly communicates, to a subservient wife who decides to follow the Buddha because her husband does. One of her later biographies even dismisses the possibility that she could have had such a profound comprehension of the teachings herself. The second account, of Bhaddā Kuṇḍalakesā, shows another way in which the stories of women's lives can change. An episode in the biography of Bhaddā Kuṇḍalakesā concerning her conversion from Jainism to Buddhism changes considerably between early and later versions. This change does not negatively reflect on Bhaddā. Both accounts portray her as a wise and intelligent woman. In the first instance she converts as a result of a realization whilst meditating in a cremation ground, and in the second instance she is defeated in debate by one of the Buddha's chief disciples, Sāriputta.[4] The third biography, of Paṭācārā, demonstrates further aspects of these stories that have come down to us. First, that the name attached to each might not have been the actual name of the nun whose life story is being told, and second, how stories of different early Buddhist women, if they had similar features, might have become confused with one another during the long transmission process of the Buddhist tradition – oral and written.[5]

Dhammadinnā

The *Therīgāthā* verse attributed to Dhammadinnā is:

> She who has given rise to the wish for freedom
> And is set on it, shall be clear in mind.
> One whose heart is not caught in the pleasures of the
>   senses,
> One who is bound upstream, will be freed.[6]

The fullest accounts of Dhammadinnā's life are based around an important discourse given by her in the canon. This discourse is a question and answer session between Dhammadinnā – as the teacher – and a male lay disciple, Visākha. There is no biographical information on Dhammadinnā in this discourse, which focuses wholly on her teaching. This discourse, however, comes to be the basis of Dhammadinnā's biography.

The discourse begins with the lay disciple approaching Dhammadinnā at the Bamboo Grove, in the town of Rājagaha. As he greets her, his actions reveal the great respect he has for her as a teacher. He pays homage to her and sits down, respectfully, to one side before asking her a series of questions. In his study of three versions of this discourse in Pāli, Tibetan, and Chinese, Bhikkhu Anālayo notes that Visākha's questioning of Dhammadinnā follows a similar pattern in all three:

> Behind these topics, a recurrent pattern can be discerned
> which proceeds from relatively simple and innocuous
> questions to intricate and profound matters.[7]

The first question Visākha puts to Dhammadinnā is about *sakkāya*, a term usually translated as 'identity' or 'personality', although neither of these terms, in this instance, fully indicate the gist of Visākha's question. Visākha is essentially asking about the nature of existence, and his question could be better rendered in English as 'Why do we exist?', 'Why do I exist?', 'Why do you exist?', or 'How and why does existence come about?'. Dhammadinnā answers that we exist because of the five aggregates that combine to enable a human being to exist: material form, feeling, perception, volition, and consciousness. These things, she says, combined with an accompanying clinging to existence, are the basis of each person's coming into being. Next, Visākha asks from where existence originated. This is a deeper 'why' question. It is as if he is asking more emphatically, in response to the answer to the first, 'Yes, but *why exactly* are we constituted of these five things combined with a clinging?' Dhammadinnā replies that the deeper basis is craving: we exist because we crave it; once we have been born into one life we long for our existence not to end, so we are reborn.[8] Visākha then inquires as to the cessation of identity, or existence, and the way leading to cessation. In order for identity to cease, Dhammadinnā tells him, you must let go, that is, essentially, ultimately, let go of your craving for continued existence. And to get to the point of being able to let go, you must follow the path set out by the Buddha; the way leading to cessation.[9]

Dhammadinnā's answer connects back to the discussion in chapter 3 on the aggregates and women's nature. The aggregates, all that make up the human being, are, essentially, mind and matter. Material form – the body – holds biological sex, and feeling, perception, will, and consciousness are aspects of the mind and mental events, or a combination of mind and body reacting to the world together. Human nature and therefore women's nature is accounted for within the aggregates. In this instance, it is the female teacher who knows and comprehends the meaninglessness of categorizing, classifying, and clinging to our categories of existence, which implicitly includes the categories of sex and gender.

The remainder of the discourse involves Visākha posing question after question to Dhammadinnā on equally central points of doctrine and practice. Dhammadinnā answers each one fully, completely, comprehensively. Finally, Visākha brings up the topic of nirvana, at which point Dhammadinnā stops his questioning, telling him he has reached the limits of his line of questioning without realizing it. The reason he does not realize it is because he does not comprehend nirvana, which is the end of the path and about which nothing can be said.

In the earlier biographical accounts of Dhammadinnā her authoritative discourse with Visākha is mentioned, not by name, but by recounting that she answered questions from a lay follower. This discourse is said to be the reason the Buddha describes her as the best teacher amongst all the nuns who are teachers. The biographical accounts begin by tracing Dhammadinnā's previous lives during eras of previous Buddhas. They begin in the time of the first Buddha, Padumuttara. She was born a servant in a household in a town called Haṃsavatī. One day, when going about her chores, she made an offering of some food to one of the Buddha's disciples. After the disciple accepted this from her, she offered more. Seeing this, her master was impressed with her kindness and so made her his daughter-in-law, marrying her to his son. Some time after her wedding, she accompanied her new mother-in-law to see the Buddha, who praised a nun as an excellent teacher. Hearing this, Dhammadinnā was moved and aspired to one day receive such acclaim herself. Buddha Padumuttara predicted this would happen to her as a result of her devotion.

Following her birth under Buddha Padumuttara, Dhammadinnā then journeyed on through lifetimes and was born during the era of Buddha Kassapa. At that time, she was one of the seven daughters of a king. All seven desired to follow the Buddha and renounce the world, but were prohibited from doing so by their father. Instead, they practised the holy life at home.[10] Her final birth was during the era of the historical Buddha Gotama. She was born in the town of Rājagaha into a merchant family. She was married young, and her husband, hearing a discourse by the Buddha, attained to an exalted religious state. She then decided to renounce the world and follow the Buddha herself, and soon attained the higher state of nirvana.

Up to this juncture the biographies of Dhammadinnā are fairly consistent. At this point, however, they diverge, and we begin to see how portraits of women can change. In biographical accounts composed centuries later, Dhammadinnā changes from the exemplary teacher to a subservient wife. The later accounts go into great detail on her relationship with her husband.

After her husband Visākha had seen the Buddha, he returned home. Usually, if Dhammadinnā was looking out of the window upon his arrival, he would smile at her. But on this occasion, he passed by without smiling. She wondered what she had done. She asked Visākha if she had done something wrong. He told her she had not, but that he had realized the truth taught by the Buddha and so they could not live together in love anymore. He said, 'Having heard the dispensation of the teacher, I understand the supreme dharma.'[11] In response to her husband's religious experience she decided that she would renounce the world herself. Visākha then prepared her and sent her to the nuns in a golden palanquin:

> Having bathed her in perfumed water, adorned her
> in all her ornaments, sat her in a golden palanquin,
> surrounded her with a group of relatives, he took her
> to the convent [ceremonially], as a citydweller doing
> veneration with perfumed flowers. 'Noble Ones', he
> said, 'Dhammadinnā wishes to go forth'.[12]

But Dhammadinnā was not happy living amongst the nuns. After a short time, she decided to go to the village to live in seclusion. There she soon attained nirvana. After this, she decided to return to Rājagaha, accompanied by the nuns' community. Visākha, hearing of this, wondered why she had come back so soon. So he decided to test her level of attainment.

This decision leads to the famous discourse. She easily answered all his questions 'as if cutting a lotus stalk with a sharp knife'. The biographies then all end in a similar vein to the original canonical discourse; the exchange was reported to the Buddha and he praised Dhammadinnā and heralded her pre-eminent status as accomplished teacher. The Buddha tells Visākha that he would have answered his questions just as Dhammadinnā did, which is a motif used in the canon to authorize disciples as teachers. One commentary, however, puts in a caveat that destabilizes this exposition of Dhammadinnā as wise teacher. According to this commentary, the Buddha had used his omniscience to enable her to know the answers to the questions.[13]

The accounts paint different pictures of Dhammadinnā's initiative and intelligence. In the later biographies, her husband is the first to follow the Buddha and attain great religious insight. In all later versions, upon hearing a discourse by the Buddha, Visākha experiences religious insight. Then he shuns Dhammadinnā when he returns home. She stands as a woman rejected by her husband, not comprehending what she might have done wrong. It is Visākha's role to explain the situation to her. In a thoroughgoing reversal of the original canonical discourse, he is the one with knowledge and understanding while Dhammadinnā is ignorant. Dhammadinnā understands but then asks whether the Buddha's dharma is open to women as well, further showing a deference and reversed hierarchy of knower/questioner. Once she decides for herself to renounce the world and follow the Buddha, the texts record that Visākha *took her* to the nuns, sometimes ceremonially. In this case, her husband is very much the agent; he bathes and dresses her in her finery and brings together relatives for the ceremonial journey. It is only once ordained, and when the commentarial biographies begin to mirror the canonical text, that Dhammadinnā regains full agency. And this only in some accounts, since in one commentary it is the Buddha's omniscience, rather than her own individual intellect, that produces her insightful answers to Visākha's questions.

Bhaddā Kuṇḍalakesā

Bhaddā Kuṇḍalakesā was a Jain convert. The *Therīgāthā* verses attributed to Bhaddā Kuṇḍalakesā refer to this feature of her biographical account, her history as a Jain practitioner. Although her conversion is mentioned in all accounts that follow, how her conversion came about is recorded differently in the various biographies. And these differences are noteworthy. Her *Therīgāthā* verses are as follows:

> Hair cut, wearing dirt,
> with one robe, I wandered previously,
> thinking there was fault where there was no fault,
> and that there was no fault where there was fault.

Leaving from my daytime dwelling on Mount
    Gijjhakūṭa,
I saw the stainless Buddha, attended by his community
    of monastics.

Having bent my knee, having paid homage,
I stood face to face with him, hands in the gesture
    of respect.
'Come, Bhaddā,' he said,
that was my ordination.

I travelled over Aṅga and Magadha, Vajjī, Kāsi, and
    Kosala.
for 50 years I enjoyed the alms of the kingdoms,
free from debt.

Indeed, that lay disciple is wise and has produced
    much merit,
that one who gave a robe to Bhaddā who is now free
    from all bonds.[14]

The first verse is describing Bhaddā Kuṇḍalakesā's life as a Jain. Jain
nuns, like Buddhist nuns, shaved their heads and wore robes as a
symbol of their renunciation. The description of her lack of ability
to really see and understand the truth is a reference to her former
adherence to Jain doctrine and practice. In these verses, her conversion
happens as soon as she comes into the presence of the Buddha. This
alone is enough for her to realize that he is the leader she wants to
follow. Bhaddā is not alone in having this experience; in the accounts
of lives of monks and nuns and recounting of episodes of the life of
the Buddha as he wanders the forests and plains of north India, others
too convert through having met him, or even just from hearing his
name. Bhaddā's biography begins, like Dhammadinnā's, with her
previous lives. She, too, was born during the era of the first Buddha,
Padumuttara. Unlike Dhammadinnā, in this first life, she was born
into wealth and luxury. Her father was a merchant in the town of
Haṃsavatī. Again, like Dhammadinnā, she experiences another being
praised by the Buddha for an attribute and she then herself decides

she wants to attain. In Bhaddā's case, her ambition is to become skilled in quick realization, and Padumuttara predicts she will attain that during the time of Gotama Buddha. Following her birth under Padumuttara, she journeyed on in worlds of gods and men for a hundred thousand aeons. She was then born during the era of Buddha Kassapa, as another of the seven daughters of the king. They wished to renounce but were not allowed to do so.

In the era of Gotama Buddha she was born in Rājagaha, and again as a daughter of a wealthy merchant. At this point, one biography digresses into a narrative about Bhaddā's husband-to-be. On the very same day that Bhaddā was born, in the same city a son was born to the king's priest. At the moment of his birth, all the weapons in the city, including those in the royal palace, began to glow. This alarmed the king, who discovered the next day the cause was the birth of this boy 'born under the robber's star'. The priest advised the king that there was no particular harm foretold for the king due to the birth of this boy, but that he could send the boy away if he so wished it. The king did not, so the boy grew up in the priest's house, while Bhaddā grew up in the merchant's house. As soon as this boy, Sattuka, could walk he took up the art of stealing, always bringing things back from wherever he went until his parents' home was full.[15] Once he grew up, his father, seeing that there was no way to keep him from his destiny, provided him with suitable attire and tools for housebreaking and sent him on his way! Soon, there was no house in the city that had not been penetrated by him, and when this came to the king's attention he demanded the thief be caught. It is here that the other texts pick up the story, introducing Sattuka only as an adult.

Bhaddā's father was a rich merchant from Rājagaha. When Bhaddā was sixteen years old, as women of this age 'burn and long for men', her father confined her to the top storey of the house. One day, as Sattuka was being led away to execution, Bhaddā glimpsed him out of a latticed window and immediately become infatuated. She threw herself on her bed and cried 'If I have him I will live, if not I will die.' Given the intensity of Bhaddā's infatuation her parents, unusually, relented and decided to grant their daughter what her heart desired. He father paid a thousand coins to have the thief released. After Bhaddā and Sattuka were married, he soon connived to steal her jewellery. Sattuka persuaded Bhaddā to go to a mountain, known as the 'thief's precipice', apparently to make an offering to the goddess dwelling there, but in reality to steal her jewels.

When they had arrived at the foot of the mountain, Sattuka realized he must stop their entourage going up with them, in order to successfully accomplish his task. On their walk up the mountain Sattuka uttered no loving word to Bhaddā, and because of this she began to understand his real intention. Once they reached the summit, Sattuka made his true intentions clear and demanded she remove all her jewels and pass them to him. Bhaddā agreed to this, but by then was plotting herself. She asked if he might allow her one final embrace before he ended her life so that he could run off with the jewels. He agreed to this fatal deed. She went to embrace him, but instead pushed him over the cliff and he fell to his death. The goddess dwelling on the mountain then recited two verses on how a woman can be wise and astute, as Bhaddā was, realizing her impending fate and acting to subvert it. Having done this deed, Bhaddā realized she could not return home, and instead her only real option was to renounce the world and become some sort of religious ascetic. She decided to join the Jains. As part of the ordination procedure, her hair was pulled out, a usual feature of the ceremony. When her hair grew back it grew curly, and this is why she was called kuṇḍalakesā ('curly hair'). She became adept amongst the Jain community, quickly comprehending the teachings.

At this point the early and later biographies highlight different reasons for Bhaddā's religious conversion, when she becomes a follower of the Buddha. This is the next episode in the story. Unlike the changes we see with Dhammadinnā's biography, in this case, even though the recounting of the detail of how her conversion happened changes, it in no way changes the positive portrayal of Bhaddā. In both accounts she is an adept and accomplished Jain practitioner who sees the error of her ways; the inadequacy, that is, of Jain teachings. According to the canonical account, she learned Jain doctrine and lived alone. Then, in a somewhat ambiguous verse, it narrates that one day, whilst meditating in a cremation ground, a dog dropped a rotting hand by her, and she had a realization that Jain doctrine, like the rotting flesh, was full of maggots. Stirred by her experience and seeking answers, it was recommended to her that she go to the disciples of the Buddha. The disciples took her into the presence of the Buddha who taught her the dharma. She requested ordination, and was ordained by the Buddha with the words 'Come Bhaddā'. The Buddha proclaims her as foremost of those with quick realization, and then, in the concluding verses, she voices her attainments won through religious insight:

> In meaning and teaching,
> Etymology and preaching.
> My knowledge is vast and flawless
> Through the Great Sage's majesty.
>
> My defilements are [now] burnt up;
> All [new] existence is destroyed.
> Like elephants with broken chains,
> I am living without constraint.
>
> Being in the best Buddha's presence
> Was a very good thing for me.
> The three knowledges are attained;
> [I have] done what the Buddha taught!
>
> The four analytical modes,
> And these eight deliverances,
> Six special knowledges mastered,
> [I have] done what the Buddha taught![16]

The commentaries begin with this same point of departure: Bhaddā learned and mastered the doctrines of her Jain renouncer community. Once she became an accomplished and renowned Jain, she took up wandering from village to town, seeking to debate. Once she arrived at a new place, she would position a rose-apple branch in a pile of sand near the gate to the town or village, and make it known that anyone who wished to challenge her in debate should trample down the branch. She became a skilled debater and soon found none could match her. Whenever men knew she was in town, fearful of being drawn into debate with her, they would run away. One day, she arrived at the town of Sāvatthī. She placed the rose-apple branch in a pile of sand as before. One of the Buddha's chief disciples, Sāriputta, who was in Sāvatthī at that time, saw the rose-apple branch she had set up. He decided to have it trampled down, so that he could enter into a contest with her. Learning of Sāriputta's challenge, Bhaddā went to meet with him, accompanied by a large crowd from the town. The two began to debate, with Bhaddā questioning Sāriputta on all matters of doctrine in which she had expertise. To her surprise, she found he could answer them all. When she had exhausted her best efforts and not defeated him, it was Sāriputta's turn to question her. He asked her a single, simple question, 'What is one?' She could not answer. She was defeated. Acknowledging the greater insight and skill of her opponent, she requested Sāriputta become her teacher. Instead, he advised her to become a disciple of the Buddha, as he was. Very soon after this she attained nirvana.

The question that sees Bhaddā outsmarted is the enigmatic 'What is one?' This is recorded in other parts of the Pāli canon as one of the ten questions for novices. The answer to the question is not profound, and not important. The point is rather that Sāriputta demonstrated an ability to outwit Bhaddā in debate, and by doing so was the catalyst for her conversion.

Paṭācārā

Like Bhaddā, Paṭācārā was an accomplished practitioner who achieved liberation. Her own verses in the *Therīgāthā* describe the day she had her realization:

> Ploughing the field with ploughs, sowing seeds in
>   the ground,
> nourishing wives and children, young men find
>   wealth.

Why do I, possessed of virtuous conduct, complying
with the teachings of the teacher, not obtain nirvana?
I am not lazy, nor proud.

I washed my feet in the water and paid attention,
observing the water for the feet flowing from the high
to the low ground.

Then I concentrated my mind,
like an experienced, well-trained horse.
I took a lamp, and entered my dwelling.

I inspected the bed and sat on the couch.
Then I used a needle and drew out the wick.
The liberation of my mind was like the extinguishing of
    a lamp.[17]

Prior to her life as a nun, Paṭācārā experienced great sorrow,
living through the grief of losing her children. Aspects of Paṭācārā's
life story resemble the well-known and often told story of another
Buddhist nun, Kisā Gotamī. Both tell of the suffering occasioned by
the death of a child or children. The biographies of the two women
are different stories, but they become mixed up and confused as
the Buddhist canons are transmitted down the generations. In one
tradition, the story usually associated with Paṭācārā is said to be
that of Kisā Gotamī, and vice versa. It is also the case that the
poems of Kisā Gotamī, in the *Therīgāthā*, appear to be telling the
story of Paṭācārā.

The accounts of Paṭācārā's previous lives mirror those of
Dhammadinnā and Bhaddā Kuṇḍalakesā. She was born during the
time of Buddha Padumuttara, in the town of Haṃsavatī, to a wealthy
merchant. Having seen another nun declared to be foremost of those
who know the *vinaya*, the monastic code, she herself aspired to that
position. Padumuttara predicted that she would attain that position in
the future, as a disciple of Gotama Buddha. She journeyed on through
realms of gods and men and was then born during the era of Buddha
Kassapa, as one of the seven daughters of the king. In her present
life, she was born in Sāvatthī, into the family of a wealthy merchant.

When she grew up, she became attracted to a man her parents did not approve of. Her canonical biography recounts:

> When, as a young woman, I saw a man from the country, under the influence of impetus thoughts I went with him.[18]

This man was considered unsuitable for her because of his low status. In some accounts he is described as a servant in her father's household. Paṭācārā had fallen in love, so when she learned she was to be married off to a suitable match, she decided she must take matters into her own hands. She decided to run off with her love, the servant. Paṭācārā told him that if she was married they would no longer be able to see each other:

> After tomorrow you will be kept from seeing me by a hundred warders. If you are able, go now and take me with you![19]

The couple decide to leave Paṭācārā's family and live a quiet remote life together in the forest:

> The husband sowed the field in the forest, bringing collected sticks and wood etc. The woman fetched water with the water-pot and with her own hand pounded the rice, did the cooking and other domestic chores.[20]

After some time with her husband, Paṭācārā became pregnant and this gave rise to a desire to return home, to see her parents. When she tells her husband of her wish, he becomes fearful of torture at the hands of her parents should they to return. Paṭācārā tried to persuade him to take her, but upon umpteen prevarications of 'we'll go tomorrow' she realized 'this fool will never take me',[21] and so she set out alone. Her husband caught up with her on the road just as her labour pains began. She gave birth on the road, and he persuaded her to go back home with him.[22] This was repeated with the pregnancy of the second child, but with different consequences. This time, labour pains began just at the moment a storm broke. Then, all manner of misfortunes began to befall Paṭācārā and her family. First her husband was killed by a snake, his body turning blue as the poison engulfed him. Trying to cross a flooded river, Paṭācārā took one child in her arms. As she was returning for the other a bird of prey swooped down and took the first. Whilst she was waving her hands around in anguish midstream, her other child saw her and attempted to go to her, but was instead carried off by the current.

Finally, bereft and distraught at her loss, Paṭācārā made her way to Sāvatthī only to discover more sorrow ahead. She met a man on the road coming from Sāvatthī, who told her her family home had been destroyed by the storm that night, killing all within. The bodies of the three occupants – her mother, father, and brother – were burning upon a funeral pyre. The man told her the pyre was still burning and pointed out that if she looked she could see its billow of smoke. Paṭācārā's grief reached its climax at this point. And it is here that the canonical account and the commentaries diverge. In the canon, overwhelmed with the intensity of her sorrow, she uttered:

> Both of my sons have passed away,
> my husband is dead on the road;
> mother and father and brothers
> are being burnt on a single pyre.
>
> Then [I grew] pale and thin, helpless;
> [I was] in a low state of mind.
> After that, while roaming I saw
> [him], the Charioteer of Men.
>
> Then the teacher said [this] to me:
> 'Do not grieve, child; breathe easily.
> You should search after your [own] self;
> Why uselessly torment yourself?
>
> There are no sons to [give] shelter,
> Not fathers nor even kinsmen.
> There is no shelter with kinsmen
> When one's seized by the end-maker.'

After hearing the Sage's speech,
I realized the first [path] fruit.
Having gone forth, in no long time,
I achieved [my] arahantship.[23]

In this canonical account, Paṭācārā is grief-stricken but nonetheless rational. The commentaries, however, dramatize and embellish these now colourful scenes. At the moment of realization that all her family are gone and overwhelmed with the grief of losing so many loved ones, her clothes fell to the ground. The devastating grief sent her reeling. In this newly disturbed state of mind she did not realize her clothes had fallen from her body. This naked and crazed state engendered a period of vagrant wandering. When people saw her they threw rubbish and earth at her, shouting at the 'crazy woman' to go away. Then, one day, Paṭācārā met the Buddha, coming upon a monastery in which he was teaching. Due to the Buddha's omniscience, he 'sees' Paṭācārā is one who has made an aspiration during the time of Padumuttara Buddha. The Buddha's disciples, seeing this crazed woman approaching, tried to shield the Buddha from her, but he allowed her through. The Buddha then spoke to Paṭācārā, comforting her, but offering words that resonated. The Buddha simply said, 'Sister, regain your senses',[24] and she was instantly revived from her grief-stricken, deranged state. She became aware of her nudity at this moment, was embarrassed and then quickly thrown a garment by a bystander.

Paṭācārā requested ordination, and the Buddha took her to the nuns. She subsequently attained nirvana, as in the canonical account. In her own words, she then 'learned all the discipline in [the Buddha's] presence, perceiving all, all the detail, I recited it as it was'.[25] With this, the Buddha acknowledged her as foremost of those who know the discipline and said 'Paṭācārā is unique'.[26]

Women in Early China

When Buddhism travelled to China, many of the same texts with the accounts of these early nuns were transmitted. The same and similar women were named, and the same and similar stories told, yet many aspects of the accounts, depictions, descriptions, and other information changed. We have seen above dramatic changes to biographies even within accounts transmitted by the same tradition. Similar shifts in interpretation take place between traditions, countries, continents, and languages. For example, as noted in the Introduction, there exists a canonical list of pre-eminent Buddhist nuns, revered for certain qualities, and in the Chinese version of this list fifty-one nuns are listed, whilst in the Pāli version there are only thirteen nuns. Exactly why this is the case is unclear; it must either be that in one list some were added or in the other some were removed.

The Buddhist canons in China, now serving a community in a country very different to India, contain stories of the same Indian women: the early disciples. There are, however, also records of some prominent Buddhist nuns from medieval China. One biographical source composed in the early sixth century provides us with insight into the lives of early medieval Buddhist women in China. There are also inscriptions, some of them lengthy, that give us a potted history of a few nuns.[27] There are also other texts that provide glimpses into the lives of Buddhist women from this period.[28] The nuns who are the subject of the biographical work lived between the fourth and sixth centuries, that is, not long after the arrival of Buddhism in China in the second century. These nuns were highly esteemed within the Chinese tradition, to the extent that the author could not hold back and had to set brush to paper to record their lives for us. We are fortunate that this author, Baochang, thought of us, and decided that writing about these women might be beneficial:

> These nuns then, whom I hereby offer as models, are women of excellent reputation, paragons of ardent morals, whose virtues are a stream of fragrance that flows without end.
>
> That is why I take up my ink brush . . . to record the women's biographies to hand on to later chroniclers, that they in turn might use the material I provide to encourage and admonish generations to come. Therefore, although I might wish to teach wordlessly [as the sages do], in this case I cannot refrain from using words.[29]

Buddhist texts reached China in rather a piecemeal way, and this was true of the monastic rules on codes of conduct for monks and nuns. By the sixth century, a comprehensive set of rules existed for monks in China, but not yet for nuns. So, during this early period, the rules intended to govern the lives of ordained women following the Buddha were not clear, and neither was the ordination process itself, as one of the stories below demonstrates. The Chinese also began to adapt and modify the monastic code: in certain aspects it was more fit for Indian communal life than Chinese. Further, quite early on in the history of Buddhism in China, other texts began to be written locally. Some of these were positive about women, saying they were all able to make good progress on the path, and attain what the Buddha attained. According to one text, in the future, women will be more fervent practitioners than men:

> When the Dharma is about to be extinguished women
> will be zealous, constantly doing meritorious deeds,
> [while] men will be lazy and indifferent, will not engage
> in religious discourse, will look on monks as manure,
> and will not have believing minds.[30]

Zhu Jingjian

According to the records, the first Chinese woman was ordained in 317 CE. Her name was Zhu Jingjian (Pure Example). As a child Zhu Jingjian had enjoyed learning and when her father died whilst she was still young, she taught the lute and calligraphy to other children to support her family. Feelings of faith and joy arose in her when she first heard of the Buddhist teachings. At first she found it hard to find a teacher, but as a young woman she met a teacher who was able to provide her with good instruction. As a result of the teaching, she grew firmer in her commitment, and began to read scripture herself. Zhu Jingjian learned that both men and women could be ordained as followers of the Buddha, but her teacher had reservations about attempting to ordain her, not clear if the rules governing ordination for women could be met, and also concerned that there was not, as yet, in China, a full set of monastic rules for nuns. Replying to Zhu Jingjian's questions on this, he said:

> Foreign Buddhists say that nuns have five hundred rules to follow as compared to fewer for monks. . . I asked the instructor about this, and he said that the rules for nuns are highly similar and only slightly different from the monks' regulations, but, if I cannot get the complete texts of these rules, then I certainly cannot bestow on women the obligation to observe them. A woman aspiring eventually to become a nun may, however, recite the ten fundamental precepts from the Assembly of Monks only, but, without a female instructor to train her in the practice of all the rules a woman has no one on whom to rely [for that training which prepares her to accept the obligations to observe all the rules of monastic life].[31]

Zhu Jingjian nonetheless renounced the household life and, along with other women who wanted to commit and become followers, set up the first nunnery in China, the Bamboo Grove Convent. They had no female instructor, so all the others consulted Zhu Jingjian, whose instruction, the author writes, 'was superior to all those already recognised as accomplished'.[32] So accomplished was Zhu Jingjian as a Buddhist teacher her teaching was said to be 'like wind moving grass'. This is a reference to Confucian ideas about the moral person whose virtue is compared to the wind that can bend grass, that is, can impact many.[33] Eventually, a set of nuns' rules was obtained by a Chinese pilgrim travelling in Central Asia, and translation of this was completed in 357 CE. A ceremony was performed so that Zhu Jingjian and her disciples could commit to follow the rules of the newly translated text. Resistance to this continued, as questions were raised about this as an ordination, because no elder nuns were present – nor available, as there were none in China – to make this a true ordination according to formal monastic organizational procedures. Nonetheless, Zhu Jingjian is considered the first Buddhist nun in China. The ceremony was a spectacular event:

I Hear Her Words

On the day of that ritual, remarkable fragrance and perfume [filled the air]. Everyone smelled it, and there was none who did not rejoice and marvel; respect for her increased all the more. Zhu Jingjian well cultivated the monastic rules and resolutely studied without ceasing. Although the gifts of the faithful were many, she distributed everything she received, always putting herself last and others first.[34]

When Zhu Jingjian died, aged seventy, the same fragrance could be smelled again, and a red, misty cloud appeared, out of which a woman holding a five-coloured flower descended, and Zhu Jingjian said her farewell to her followers.

An Lingshou

The other religious traditions of China at the time impacted on the lives of the Buddhist nuns. The tradition of Confucius, the ancient sage of China, underpinned the sociopolitical and religious landscape of the time. Central to Confucian ideology is the importance of family, and respect for one's elders and ancestors.[35] An Lingshou (Esteemed Leader) is another nun whose story is told in the collection. Although devoted to Buddhism at a young age, she was pressured by her family to marry:

When she was young, Lingshou was intelligent and fond of study. Her speech was clear and beautiful; her nature modest and unassuming. Taking no pleasure in worldly affairs, she was at ease in secluded quiet. She delighted in the Buddhist teachings and did not wish for her parents to arrange her betrothal.[36]

Nonetheless, her father tried to insist. He said:

'You ought to marry. How can you be so unfilial?'
Lingshou said, 'My mind is concentrated on the work of religion, and my thought dwells exclusively on spiritual matters. Neither blame nor praise moves me;

purity and uprightness are sufficient in themselves. Why
must I submit thrice [to father, husband, son], before I
am considered a woman of propriety.'[37]

Her father said, 'You want to benefit only one
person – yourself. How can you help your father and
mother at the same time?'

Lingshou said, 'I am setting myself to cultivate the
Way exactly because I want to free all living beings from
suffering. How much more, then, do I want to free my
two parents!'[38]

Not knowing what to do, her father consulted a magician monk,
who instructed him to perform certain actions, then return after three
days. This he did, and the magician then spread his hand with oil
of sesame and safflower. Her father had a vision on his hand of his
daughter dressed in Buddhist monastic robes preaching the Buddha's
teachings to a large crowd. The magician also predicted that Lingshou
would guide her family to nirvana. Her father then permitted her to
become a nun. She cut off her hair, donned robes and set up her own
monastery. She became a renowned Buddhist teacher and leader:

Lingshou widely perused all kinds of books, and, having
read a book through only once, she was able to chant
it by heart. Her thought extended to the depths of the
profound; her spirit intuited the subtle and divine.
In the religious communities of the time there was
no one who did not honour her. Those who left the
household life because of her numbered more than two
hundred.[39]

Daoxing

During the lives of these first Buddhist nuns in China, between the
fourth and sixth centuries, they resided alongside female practitioners
of the Daoist religion. Some Daoists were hostile to Buddhism,
believing that Buddhist monks and nuns might convert some of their
own followers, given the apparent overlap between some of the key

doctrines and practices of the two traditions.[40] For one nun, a gentle, popular character, this rivalry proved deadly:

> Daoxing was both scrupulous and firm in character, and she was able to get along with everyone. During her probationary period before becoming a fully-fledged nun, she practiced chanting the scriptures while running errands and performing other duties. Therefore, by the time she was twenty she could recite from memory the *Flower of the Law*, the *Vimalakirti*, and other scriptures. After she had accepted full obligation to the monastic rule and become a nun, she pursued her study of Buddhist teachings while continuing to maintain her vegetarian diet and her practice of austerities. As she grew older, rather than taking more ease, she intensified her rigorously ascetic way of life.[41]

She was known for her intellectual prowess, especially in relation to the *Smaller Perfection of Wisdom* text. Within the region, all students who followed the teachings of the Buddha considered her their teacher. Daoxing lived in north China, in a convent on the south bank of the Yellow River. A female Daoist teacher also lived in the region, and had been a popular teacher until Daoxing arrived, and Daoxing's 'way of Buddhism eclipsed her own arts'.[42] This female Daoist teacher cultivated a friendship with Daoxing, but secretly despised her, and used the opportunities afforded by the friendship to poison Daoxing, putting poisonous herbs in her food. Medicines were not enough to save Daoxing, who never recovered from the toxin. When her disciples asked her the cause of her illness, she refused to tell them, and died not revealing the truth, although it was clear she knew who was responsible.

Women in Modern East Asia

As we will see in the next chapter, in the Theravāda tradition the nuns' Order died out in some countries. It may never have ever existed in others, and was not reinstated until recently, and only partially.

By contrast, the nuns' Order in East Asian countries continued and continues to exist today, with many convents, women practitioners, and prominent female teachers. In the Chan (or Zen) school in East Asia, within which transmission lineage is of crucial importance, there is evidence that women were involved from the fifth century. There were also female Chan masters (esteemed and influential teachers) and women were leaders and devoted participants in lay Buddhist communities. Although, as we have seen above, nuns did live in convents, many nuns also stayed in the family home and practised at home. It's possible that from the time of Buddhism's arrival in China there existed popular lay religious movements largely operating at local and regional level that were an admixture of Buddhist, Daoist, and Confucian beliefs. These movements consisted of predominantly female practitioners, and produced the three popular goddesses of medieval China. One of these three, Guanyin, is Buddhist in origin but the other two, Mother of the West and Mazu, are not.[43] Initially, women were restricted within these movements, but from the fourteenth century onwards women were allowed to be leaders and teachers of such movements, which had, by then, become more wide scale and organized. Women's leadership within these movements was supported by their scriptures, such as the *Baojuan*, 'Precious Volumes', which contains narratives on religious and moral conduct within which women are the chief protagonists.

By the early modern period, women could and did become prominent leaders and teachers in East Asia. Significant evidence for this comes down to us in the form of compositions written by these women themselves, and their female disciples.

Qiyuan Xinggang

Qiyuan Xinggang (1597–1654) is one of the best known of the seventeenth-century female Chan masters.[44] She had many disciples, one of whom composed a long and intimate biographical portrait of her in 1655, the year after she died. This portrait has been preserved in the Ming Dynasty edition of the Buddhist canon. Qiyuan Xinggang was the only child of a retired scholar. Like other women of her class, she received a good education, and may have been tutored by her father. Like her earlier Chinese monastic counterparts, Qiyuan Xinggang displayed a fondness for Buddhism as a child, but was pressured into an engagement to a man in her teenage years. This man died before they married, as a result of which Qiyuan Xinggang urged her parents to let her become a nun. As her biographer, Yikui Chaochen, puts it:

> One day, she suddenly began to think about how quickly time was going by and that she was not making good use of her floating life in this world of Jambudvipa. When death arrived, how could she be its master? She became more and more depressed every day and was ashamed of being unable to seek out guidance from knowledgeable teachers. Day and night she earnestly prostrated herself in the front of the statue of the Buddha and vowed that she would realize the true fruit of enlightenment in this very lifetime. Our Master was her father and mother's only child, and they cherished her as they would a pearl in the palm of their hands. However, when they forbade her to eat only vegetarian food, our Master simply stopped eating or drinking altogether. Her father and mother felt pity for her and finally went along with her wishes.[45]

Given the normative Confucian commitment to family and filial responsibilities at this time in China, as well as Qiyuan Xinggang's daughterly duties relating to her parents, she now also had obligations to her prospective parents-in-law. It was considered the duty of the wife of a deceased man that she live with his parents and devote herself to a life of service to them. Instead, Qiyuan Xinggang composed a long, careful letter to them, expressing her regret that, as she had now renounced the worldly life, she was no longer able to carry out the ancestral rituals and more mundane duties incumbent upon her as the (potential) widow.

Now that Qiyuan Xinggang was free to practise, what she most desired was fuller and more complete knowledge. Following the death of her own father, after a period of mourning, she sought out a Chan master for herself. This teacher told her a story about a determined female practitioner of the past – a common strategy, intended to inspire the listener. The young woman at the centre of the story demonstrated great fearlessness and confidence in her understanding of Chan when going to meet her own master. The teacher sent Qiyuan Xinggang away with the instruction to meditate on the question 'Where is the place where I can dwell in peace with the will of heaven?' Qiyuan Xinggang was not able to make much progress with this practice, although she tried for many years. Eventually, she returned to the same teacher to request further instruction, which he granted her. She, however, was not in the end satisfied with this teacher, so sought others. She tried other teachers, who provided her with different questions to contemplate, but after some years of making little progress she became immensely frustrated:

> Hating herself for being so stupid and clumsy . . .
> she faced the statue of the Buddha and wept bitterly.
> Plagued by nightmares, she took her ordination robes,
> and placing them on the top of her head, she knelt in
> front of the statue of the Buddha [, saying,] 'Given that
> I have found that for which I have an affinity, I will not
> let it go.' Day and night she labored and toiled, but still
> did not succeed in having a breakthrough. One day, just
> as she was seated in meditation, it was as though in that
> dark room she had a glimpse of a white sun, which was
> a second later obscured again by floating clouds. Her
> efforts were very strenuous, and she paid little heed to
> her physical body. Even though one day she spat up
> three bowls of red [blood] and could neither eat nor
> drink, yet still she refused to let up on her efforts.[46]

This intense effort began to pay off, and gradually Qiyuan Xinggang began to make progress. Finally, she began to experience realization after realization into the true nature of things. In the end, her advancement on the path and accomplishment as a practitioner moved her teacher to acknowledge her as his dharma heir; that is, as a Chan master who continues the transmission lineage. That she was a woman in this position was unacceptable to some, as in being bestowed this honour she was taking an official position traditionally reserved for men. According to her biographer, Qiyuan Xinggang was moved by this acknowledgement of her profound comprehension of the teachings, because for her the accolade represented religious achievement and was not, as for many of her male counterparts, gained for political or polemical reasons.[47]

Following her receiving the formal dharma transmission, Qiyuan Xinggang decided to undertake a solitary retreat, which was a common practice at the time. She spent nine years in retreat, engaging in ascetic practices, and her own words tell us of some of the insights she won as a result of this experience:

> I lived in deep seclusion with few comforts but
> determined to persevere. My body [seated upright]
> with grave dignity, [I made no distinctions between]
> inner and outer. I pushed against emptiness, cutting off
> entanglements. Once the [distinction between] inner and
> outer [was gone] then all entanglements were dissolved.
> When there is neither shape nor form, one sees oneself
> face to face, and can gather up a *mahakalpa* in a single
> point and spread a speck of dust over the ten directions.
> [Then one experiences] no restrictions, no restraints,
> [and is] free to go where one pleases.[48]

Following her period in solitary retreat, Qiyuan Xinggang was invited to become the abbess of a fledging convent, a project begun by a devout Buddhist family to transform their own family estate into a larger-scale nunnery. Qiyuan Xinggang was initially reluctant to go, but eventually accepted the invitation as, it seems, she considered it her duty to do so. By this stage in her life and practice, Qiyuan Xinggang had gained a solid reputation; therefore she quickly attracted many disciples to the convent. Nearly one hundred nuns came from all over China to reside there. She was indeed, by now, a true Chan master. Some of her own teachings to her students included the following:

Qiyuan knows nothing of Chan: when hungry, she eats; when tired, she sleeps. When people come to ask her about the Way, she has nothing to say: thrusting forth her hand and clenching her fists, the marvelous mystery is complete.

In my hand I grasp the scepter,
Totally at ease, without a care.
As pure as jade, virtuous as ice,
The winter plum puts out buds,
Ah! The endlessly fragrant breeze stirs!
There is nothing that I am concealing from you.[49]

There is no greater suffering than to be caught up in the bustle of worldly affairs, there is no greater joy than cultivating the way with a one-pointed mind. The Way is no other than the greatest joy in this world. Abandoning the Way in order to seek out pleasure is like throwing away food and seeking hunger![50]

Raising a flower with a smile: before a single word is
    uttered:
Lightning flashes and stars fall: before a single text is
    written.
Face to face with a white staff of the most marvelous
    means
One lamp lights the next as the past is continued into the
    present.[51]

Chiyo-ni

Buddhism arrived in Japan in the sixth century and between the sixth and eighth centuries many women followed the tradition, being ordained as nuns alongside monks. After this period, however, and continuing down the centuries, nuns were continually less valued, and as a result fewer women decided to dedicate their lives to Buddhism by taking up robes.[52] Aristocratic women in particular did continue to practise, but renounced the world without formally becoming nuns. Such women are depicted in stories from a text entitled 'A Record of Japanese Born in the Pure Land' (*Nihon ōjō gokuraku ki*), complied in the tenth century.[53] It was not until the time of Nichren (1222–1282), a progressive thinker who championed women, that things began to change.

One of the best-known forms of poetry in the modern world, haiku, originated in Japanese literary culture of the seventeenth century. Traditionally, a haiku is a poem of seventeen syllables structured in three lines of five, seven, and five syllables respectively. Bashō is the best known of all haiku poets. Yet with good reason the female haiku master Chiyo-ni, who became a Buddhist nun, was as well known as Bashō during her lifetime in the eighteenth century, and into the nineteenth century. Since then, however, her work has not enjoyed the continued fame of the works of Bashō, as influential male haiku masters of subsequent centuries maligned and disparaged her poetry. In 1998, Patricia Donegan and Yoshie Ishibashi published a book of her life and works, which contains a hundred of her haiku. This book is significant as it begins to restore knowledge of Chiyo-ni for the modern English-speaking world, although it only scratches the surface of Chiyo-ni's extensive collection of 1,700 haiku. In other ways, as well, Chiyo-ni is becoming known again: there are paintings of her now housed in the Museum of Fine Art in Boston and the British Museum; in north Japan, near her hometown, a museum is dedicated to her.

Chiyo-ni was born in 1703 in Kanazawa, and named Chiyo. The -ni means 'nun' and was added after her ordination. Her father earned a living mounting pictures on scrolls and screens, a profession she would take up herself after his death. When she was sixteen, a well-known haiku master visited her house and wrote with her, immediately recognizing her talent, and this was the catalyst for the launch of her career. Her best-known poem is 'Morning Glory', and she wrote many about women. It was only later in life, when she was in her fifties, that she became a Buddhist nun. This did not halt her creative output and she continued to compose many more poems. *Chiyoni kushū*, 'The Collected Haiku of Chiyoni', was published ten years after her ordination, and when she died, in 1775, she left behind more haiku than any other premodern Japanese woman poet.[54] Here is a selection of her Buddhist poems, with the most famous first. I include interpretations of the poems by Donegan and Ishibashi:

> morning glories –
> the well-bucket entangled
> I ask for water[55]

This poem is about compassion; Chiyo, not wanting to disturb the flower, asks for water from a neighbour instead. The boundary between self and other disappears, she is able to see the world through the eyes of the flower.[56]

> anyway
> leave it to the wind
> pampas grass[57]

Another haiku about compassion, but included here as well, is a reflection on letting go of self-centredness and becoming empty, like grass blown in the wind.[58] Although it is not clear if, during her life, Chiyo-ni ever lived in a convent, this next haiku is about a silent meditation retreat:

> even
> the flowing water
> doesn't say anything[59]

Impermanence of all that exists is generally reflected in the vision of poets, and with haiku it is no different. Three of Chiyo-ni's poems that beautifully distil the impermanence of the natural world are:

> traces of a dream –
> a butterfly
> through the flower field

> clear water is cool
> fireflies vanish –
> there's nothing more

among a field
of horsetail weeds –
temple ruins[60]

Women in Modern Thailand

Biographies of Buddhist monks are very popular in modern Thailand, and easy to come by. Some are even sold in 7/11 convenience stores.[61] Biographies of Buddhist women, however, are much harder to find. Because the nuns' movement in Thailand either died out or was never established in the first place, Buddhist women in modern Thailand are not fully ordained nuns. As mentioned, committed Buddhist women in Thailand, who shave their heads and wear robes, are called *mae chi*.[62] Written modern biographies of such women have, however, been rediscovered and recently brought to light. These women are known both from rare textual sources and via oral accounts. Stories of prominent and celebrated female teachers from this last century continue to be retold by their disciples and passed on down village generations.[63] One such woman was Mae Chi Kaew Sianglam (1901–1991). Details of her life story are recounted in a variety of sources. These include, for instance, sermons and talks of an influential Thai monk who knew her well, framed posters attached to the walls in a museum that commemorates her life, and oral accounts shared by her disciples. These all exist alongside her published biography.

Mae Chi Kaew Sianglam

Mae Chi Kaew Sianglam was born at the turn of the century, in 1901, in a village in north-eastern Thailand, and given the name Tapai. She was the youngest of six children and when she was still a child her mother died. At the tender age of just one year old, she had, according to her biography, her first visionary experience, the first of many to come. She saw a divine horse that tried to persuade her to accompany it to a heavenly city. As a child she was able to recollect past lives and became renowned for her ability to enter into concentrated states of mind in meditation. The motifs here are similar to those used in the accounts of the early Chinese nuns above. As a result of her many visions, her father was concerned that others might perceive her as mentally unstable. She was not allowed to go to the monastery unaccompanied; only alongside her parents, who would make her sit far away from the monks.

In 1917, two influential monks visited her village, and her experience of meeting them significantly impacted upon her life and continued practice of Buddhism. One of the teachers was named Luang Pu Man. Mae Chi Kaew's biography recounts some of the intense experiences she had during this first visit:

> . . . one night, following Luang Pu Man's instruction on meditation and having developed deep concentration, Tapai had another vision, in which she watched her own body getting older and deteriorating until eventually she died. Her corpse was then consumed by maggots, and only her skeleton remained. While convinced of her own death during this vision, she worried that she would not be able to donate food to Luang Pu Man the next morning. The vision continued, however; after villagers had taken her corpse to the cemetery, Luang Pu Man arrived and touched parts of her body with a stick. Whichever body part was touched with the stick rotted away until only her heart remained. Luang Pu Man picked up her heart, saying that it was indestructible. After regaining consciousness the next morning, Tapai was disappointed as she believed she had had a dream instead of having practiced proper meditation. After having reported to Luang Pu Man the content of her 'dream', however, she was told by him that this was not a dream but a vision; instead of failing in meditation, she had actually made extraordinary progress in her meditation practice. During the rainy season of that year, Luang Pu Man paid special attention to Tapai's meditational progress and visions. When asked why Tapai was able to achieve such rapid progress in meditation, Luang Pu Man explained, 'This young girl

practiced meditation in many former lives, which is
the reason why the principle of impermanence of all
conditioned things had so deeply and completely been
ingrained in her mind.'[64]

When Luang Pu Man was preparing to leave the village,
accounts vary as to what he said to Mae Kaew (Tapai). He instructed
her to stop meditating, perhaps because without his instruction she
would not be able to make balanced progress, given the intensity of
her visions. He may have asked her if she wanted to join him as an
ordained follower, but whether this happened is unclear. She did
not accompany him, however, and stayed in the village. Following
her parents' wishes, Mae Kaew (Tapai) married, although she had
no interest in doing so herself and, after failing to conceive, she and
her husband adopted a daughter. Her husband banned her from
meditating, and only allowed her to practise Buddhist chanting
and give alms to the monks. Once their daughter was grown, and
old enough to look after herself, Mae Kaew requested that her
husband allow her to ordain as a *mae chi*. She was now thirty-
four years old. Her husband at first refused to grant this, but after
two years of repeated requests and the intervention of another
family member, he granted her temporary ordination, for one rainy
season. After the rainy season was over, Mae Kaew had no desire
to return to live with her husband, who had, after her departure
to the community, taken to bad ways. He was not pleased at this,
and became angry, following her back to the monastery with the
intention of bringing her back home. Two of her brothers had to
hold him back, to enable Mae Kaew to return to the monastery.
After that, she never went back to him.

Mae Kaew then spent a period of time living as a recluse on a
mountain near her village, practising meditation, and again had many
of the intense meditation experiences she had had whilst young. In
1945 she returned to her village to set up a nunnery. Life was hard
for the *mae chi*s who lived there, as they did not have good access
to teachers who could help them make progress. After some time,
following the death of Luang Pu Man, one of his disciples came to

visit Mae Kaew. He found her to be too wrapped up in her meditation experiences in a way that was stopping her make progress towards nirvana. He tried to instruct her in this, telling her to concentrate on her internal mental and psychical experiences, rather than to pay so much attention to the visions, but she initially refused to comply. As Seeger comments:

> The kinds of horrific deconstructions of her body Mae Chi Kaew was repeatedly experiencing during her meditation experiences are particularly remarkable and often accentuated in the hagiographies. . .
>
> In her meditation practice Mae Chi Kaew dissected the various bodily organs and parts of her body, and she thereby 'understood that the entire body was disgusting and repulsive.' These hagiographical elements are both in language and content reminiscent of the life accounts of female saints of early Buddhism. . . [65]

After some time, however, she did change her practice in accordance with what this teacher advised, and this did eventually lead to her Awakening. At dawn, on 1 November 1952, whilst resting after a walking meditation, Mae Chi Kaew attained Awakening:

> She felt tired after having done walking meditation for the whole night and therefore sat down on a bamboo platform under a phayom tree to get some rest. While reclining in order to lie down and thinking, 'I will rest for a moment and then boil rice,' she perceived a rumbling noise as if lightning were hitting the platform on which she was resting. At the same time, there was a noise saying, 'The rebirths have come to an end!' Her tears were flowing copiously in joy.[66]

After this, Mae Chi Kaew committed the rest of her life to helping others. She travelled with her teacher and helped him build his famous monastery in Udon Thani Province. She lived in her nunnery in her village but travelled with other *mae chi*s to see famous teachers and built up a strong network of *mae chi*s around the country. She died in

1991, and her cremation, at her nunnery, was attended by numerous monks, *mae chi*s, and laity.

* * *

In this chapter I have surveyed some of the biographies of Buddhist women from different time periods and different regions. These are just a few examples of a rich, preserved tradition of narratives of women who followed the Buddha; women adept at practice, who taught others, were esteemed and revered, followed the Buddha's teachings and attained Awakening. If we recall the vilifying text passages from chapter 2 and set them alongside the reality of women's lives, expressions of their talents, and biographical accounts that were transmitted down the centuries – all of this could not be further removed from characterizations of women as morally weak, intellectually challenged, and uncontrollably manipulative.

CHAPTER 5

RECOVERING A LOST PAST: SOUTH AND SOUTHEAST ASIA

Here, I profess my good works . . . I, the queen mother, Mahākalyāṇavattī Śrī Sujātā, princess of noble birth, devout great lay disciple. I prostrate myself at the noble lotuses that are the feet of the revered Triple Joy who is our Lord, our supreme refuge. . . My heart full of *dharma*, I have regularly accomplished many pious acts. . .

Inscription at Angkor Wat, Cambodia.[1]

In these final three chapters of the book, I will trace the history of women in Buddhist traditions down the centuries and across the world. In this chapter I focus on the countries of South and Southeast Asia. Each currently follows Theravāda Buddhism as the state-sponsored religion. In each of them, however, other forms of Buddhism as well Hinduism are practised, primarily as a result of past contacts with India. Also, each had its own indigenous religion. While our knowledge of these religions remains uneven, evidence shows that each impacted on the way in which Buddhism has been integrated in the respective countries.

I begin with the first country within which Buddhism was established outside of India, Sri Lanka. I then progress to mainland Southeast Asia, and discuss a period prior to the establishment of the modern nation-states. During this time, political kingdoms came and went, but some left evidence of both the arrival of Buddhism in the region and the status of women within it. Next, I take in turn three countries – Cambodia, Burma, and Thailand – and discuss more modern history. In each of these countries, as with Sri Lanka, the nuns' Order either died out at some point or was never introduced. Today, there exists no Theravāda country with an unbroken lineage of Theravāda nuns.[2] It is unclear exactly how and why the lineages were lost or disrupted. Yet, because of this history, each of these countries has developed a new system for women who wish to live a monastic life. Each allows women to renounce the world and live a life similar to that of a Buddhist nun, practising the teachings of the Buddha, but without the formal legal status of nuns. This has resulted, in many cases, both historically and today, in a great deal of economic hardship for these women, and low social status. In Sri Lanka, these groups of women are called *dasa sil-mātās*, in Cambodia *ṭūn jī*, in Burma *thiláshin*, and in Thailand *mae chi*s. Each group dons the apparel of a monastic – they shave their heads and wear robes – each follows a set of Buddhist precepts, and, at least to some degree, lives a monastic lifestyle.

In the modern histories of these countries there have been attempts to re-establish the Order of nuns, and in the last few decades international efforts as well. These international efforts, beginning in the mid-1980s, culminated in the Theravāda higher ordination for women in the 1990s. In 1996, then 1998, four Sri Lankan women were ordained in India: two at Sarnath, then another two at Bodhgaya. This was through the efforts of an organization known as Sakyadhita International, founded in the late 1980s. Following this, efforts intensified within Sri Lanka to ordain more women. The Sri Lankan Bhikkhunī Re-Awakening Organization devised a training schema to prepare *dasa sil-mātās* for ordination, and efforts intensified in other countries too.[3] This chapter discusses the extent to which the traditional monastic communities of each country accept the status of these women. Despite differing levels of acceptance, the ordained women of South and Southeast Asia have established communities within their own countries, or in international settings, and live alongside the *dasa sil-mātās, ṭūn jī, thiláshin*, and *mae chi*s. The question of the re-establishment of the nuns' Order in these countries is more complex than it might at first appear: for a variety of reasons, many of the women already living their lives as female ascetics do not wish to take on fully ordained status as nuns.

While recounting these histories of Buddhist women through the ages in this and the next chapters I try, as much as possible, to write them in the words of Buddhist women themselves, or to include something of their voices. In these ensuing three chapters we will meet with many more women who, like our queen mother from Angkor Wat whose words open the chapter, profess either their own good works or those of others – their sister, female teacher, disciple. Many whose own hearts, alike, are 'full of dharma'.

Sri Lanka

Sri Lanka was the first place within which Buddhism was established outside India. There are chronicles that relate how and when Buddhism arrived in Sri Lanka, but these accounts are more legend than historical fact. According to the chronicles, an Indian king, Asoka, sent a mission to Sri Lanka that included his son and also, eventually, his daughter, Saṅghamittā, who established the Order of nuns on the island. Asoka, who ruled during the third century

BCE, famously converted to Buddhism during his reign and was a significant figure in promoting the establishment of Buddhism outside of India. Importantly, both monks' and nuns' Orders were established in Sri Lanka. Both from textual and epigraphic evidence we have knowledge of women who practised on the island. As in India, inscriptions record the names of Buddhist women, although there are far fewer. Unlike in India, we do not know the status of the women; that is, they do not identify themselves as nuns. Still, the chronicles themselves include a great deal of evidence of nuns. One in particular, the *Dīpavaṃsa*, focuses more on nuns than on monks, recording, for instance, that kings listened to their advice. This has caused some to wonder whether this text was authored by nuns.[4] Not only is there a focus on nuns within the text, but it is also stated that 'they were the first on the island to obtain the fruits of the Buddhist path'.[5] One long section of the *Dīpavaṃsa* details the names of many of the most eminent nuns in Sri Lanka, past and present. It is a record of esteemed named Buddhist women who were instrumental in the spread of Buddhism in Sri Lanka. It may be, as well, that this chronicle represents an attempt to trace an ordination lineage for nuns in Sri Lanka, an authoritative lineage that reaches back to India and the time of the Buddha.

The section on nuns begins with an acknowledgement of the Buddha's stepmother and aunt, Mahāpajāpatī Gotamī. As we have seen, according to traditional accounts she was the first in the nuns' Order. After extolling her virtues, the text celebrates other women who were direct disciples of the Buddha, some of whom we met with in chapter 4 of this volume. Well-known figures are listed: Khemā, Uppalavaṇṇā, Paṭācārā, and Dhammadinnā. These are listed alongside lesser-known nuns known from Indian sources. Each is lauded as a 'guardian of the teachings' and said to be well versed in the monastic code. These nuns lived in India, which distinguishes them from those who follow, some of whom came from India to Sri Lanka, and others who were native to the island. Those who travelled from India, along with Saṅghamittā, are listed next. The text states that these nuns taught the teachings of the Buddha and the monastic code in Sri Lanka. Next, women who received ordination in Sri Lanka are extolled, who we assume were taught by, and ordained by, the nuns from India. These nuns were said to be well-versed teachers as well as adept practitioners, exemplifying passionlessness, calm, and resolve. These nuns, honoured by the king, headed up a group of twenty thousand nuns. Then follows a roll call of the daughters of another king and his priest, who headed up a further group of twenty thousand. Next are the leaders of another group of twenty thousand, then nuns most able in reciting the *vinaya*, followed by names of some of the best teachers. Another two who converted many in India are acknowledged, who came to Sri Lanka with twenty thousand nuns. Then others who were ordained in Sri Lanka. Finally, the section concludes with a few other nuns, named in a similar fashion, with accompanying praise. Each of these on this extensive list, the text concludes, attained nirvana.[6]

The biographical text by Baochang discussed in the previous chapter records that nuns came to China from Sri Lanka to establish the first community of nuns. This is recorded in the Chinese source but not in Sri Lankan sources. Generally, for the early medieval period we do not have much information on nuns or other female Buddhist practitioners in Sri Lanka. Some inscriptions demonstrate that royalty – both kings and queens – patronized Buddhism. For instance, one text dated to the eleventh century states that the king had an alms hall and other buildings built for the nuns.[7] There is also a Sinhalese text, the *Saddharmaratnāvaliya*, that dates to the thirteenth century. This text retells the biographies of some of the early Buddhist nuns that we met with in chapter 4, amongst others. This indigenous Sri Lankan version, though, casts the nuns in a less favourable light.[8]

It is well known that the nuns' Order died out in Sri Lanka during the eleventh century, possibly as a result of the invasions of a South Indian dynasty. There is no witness to its disappearance, nor are there later sources that reveal any attempt to reintroduce the now defunct Order of nuns.[9] It is not until the last decades of the nineteenth century that we once again begin to see accounts of committed female Buddhist practitioners on the island. In the 1890s and then more fully in the 1900s, the system of the *dasa sil-mātās* or *sil-mātās* began. These are women who live an ascetic life but are not fully ordained. The term *dasa sil-mātās* means 'ten precept mothers', to indicate that upholding precepts is central to their lives.[10] As well as maintaining their own practice and living a monastic lifestyle, many *sil-mātās* teach and also seek to raise awareness of women's issues in modern Sri Lanka. Although there have been several in-depth studies of *sil-mātās* published in recent decades, these have tended to focus on the social history of the group and biographical information about the women themselves, rather than on the ways that they practise or on what they teach.

In her seminal work on women in Buddhist Sri Lanka, Tessa Bartholomeusz recounts partial biographical narratives of many *sil-mātās*, highlighting difficulties the women had after making the decision to commit to the Buddhist path. One such woman whose circumstances she relates is Kotmalee Dhīrā Sudharmā, founder of a lay nunnery in the Colombo district.[11] At the time of the interview, Kotmalee Dhīrā Sudharmā was fifty years of age. Many of her family lived near the nunnery and had been a great support to her. Yet this positive relationship she was enjoying with them had been problematic in the past. Her family's initial response to her vocation mirrors the reactions of close relatives from accounts in chapter 4:

> I was ordained even though my parents tried to stop
> me in every way possible. After spending days, and
> then weeks, crying and moping and not doing much of
> anything else, my father permitted me to leave home.
> I was twenty-two years old and it was time for me to
> think about marriage. . . Having put only a few things in
> my suitcase, I went to the temple in my village.
>
> The day I left home, I had an inexplicable feeling
> of joy, even though I was leaving my ten brothers and
> sisters, and my property. I have had many experiences
> in past lives which have prepared me for the difficult life
> which I now lead. The training is a long process and it
> carried over from one life to another. Not just anybody
> can become a *sil mātā* and maintain the lifestyle without
> acquiring the proper disposition from previous births.

The monk who ordained me knew that I would be a good *sil mātā*. In the ordination service for the monk, the senior monk asks the initiates to say the Three Refuges in the following way: '*Buddhaṃ saranaṃ gacchāmi, dhammaṃ saranaṃ gacchāmi, saṅghaṃ saranañ gacchāmi.*' I, too, recited the refuges this way. When lay people recite the Three Refuges, they say '*Buddhañ saranañ gacchāmi, dhammañ saranañ gacchāmi, saṅghañ saranañ gacchāmi.*' That priest considered me to be no different from a *sāmaṇera*. In fact, the day I was ordained, I preached *bana* and loads of people came to listen. My family all came, too; there were so many of them it took a mini-van and a car to transport them all![12]

In this extract Kotmalee describes herself as ordained, as having had an ordination no different than that of a novice monk (called a *sāmaṇera*). It is also evident from the quote that Kotmalee is a teacher, and this is the case with other *sil-mātās* as well.[13] Although they are not fully ordained like their monk counterparts, their leadership, teaching, and other activities are often appreciated by local communities, on occasion more so than that of monks. Ranjani de Silva, also known as Kusuma, has set up training centres for *sil-mātās* in Sri Lanka, from which they are able to go out into villages and be of service. In a recent interview she reflects on her efforts during the time of civil war:

I went into the field, all ten districts, at that time we couldn't cover all of them because of war. After training, we spoke to the villages and told them that the nuns had received this kind of training and that they are your leaders and they will be helping you, so they were very happy. Everywhere we got a very good response, and sometimes we invite the head village member, the school principal, and people like that, they always say that these *sil-mātās* are good. In some places they say they need the monks, but there are some places there are no monks who can serve the community. It's sad to say that

sometimes they don't keep to the precepts. . . So this is
why nuns are doing a great job.[14]

Other studies of life in modern Sri Lanka have similar findings;
villagers appreciated the efforts of the *sil-mātās*. One villager
commented on the way that *sil-mātās* encouraged dual parenting
responsibilities, to good effect:

> It was really good to have the dasa sil matas teaching us
> meditation in the village. We help each other now. It is
> good that our husbands share the housework and child
> care with us. My husband brings the water from the well
> nearly a mile away, as our well has dried up. He also
> helps with the cooking in the mornings (Sudu Menike,
> interview, 27 July, 2000).[15]

As indicated, the community of women in modern Sri Lanka
living ascetic lives comprises two groups, *sil-mātās* and now
some fully ordained nuns. Still other women choose to practise
as lay devotees. In 2001 Helle Snel published a book in which
she recounts interviews with Sri Lankan women asking them
what their Buddhist meditation practice means to them. As Snel
notes, these women do not make up a representative sample.
Nonetheless the book provides insights into the lives a selection
of modern Buddhist women in Sri Lanka, and highlights some of
their personal motivations for continuing to practise Buddhism.[16]
Snel first introduces each of the women, then questions them about
their meditation. The answers reveal a group of women dedicated
to their Buddhist practice, knowledgeable about and reflective on
the basics of Buddhism and the vicissitudes of modern life. The
interviewees' responses demonstrate that, whether ordained or not,
Buddhist practice remains an important part of the lives of many
women in Sri Lanka today. Here are a few excerpts:

Ms Agnes Abeysekera was an eighty-year-old former school teacher
who, at the time of the interview, was continuing to do some part-
time tuition. Snel writes that she

. . . is a member of a group of mostly elderly women
(60–80 years) who meet two hours every week to treat
some subject of religious and/or moral importance,
a sutta(discourse of the Buddha) for instance, under
the leadership of a teacher. The regular teacher of this
group of 30–40 ladies is an 81 year old woman, a retired
teacher, but sometimes the teacher is a monk.[17]

Mrs Abeysekera comments on her practice:

I practise meditation by trying to be mindful during the
day. I have a mind that keeps wandering – past, future
– I try to bring it back to breathing. In the morning, first
thing, at 3 or 4 o'clock, I meditate. I take a glass of water
and then I sit on the stool for *mettā* a half-hour or an
hour in my bedroom. I take the five precepts whenever
I sit on the stool. First I do the *mettā-bhāvanā* (meditation
on loving kindness) – being compassionate even to ants
– then I think: what is it that I call 'me'? Then I think
of my body. I do no standing or lying meditation, but
sometimes in the evening I do walking meditation – I
do a lot of gardening. Happiness is very important. At
night, before I go to sleep, I think, 'If I don't wake up
again, I must at least be happy now.'[18]

The next quotes are from Mrs Violet, a married woman, aged 64
at the time of the interview, a former principal of a primary school for
girls. In response to Snel's question, 'Please tell me why you meditate',
Mrs Violet answers:

I firmly believe that if you improve the quality of your
mind, you will achieve good results. And I believe that
you are being reborn every single moment of your life.
Every moment is a little life. Experiencing every day like
that, is being free. Meditation is like an immunization:
when you meditate, you can exist anywhere, but you
don't get yourself involved. Like because you have to
eat, you eat.

I always had a strong belief in duty. Doing your duty is a good thing. Not demanding your rights, but doing your duties – that will give you your rights. Once you do your duties, your rights come automatically. You don't have to fight for them. I feel that this is living Dhamma. And this is what Vipassanā has done to me. Vipassanā is knowing the mind through the mind – not through the five senses. The senses distort. Feelings don't count. That leads to 'right seeing' (*sammā diṭṭhi*), the first step of the Noble Eightfold Path. And then the other steps follow automatically.

To me talking and teaching is also meditation – it leads to right thinking and right speech. I used to think that I was a good Buddhist. Now I know that I am only learning to become a Buddhist – by living the Dhamma.[19]

Mainland Southeast Asia

According to the Sri Lankan chronicles, Asokan missions were responsible for the transportation of Buddhism to Sri Lanka, and they were also the source of Buddhism's arrival on mainland Southeast Asia. The chronicles and a few other sources mention a 'Land of Gold' to which Asoka sent two monks – Soṇa and Uttara – who established Buddhism there. Many modern-day Buddhist countries in the region claim this as their origin myth, and as the way Buddhism first arrived in their country. Exactly which part of ancient mainland Southeast Asia comprised this so-called land of gold remains at issue. For example, a well-known royal inscription from Burma dated to 1476 describes the arrival of Soṇa and Uttara and the establishment of Buddhism in the region that became Burma. This inscription records that both men and women took up monastic life when Buddhism was established there. After Soṇa and Uttara taught the inhabitants the dharma:

> . . . 60,000 people attained to the comprehension of the truth; 3,500 men and 1,500 women renounced the world, and the rest were established in the three refuges and the *sīlas* [ethical principles].[20]

The validity of this claim to the origins of Buddhism on mainland Southeast Asia can be called into question. The region was certainly influenced by the neighbouring Indian society and culture during this period, and both Hinduism and other forms of Buddhism as well as Theravāda were prevalent in the region.[21]

The modern nation-states of Cambodia, Burma, Laos, and Thailand did not begin to establish their current boundaries before the eleventh and twelfth centuries. Prior to that, there were smaller centres of power which were eclipsed by two significant kingdoms in the eleventh and twelfth centuries – the Pagan kingdom, which was to become modern Burma, and a kingdom centred around the Angkor plain, known as the Angkorian Empire or the Khmer Empire. This kingdom spread over most of modern Cambodia and parts of Thailand and Laos.

Three kingdoms were situated in the area that was to become Burma, along the central Irrawaddy River. Colonial historians classified these in ethnic terms, although noted historian Michael Aung-Thwin has questioned these classifications as appropriate ways to view the history of the region.[22] We do not have much evidence of these kingdoms, and only a few examples of their practice of Buddhism. The ancient Pyu kingdom (second–ninth CE), for example, left a corpus of inscriptions, but these are yet to be satisfactorily deciphered. Chinese travellers did report, in the third century and in the ninth, that the Pyu were followers of the teachings of the Buddha, and that is certainly confirmed by the archaeological evidence. Sri Ksetra is the best-known site, where the archaeological remains include not only stupas and Buddha statues but also gold plate manuscripts with extracts from various books of the Pāli canon.[23] The Mons, a different group at another centre along the Irrawaddy, are believed to have produced chronicles, though many no longer exist.[24] With such limited evidence for Buddhist practice overall, it will come as no surprise that information on women is scarce. Some of the Pyu inscriptions do appear to have been made by female donors but, until more work is done on the language, the potential words of this group of women are the only ones – in this entire book – that we are not, as yet, able to hear.

Between the tenth and twelfth centuries, two larger centres of power emerged in the region. First, the Bamar eclipsed the other two groups along the Irrawaddy River and from this began the Pagan period. Pagan remains a famous Buddhist site to this day. Popular with tourists, it is the largest Buddhist site in Asia, with more than three thousand monuments. We have some evidence of female practice of Buddhism from the Pagan period. There are images of two of the early Indian nuns, Uppalavaṇṇā and Kisā Gotamī, that are part of a panel in one Pagan temple.[25] These are accompanied by label inscriptions that identify the figures by name. As such, these are the first confirmed images of early Buddhist nuns known to exist.[26] We should not assume, however, that nuns existed at the time, only that the narratives about the early Indian nuns were circulating (and popular) during this region and period.

The second larger power was the Angkorian Empire (ninth–thirteenth CE), centring on what is now called the Angkor plain in northern Cambodia, which includes the well-known Angkor Wat. It is from another temple, one of hundreds of Hindu and Buddhist temples dotting the Angkor plain, that we have a significant piece of evidence for women practising Buddhism in the region. This is in the form of an inscription made by a royal woman about her sister, both of whom followed the teachings of the Buddha. This inscription is unique in Southeast Asian history as being the only inscription written by a woman about another.[27] Dated to the twelfth century, the inscription was made by Indradevī about her sister Jayarājadevī. Indradevī says of her sister:

Instructed by her elder sister, Srī Indradevī and
beholding the Buddha as the beloved to be attained,
she walked the calm path of Sugata [the Buddha],
which passes between the fire of torment and the sea of
suffering.

... she worshipped the Buddha ... desiring
emancipation ... following his own path. . .

. . . her good deeds accomplished . . . her conduct
prescribed by tradition and the engendering of
her acquired merits earned her glory resplendent
throughout the world.

Having adopted by the hundreds hosts of young girls,
injured and abandoned by their mothers, as if they
were her own, she raised them in [a village] called
Dharmakīrti renowned for its dharma, rich in happiness
and wealth.

In this way, she brought into religion, with clothing,
gifts and prescribed ritual, the village of Dharmakīrti,
transformed with its established boundaries, famed for
its religious teachings, forever maintaining the honour of
dharma.[28]

In these short extracts from the longer inscription, we can see that
not only were both sisters devoted followers of the Buddha, but
Jayarājadevī also set up a convent for girls within a village, with the
intention that it become the hub of village life. Following the death
of Jayarājadevī, after 1190, the king made Indradevī his queen, and
put her in charge of multiple centres of Buddhist learning, at which
she taught other women.[29]

Cambodia

There has long been an understanding that women enjoyed a certain
degree of power in ancient Cambodia. The exact parameters of this,
and the extent to which it was symbolic or social power, have yet to
be established.[30] Some scholars have interpreted the data to indicate a
major shift in the situation for women with the advent of colonialism
in the nineteenth century. Jacobsen speculates that though any
Cambodian Order of nuns would have died out in precolonial times,
women retained power until then, citing passages in post-Angkorian
Cambodian Buddhist didactic literature which seem to suggest a kind
of equality between the sexes:

In being born human, *dharma* is the only concern to men and women. . .

Whether you are born male or female in this world, the wise say to obey your masters, to ensure that unclean substances do not touch you and contaminate you, and that you must endure the consequences of your actions.[31]

The inscription that begins this chapter is one of several dating from the post-Angkorian period that record a history of female practice in Cambodia. The devotion of women in these sources is notable. An exceptional long verse inscription from the early eighteenth century details the virtuous life of a woman named Paen. She is said to have performed many meritorious acts including the commission of statues and paintings of the Buddha, numerous stupas, as well as religious texts, the purchase of robes and candles, and the sponsoring of ordination ceremonies for young monks-to-be.[32] As well as this, there appears to be some inscriptional evidence that women may have 'entered the religious life', although the validity of this turns on some lesser known and little understood terms.[33]

Following the demise of the presumed nuns' Order, whenever that may have been, the subsequent beginnings of Cambodia's version of modern female asceticism are the *ṭūn jī*. Unlike Sri Lanka, little is known about the advent of this movement of female asceticism in Cambodia. Also, unlike Sri Lanka, although the nuns' Order has begun again for Sri Lanka and Thailand this is not the case for Cambodia. Nonetheless, we continue to find, in the modern period, inspirational and pioneering Buddhist women, such as one nun who until her death in 2008 ran a meditation centre near Angkor Wat. This woman made a choice to become a *ṭūn jī* after attending the inaugural conference of the Association of Nuns and Lay Women in Cambodia in 1995. Following this, she learned and practised meditation and then:

Loak Kruu ... began teaching others back in her home village, including monks from the local temple. Soon grateful learners started to make donations. In 1997, the head monk of the local temple donated an area of temple land adjacent to the temple area for her to use as her meditation centre.[34]

This donation enabled this venerated nun to build cottages and a meditation hall. She had many disciples and some monks named her as their teacher. This demonstrates that, although women cannot gain the full ordination status that men can, nevertheless they can make significant progress in their practice of and understanding of Buddhist teachings. When they do, this can be – although it is not always – valued by their communities, such that they are considered on a par with esteemed monks.[35]

Another inspirational woman who, like the nun above, lived through the period of the Khmer Rouge, is Thavory Huot. Thavory herself remained a lay practitioner, but has been involved in human rights and peacebuilding efforts within Cambodia for most of her life. She is currently the executive director of the Khmer Ahimsa Organization. Her life story is available to read online.[36] I also include here an extract from an article penned by Thavory Huot for the Sakyadhita International newsletter in 2015. Here, once again, we are offered some insight into the activities of a temple in Cambodia within which there is a female teacher, who teaches alongside monks:

> Wat Sampov Meas (Golden Ship Temple) in Phnom
> Penh is out of the ordinary. Typically, temples in
> Cambodia provide housing and education for boys
> and young men, but not for women. Sampov Meas
> Temple sets a groundbreaking precedent by providing a
> Buddhist study program for laywomen and nuns. Even
> more extraordinary, one of the teachers in the study
> program is a nun. Her name is Heang Kim Yun, but
> everybody calls her Donchee Kea.

Huot continues, detailing life at the temple and providing more insight into the work of the teacher, Kea:

> Wat Sampov Meas is unusual both because it provides
> rooms for a small group of nuns and because it
> provides classes on Buddhism for both laywomen

and nuns. Currently, the temple offers two different classes on Buddhism. One class is for monks, taught by the abbot of Wat Sampov Meas. The other class is for nuns and laywomen, taught by Nun Kea. The laywomen who join the classes are devout practitioners who work during the day as teachers, nurses, and shopkeepers. Many more women would like to join the classes, but are unable to read. Nun Kea teaches these women how to chant, the meaning of the chants, and about the qualities of the Buddha. The curriculum for the class taught by the monk abbot includes Dhamma and Vinaya (monastic discipline). He focuses on kammathan: how to develop awareness, let go of delusions, and develop wisdom. The curriculum for the class taught by Nun Kea is based on the tripitaka (the 'three baskets': Vinaya, Suttas, and Abhidhamma). She focuses on apithorm: how to better understand the nature of the mind and its unsystematic way of seeing, listening, tasting, speaking, and thinking. She teaches that, through awareness and understanding, the uncontrolled mind can be trained. She expects that the participants will become educated, train their minds, and develop wisdom. Along with their scriptural studies, the students train in mindfulness, so they can avoid negative responses and contribute to building peace within themselves, their communities, and society as a whole. Nun Kea teaches that when human beings are mindful, they are able to realize whether their daily activities are wholesome (kusala) or unwholesome (akusala), meritorious or demeritorious. With the insights the students gain through their studies, they come to realize that the quality of their actions depends on the quality of their mental states. With practice, they learn to let go of habitual tendencies that create suffering.[37]

Burma (Myanmar)

Modern accounts of women in the history of Burma are commonly shaped by skewed impressions dating to the colonial period. These suggest that women in Burmese history enjoyed a much higher status than that usually accorded to women in ancient and medieval societies. Although British colonialism is most often associated with India, Burma suffered a longer period of British colonial rule, lasting over one hundred and twenty years. When colonial administrators first arrived in Burma in the early 1800s, they were astonished to see that women were the main workers in the marketplace, doing the buying and selling and trading. This led colonial writers to assert that Burmese women, traditionally, unlike their 'sisters' in other parts of Asia, enjoyed great independence, autonomy, and liberty. Yet the historical evidence does not support such an interpretation. While women were actively involved in economic spheres, they were subordinated to men within the domains of religious life.[38]

Inscriptions from the twelfth century onwards attest that women had significant wealth. During the Pagan period we have inscriptions that mention names of both female ascetics and other women. One royal woman, who makes no secret of the pleasures derived from having money, nonetheless donates it. Her inscription reads, 'I have offered so much wealth not because I do not love it, but because I love Buddhahood more than wealth.'[39] Also from this region is an inscription of a queen regent, Bañā Thau, which is a Buddhist donor offering dated to 1455.[40] After listing the offerings made, the inscription states that those who uphold the offering, 'whether men or women', should enjoy good births as a result. Despite this being an inscription of a queen who is ruling independently, the good births that she highlights are all births as men – as rich men, kings, male gods, or (male) Buddhas.[41] The inscriptions also reveal that women were literate, engaged in other professions, and keenly devoted followers of the Buddha. Several inscriptions also mention one female ascetic in particular, Ui Chi Thaw, who was the head of a convent. Despite the record of Ui Chi Thaw, the extent to which a nuns' Order existed, and its parameters, is unclear.

Laywomen during this period made many donations that resulted in monasteries and temples being built. They gave silver and land to Buddhist establishments.[42] Female donors did not always have their own names recorded in the inscriptions, instead defining themselves by relationship as a wife, daughter, mother. The same occurs in royal orders from a later period. Here we find that although by this time women could not become fully ordained nuns, they could still use their wealth to their advantage. They could make donations that would lead to nirvana. This is illustrated in a royal order, dated to 1642, concerning a laywoman who donated money to enable a monastery to be built for monks:

> Order: Send for the Lady Donor of a monastery for Saramancu at the Winido Monastic Establishment to appear at the court and tell her that she could not reap the full benefit of building a monastery a.) if she had allowed any propriations made to spirits to avert any harm to workers during the constructions, b.) if she had used part of the monastery as her own store house, c.) if she had made use of the services of the monks in any of her various businesses, and d.) if she has been using one of the monks of the monastery as her medicine man; and also tell her that nirvana would be the ultimate reward if she continues supplying the four requisites of the monks to her monastery so that the monks who come to reside there could carry on with their own work without any difficulty.[43]

In this king's edict, which may sound humorous to modern ears, this female donor would be able to attain nirvana if she demonstrated that her donation was made from a wholesome motivation. Sadly, the woman's lay name is not recorded, but as a result of her donation she is given the name Saddhadhamma.[44] She is also given other material things in gratitude for her donation, such as copper, red ochre, and perfume. In other royal orders she is praised by chief monks.

For the more recent past, the 1800 and 1900s, I want to first focus on a pioneering laywoman known as Independent Daw San

(1887–1950).[45] In Burma and elsewhere, the long years of colonial rule resulted in the politicization of Buddhist monks. Many advocated that the Burmese people stop cooperating with British forces. In the 1920s and 1930s women too began to become involved in political activism. Daw San was one such woman. She was raised in a well-to-do family during the beginnings of British colonial rule of Burma. Her mother, Daw Su, supplemented the education Daw San received under the British system with 'traditional Burmese metaphysics, history, poetry and Buddhist scriptures'.[46] As a result of Christian missionaries, some of whom were women, the education of women and girls received a boost under the British. Daw San became one of a new generation of educated Burmese women.

Daw San became a teacher, and met and married a fellow teacher with whom she had four children. Her husband, sadly, contracted malaria and died at the young age of twenty-six. This was followed, just two years later, by the death of two of her children. Seemingly motivated by her grief to write, this period in her life resulted in the publication of her first major work, *Khin Aye Kyi*, a short story with a female Buddhist protagonist. In its advocacy of the importance of women's place in Burmese society, the story was both radical and groundbreaking for its time. At one point in the narrative, it is proclaimed that if women had been paid more attention, the Burmese would not be suffering under colonial rule![47]

Daw San's second marriage ended in divorce, and she moved into the world of publishing. Eventually, she set up her own newspaper, *Independent Weekly*, modelled on the Irish nationalist newspaper, *Irish Independent*. Daw San ran the entire enterprise, managing day-to-day operations as well as writing many pieces for the paper. Simultaneously, she became the leader of the first Burmese Women's Association, which played a role in the anticolonial struggle.

In modern Burma, education was important for monastics as well. Initially, this was the preserve of monks rather than *thiláshin*. But this has now changed. *Thiláshin* in Burma can commit to a career of study, taking monastic exams, teaching, and becoming state-certified dharma teachers. The first two women known to have taken up this lifestyle were Me Kin (1814–1882) and Me Natpeì (b. 1804). It is not clear whether other Buddhist *thilāshin* initiated or guided these two. Me Kin had a monk teacher who taught her Pāli grammar and with whom she studied many aspects of Buddhist teachings. Both Me Kin and Me Natpeì were appointed as private tutors and lived in the capital. Me Kin took up residence in a nunnery on the north side of the Mandalay Hill. There she taught philosophy, literature, and meditation. She was known for her charisma and flair as a teacher, and highly respected. She eventually became disillusioned with life in the capital and moved to a quiet village, where she continued to teach. Many of her female students became notable teachers in their own right, and her legacy and lineage remain strong.[48]

Since then many nuns have pursued this lifestyle, some becoming known for outstripping the monks in their ability in monastic exams. One of the best known of the scholarly nuns is Daw Dhammasari (1878–1971). She was born to a merchant's family and from a young age worked in the family silk trade. Her family were religious, so she was raised schooled in Buddhism. She had a desire to become a nun from a young age, and was easily bored helping out at the family market stall. When she told her family she wanted to become a nun they were angry. Her brother told her he would rather die than be known as the brother of a *thilāshin*. Her resolve was firm, nonetheless, and she ran away from home and shaved her head. Eventually the family relented, and she became a nun aged seventeen.

She studied with many *thilāshin* teachers and then set up her own nunnery school. She spent time in Sri Lanka and studied Sinhala, Pāli, and Sanskrit and Buddhist philosophy. After returning to Burma, she continued to attend lectures given by monks. Few women did this, and she found the environment hostile. At times, she was asked to leave the classroom, and at others had to sit behind a screen so that the monks did not know she was there. She continued to teach, both about Buddhism and language studies, and it is said junior monks would go to her classes. Eventually, her scholarly abilities were recognized. She spent the rest of her life working to improve education standards for women, writing textbooks and raising awareness. She was an informal mentor to a monk who became one of the most respected monk scholars of the twentieth century.[49]

A life devoted to studying and teaching is not the only path available to women in modern Burma who wish to commit to the Buddhist path. A range of options are available. Women can be lay followers, or choose a role that is more committed than regular lay life, but does not involve the level of engagement in practice that is expected of nuns. Often, this type of role is taken up by women later in life. Also, *thiláshin* can choose from a range of options. As well as a path of study and teaching, they can choose to focus on meditation. Or they can choose social work. A *thiláshin* can decide to follow the eight precepts, and be an eight precept *thiláshin*, or can become a ten precept *thiláshin*. Often, the goal for women, or the preferred option, is to become a ten precept *thiláshin*. But it is not always possible. A ten precept *thiláshin* is the highest status. A ten precept *thiláshin* does not engage with money and follows a more ascetic path. She will often be vegetarian, only eat raw food, reduce sleep, and observe silence. Most women are not able to practise in this way because of financial constraints. As is typical of monastic life, they rely on donations. Ironically, a woman needs to have a certain level of financial security and stability in order to become more of a renouncer.[50]

Despite the options for women, the decision to commit to following the path of the Buddha and renouncing the world can, as in the case of Daw Dhammasari, create personal hardship and tensions with families:

> Many nuns I interviewed told me about their personal
> trauma when their families found out about their
> decision to become one, as becoming a Buddhist nun for
> a daughter is not celebrated as it would be for a son.[51]

In 2003, a *thiláshin*, Ma Thissawaddy, travelled to Sri Lanka to receive ordination as a nun. Provoked by her ordination, the government of Burma published a statement. They declared the official position of the Burmese monastic community is that it is not possible to reinstate nuns as part of Theravāda tradition.[52] Nonetheless, many women continue to work to advance the situation for women in modern Burmese Buddhism. These include Ketu Mala, a young *thiláshin* who is gaining international recognition for her efforts. In an interview with *Tricycle* magazine in 2017, Ketu Mala comments on similar issues to those posed in Part I of this book, on how to engage with monks who hold certain views:

> 'If I am talking to the monks, I have to move wisely and carefully,' said Ketu Mala, explaining that she must bow when she speaks to the *bhikkhus* and sit below them. 'Some of them think that if I am talking about the gender issue, I am in competition with them. So I just have to explain to them: "This is not to compete with you. This is just for our confidence, for women."'[53]

Thailand

Until recently, scholars of Thai history tended to agree that no evidence existed for any heritage of a community of nuns in the region.[54] This has now begun to change, as a few 'glimmers' have come to light of scant evidence that suggests there may have been a nuns' Order in the region in the past.[55]

If there was a community of nuns in Thailand in earlier centuries, at some point this community ceased to exist, and during the modern period, as with Sri Lanka and Burma, there has been no nuns' Order. Martin Seeger's work, discussed in the previous chapter, highlights the lives of Thai Buddhist women during the nineteenth and early twentieth centuries. Although some of these women were, as we have seen, esteemed teachers, they were not fully ordained nuns, but rather *mae chi*s. Unlike with the *dasa sil-mātās* in Sri Lanka, it is unclear exactly how and when the institution of the *mae chi*s began. Like '*mātā*' in Sinhalese, '*mae*' means 'mother' in Thai.

In the decades or centuries prior to the nineteenth century Buddhism itself seems to have suffered a period of decline, during which it became diluted via influence from indigenous Thai religions. This decline can be adduced from the Sangha Act of 1902, a government initiative intended to revitalize and renew Buddhism, which also attempted to separate it from the influence of Thai spirit cults. Reform movements grew from the Sangha Act, some forming soon afterwards and others decades later, some advocating a traditional, back-to-basics Buddhism, and others proposing more radical reform.

Despite reforms, the traditional monks' sangha remained largely hostile to the idea of full ordination for women. Such a situation is exemplified in the story of two sisters, Sara and Chongdi Basit, whose father had them ordained in 1927. This is the first known modern case of women being ordained as nuns in Thailand. Their father, Narin Basit, a former government official and lay Buddhist, arranged for a monk to ordain his daughters. The identity of the monk was kept secret, for fear of retributions against him. One monk was suspected as the culprit, and was asked to disrobe. He denied that he had performed the ceremony. The father was accused of 'wanting to destroy Buddhism' and the daughters ordered to disrobe. Narin appealed to the king for help, but this was not forthcoming. One sister, Sara, was sentenced to jail time and fined, as she refused to comply with the order to disrobe. Because of these attempts to enable women to become nuns, monks were forbidden to ordain nuns by a specific regulation imposed in 1928.[56]

Some monks, however, even high-ranking ones, were supportive of the idea of female ordination, especially if the ordination was as part of a non-Theravāda tradition. The next well-documented case of a woman seeking ordination was Voramai Kabilsingh in 1956. She was ordained into a Taiwanese tradition. As her ordination was not as a Theravāda nun, it caused less controversy. The ordination of her daughter Chatsumarn Kabilsingh, in 2003, was within Theravāda tradition. Chatsumarn Kabilsingh, whose ordination name is Dhammananda, has been known as the 'rebel monk' in Thailand. She currently lives in a temple in Thailand with fifteen disciples, all of whom are women who have followed her example and taken full ordination. In 2019 she was honoured by the BBC News World Service's *Heart and Soul* programme as part of their series of a hundred influential women in religion. In her BBC interview, she commented on how, even today, she is often asked, 'How dare you as a woman put on the robe?'[57] In her 1991 book *Thai Women in Buddhism*, she addressed some of the same issues discussed in this book:

Local Thai beliefs and customs reinforce the negative perception of women. Some of these attitudes are regarded by the population as coming from the Buddhist teaching and are believed to reflect Buddhist attitudes, and this has lent them greater credibility and increased influence. It is frequently said, for example, that 'women were born from their bad karma.' This assertion that being a woman is in itself negative does much damage to woman's self-image and creates obstacles to her spiritual and social development. According to Buddhist teaching, everyone is born according to his or her karma. The present situation of one's life is a direct reflection of one's actions, whether good or bad. The belief that one's gender is the result of 'bad karma' does not hold any meaning. Yet many monks, whose principal source of support is laywomen, believe this idea. Many women are convinced that they carry a heavy load of karma due to the simple fact of their gender, and are therefore eager to gain merit to offset it. Making offerings to the Sangha is the primary way most laypeople hope to gain merit. Monks, being 'fields of merit', thus benefit directly from this vicious belief.[58]

As we have seen, in modern Buddhist communities, such views on women and karma can be unpopular. Despite this continuing to be a view held by many in Thailand, it is also acknowledged that gender is irrelevant in the pursuit of nirvana, and men and woman have equal capability to attain the goal.[59]

Dhammananda is an influential figure within the international Buddhist community, and the author of several books on women in Buddhism and other subjects. She continues to work to support the reintroduction of full ordination for women in Thailand. Other communities of nuns now also exist in modern Thailand, for example, a group in north Thailand who were ordained in Sri Lanka.

As well as efforts to reintroduce the nuns' community, other initiatives have been established to improve the lives of *mae chi*s and other women. For example, in the 1980s two pioneering *mae chi*s, Khun Mae Sumon and Khun Mae Pratin, started a nunnery that also incorporates the first school for *mae chi*s and girls in Thailand, the Dhammacarinii School.[60] Today there are many *mae chi*s who have received a good education and become respected teachers themselves at prestigious education institutions in Thailand. Certain of these *mae chi*s do not believe that it is either necessary, right or appropriate to (re)introduce full ordination for women in Thailand. Mae Chi Bunchuai, the respected scholar mentioned in the Introduction, who teaches at Mahamukut Monastic University in Thailand, comments:

> I do not think there should be *bhikkhunī*-s, because the lineage of *bhikkhunī*-s in Theravāda has been lost in India already. . . It is not necessary to ordain as a *bhikkhunī* in Thailand, because *mae chi* are able to study and spread Buddhism and be part of the Buddhist community.[61]

Like Mae Chi Bunchuai, Mae Chi Nathathai Chatninwat, who holds a Bachelor of Arts degree in sociology and a Master of Arts degree in women's studies, does not desire to be a nun. Unlike her fellow *mae chi*, she does not believe *mae chi* are lower than monks, but believes that if full ordination for nuns was (re)introduced, nuns would be considered inferior to monks:

> She was proud to be a *mae chi* and did not want to become a *bhikkhunī* even if it was an option. *Mae chi* were not lesser *bhikkhunī* but a particular career choice for women that permitted them a chance to study and advance psychologically; *mae chi* were not below monks, but *bhikkhunī* would be. However, she would support *bhikkhunī* ordination if it actually helped women get more opportunities.[62]

Lastly, in modern Thailand there is also an outlier, a radical Buddhist reform movement that ordains women. The Santi Ashoke movement was begun in the 1970s by Phra Bodhirak, a former television personality who, whilst a monk, became disillusioned with the traditional Buddhist sangha. The group has a radical agenda and has courted controversy throughout its existence. Surprisingly little of this, however, has been focused on the fact that women are ordained within the group alongside men. Nonetheless, because the leader split with the traditional sangha, none of these ordinations – of either monks or nuns – are accepted by the orthodox Thai authorities.

* * *

The history of women in South and Southeast Asian Buddhist traditions is a chequered one. Although we have some decisive pieces of evidence of women followers of the Buddha from the early history of the region – such as the *Dīpavaṃsa* and the inscription of Indradevī – these are few and far between. In both Cambodia and Burma, it appears that women were influential and active within political, economic, and social spheres. The available evidence for their agency and initiative clearly contrasts with colonial portrayals of Asian women as passive and docile.

In the English language there is an idiom to indicate the possibility of change: 'nothing is set in stone'. Fortunately for us, inscriptions are set in stone! Without this evidence we would know practically nothing about the lives of Buddhist women in South and Southeast Asia in the premodern period. But with this and some accompanying data in hand, we can see that there were women who were committed followers and teachers, possibly nuns, who also set up opportunities for other women and girls. Likewise, in contemporary Cambodia, Burma, and Thailand, the attitudes of women practising Buddhism, and wider attitudes about them, are multifarious. Some Buddhist women choose to devote their lives to the quest for reintroduction of full ordination for women, while others living a renunciate life prefer to remain as they are. Set against a backdrop of fully ordained, other renouncers, and lay devotees, we find a variety of characters – retired meditators, outspoken, humble 'rebels', Pāli scholars, authors, journalists, and political activists. The life of any one of these challenges Buddhist tradition and Buddhist texts that want to claim women are not men's equals.

CHAPTER 6

DEITIES, TEACHERS, LINEAGES: CENTRAL AND EAST ASIA

Women alone are the givers of life,
The auspicious bestowers of true bliss
Throughout the three worlds
. . .
When one speaks of the virtues of women,
They surpass those of all living beings.
Wherever one finds tenderness and protectiveness,
It is in the minds of women.
They provide sustenance to friend and stranger alike.
A woman who is like that
Is glorious Vajrayoginī herself.

Caṇḍamahāroṣaṇa Tantra[1]

Buddhism travelled via Central Asia to the East Asian countries in which it took root. It first arrived in China. The Chinese began to take an interest in the tradition between the first century BCE and the first century CE, coming to hear of it via merchants travelling along the well-known silk routes, and other land and sea trading routes. From there Buddhism was transported to other parts of East Asia, including Korea and Japan. The only Central Asian region within which Buddhism was established was Tibet.[2] It arrived in Tibet via two transmissions, the first in the seventh century and the next in the ninth.

In China and then in the rest of East Asia, Mahāyāna Buddhism took root. In Tibet it was tantric or Vajrayāna Buddhism that became popular. The reasons for this are historical. The modes of Buddhism transported to the new country correlate to the form of Buddhism that was either popular or had some influence in India at the time of transmission. Thus, in Sri Lanka the form that was established there was the early Indian pre-Mahāyāna form. In China it was Mahāyāna, as this had developed in India by the time of its transportation to China. In the later seventh and ninth centuries tantric Buddhism had become popular in India, so this is the form of Buddhism that was transmitted to Tibet.

In East Asian countries, a nuns' Order was established, and continues to the present day. As we saw in chapter 4, it was inaugurated in China with some initial difficulty. In all East Asian countries in which Buddhism exists there continues to be an Order of nuns. The first country outside of China to adopt Buddhism was Korea, which, at the time, was adopting other aspects of Chinese culture. Buddhism probably arrived there during the fourth century, although mural paintings in earlier tombs show some Buddhist influence in the form of lotus flowers. Korea then played a pivotal role in the transmission of Buddhism to Japan during the sixth century, with Korean monastics taking leading roles in teaching and disseminating the tradition. The first Japanese female Zen Master was Mugai Nyodai, who lived in the thirteenth century, and for whom elaborate memorial ceremonies continue to the present day.[3] Buddhism did not arrive in Taiwan until centuries after it had reached other parts of East Asia, not being established until the sixteenth century. Today, there is a vibrant nuns' community there, with nuns outnumbering monks.

Despite continued ordination, both nuns and other female practitioners have not always fared well in East Asia. The existence of ordination for women in East Asia did not amount to overall improved treatment throughout the history of Buddhism. Both with East and Central Asia, as with South and Southeast Asia, the picture is complex. Again, in both regions, the evidence about women's lives often collides with negative representations and textual prescriptions. In Tibet, a nuns' Order was never established. Nonetheless, we have evidence of some women in Tibet becoming fully ordained nuns, also of women authoring tantric Buddhist texts, of influential female teachers, such as Machig Labdrön in the twelfth century, of a female lineage being established in the fifteenth century, and of the lives of esteemed female teachers in the nineteenth and twentieth centuries.

One important difference between Mahāyāna and Vajrayāna traditions in comparison with Theravāda Buddhism is the presence of female deities. So far, in this book, we have not looked at the idea of deities within Buddhism. They are less important in Theravāda Buddhist traditions than in Mahāyāna and Vajrayāna, although not entirely absent. In Mahāyāna, two connected ideas developed. First, that there are more Buddhas than just the one historical Buddha of this era. Second, that there are concomitant beings, known as bodhisattvas. Bodhisattvas are on the path to Awakening like the Buddha, but set aside their own individual goal for the sake of other beings. The most popular of all bodhisattvas is Avalokiteśvara. His name epitomizes bodhisattva nature, meaning 'he who looks down with compassion'. Avalokiteśvara began life in India as a male bodhisattva, but, as we will see, when he travelled to China, 'he' became a 'she'; the female Guanyin, in English sometimes called the Goddess of Mercy.[4] An ever popular female bodhisattva is Tārā. Both Tārā and Guanyin are known in many parts of the Buddhist world, their popularity transcending the boundaries of Buddhist tradition. Both have been and are popular outside of Mahāyāna and Vajrayāna traditions. We have evidence of Tārā statues from seventh-century Sri Lanka, a Theravāda country, and if you take a trip in a river boat through modern Bangkok,

Thailand's capital city, you will see statues of Guanyin rising out of temple and domestic gardens that line the river bank.

To begin this chapter, I will therefore outline some of the basic features and emphases of first Mahāyāna and then Vajrayāna Buddhism.

Mahāyāna Buddhism

At first sight, Mahāyāna Buddhism appears to represent a significant and dramatic development. And when scholars began to study the tradition, it remained unclear as to exactly why such a change to Buddhism might occur in India. It is only in recent times that new clues have begun to surface that enable a viable explanation of its emergence and its links to pre-Mahāyāna doctrines and practices.

The two key features of Mahāyāna are a belief in the continued existence of the Buddha after death, and a focusing on compassion. Early Indian Buddhism is ambiguous about exactly where the Buddha goes after death. There are no definitive doctrinal formulations that are underpinned by a belief that he continued to exist, out there somewhere, accessible to practitioners and with agency in their lives. Following his death, the Buddha – now in the state of *parinirvāṇa* (ultimate nirvana) – was considered to somehow continue to 'exist' within his bodily relics. According to early tradition his body was cremated and the remaining bone relics divided up. These were then interred in monuments honouring the Buddha, known as stupas.

It is only a small step to move from a contained belief in continued existence within his bodily remains to a belief in the Buddha's more substantial continued existence. This move to rarefy the Buddha can be seen in increasing depictions of him as omniscient. One Sanskrit text that retells stories of early female disciples, companions of Dhammadinnā, Paṭācārā, and Bhaddā Kuṇḍalakesā, casts the Buddha as omniscient. With an ability to see the women going about their day-to-day lives, he is able to intervene. This he does if, for instance, they are pressured into marriage when all they desire is to become a committed follower of the path laid out by him.[5] For Mahāyāna, the Buddha is and always has been omniscient and continues to exist after death. If practitioners engage in the right way, they may be able to have access to him, perhaps in meditation. He can also have agency within their lives. Practitioners can call upon him to help with everyday problems and ongoing suffering.

Once this step is established the next step is a small one. If the historical Buddha continues to exist after death then perhaps there is not just one Buddha out there, but others as well. Beliefs develop that not only one but multiple Buddhas exist and have existed. And not only Buddhas but other beings that we can, as practitioners, have access to and that can have agency in our lives. They can help us, if they choose, to assuage our suffering or aid us on our path. Each step on the path towards these central Mahāyāna beliefs is a small one. But the transformation to Buddhism in the end is significant. Buddhism changes from what can be termed a 'self-power' religion, focusing on individual effort to achieve the goal, to an 'other-power' religion. This brand of Buddhism has a more devotional strain that looks to transcendent, omniscient beings to come to the aid of the practitioner.

As well as the various Buddhas who came to form part of Mahāyāna belief, other important figures are bodhisattvas. The word 'bodhisattva' means 'being (*sattva*) intent on Awakening (*bodhi*)'. 'For the sake of all others' is often added. Generally speaking, Buddhas are all male. However, the Introduction to this volume considers the question of whether women came become Buddhas. Importantly, bodhisattvas can be, and are, female. Tārā is the most popular female bodhisattva, known from the seventh century in India and revered particularly in Tibet. Tārā takes many forms, including wrathful tantric forms, and one text celebrates one hundred and eight forms of her. In that text Tārā says that if the practitioner simply recollects her name, she can protect and 'ferry them across' to nirvana.[6] She is best known as Green Tārā, a form that symbolizes her compassion. Rather than sitting cross-legged on a lotus flower, as is typical for bodhisattvas in Mahāyāna iconography, Green Tārā sits with one leg extended, stepping down into the world to help those who are suffering.[7] In the seventeenth century, the Tibetan commentator Tāranātha wrote a text on Tārā in which he has Tārā declare that her birth as a female was intentional.

Contrary to the prevailing notion that women are better reborn as men, this was far from her aim:

> 'In this life there is no such distinction as "male" and
> "female", neither of "self identity", a "person" nor
> any perception (of such), and therefore attachment
> to ideas of "male" and "female" is quite worthless.
> Weak-minded worldlings are always deluded by this.'
> And so she vowed, 'There are many who wish to gain
> enlightenment in a man's form, and there are but few
> who wish to work for the welfare of sentient beings in a
> female form. Therefore may I, in a female body, work for
> the welfare of beings. . .'[8]

According to Mahāyāna tradition, humans can become bodhisattvas. The bodhisattva vow, whereby a human practitioner commits to follow the path leading to bodhisattva status, is open to both male and female practitioners. As we saw in chapter 3, in the section on sexual transformation, in some Indian Mahāyāna texts women, or even girls, become female bodhisattvas. The idea that humans can and might desire to become bodhisattvas and put off their own journey to Awakening in order to aid other beings demonstrates the recentring of compassion for Mahāyāna. This emphasis on compassion originates from a particular historic situation. Institutional monasticism came under fire in India at the time of the development of the Mahāyāna. Monks were accused of having lost touch with this core aspect of Buddhism. As a response, Indian Mahāyāna texts declare that it is not only monks who can attain nirvana, laity can as well, and women and children. As this is proposed in Mahāyāna texts, this was considered significant with regard to gender. It has been seen as a symbol of respect for women. But, in reality, it was more polemic than a change heralding greater esteem.

China

The adoption of Buddhism by the Chinese was by no means straightforward but included the need to adapt certain aspects of the tradition till then infused with Indian norms and standards. This included, eventually, changes to *vinaya* rules governing monastic conduct. A nuns' Order began early on in the history of the practice of Buddhism in China, as explained in chapter 4. Initially, however, there were questions raised about whether the ordination of nuns was true ordination, as they were not carried out in accord with the rules laid down in the *vinaya*. These questions continue to reverberate today, although the community of nuns in both China and the rest of East Asia continues to flourish despite this, as it has done throughout most of its history.[9]

With the arrival of Buddhist texts into China, the Chinese learned, amongst other things, about the first female disciples of the Buddha whose stories are told in the canons. Narrative accounts, biographies, and episodes depicting the women from Indian sources – both pre-Mahāyāna and Mahāyāna – arrived in China, again in a piecemeal way. In some cases, the Chinese translations of narratives concerning women or depictions of them are more positive than what came to be the extant Theravāda accounts, in the Pāli sources. The sixth-century collection of biographies of early nuns, discussed in chapter 4, is the only text from that period that fully concentrates on the lives of nuns. Apart from this, up until the seventeenth century there is only limited evidence of Chinese Buddhist nuns available. There are a few inscriptions (such as the one that begins chapter 4), archaeological remains, often less than flattering literary depictions. There is one other source, likely dated to the eighth century, that provides a few insights into the lives of Chinese nuns of the time, and may itself have been composed by nuns. In this text, although only a few nuns are mentioned, they are praised for their worthiness in comparison with the monks. Interactions with their teacher, Wuzhu, demonstrate the power of their devotion:

> The Venerable [Wuzhu] said, 'If you are capable of such [resolution], then you are a great heroic male, why are you a woman?' The Venerable expounded the essentials of the Dharma to her: 'No-thought is thus no "male", no-thought is thus no "female". No-thought is thus on-obstruction, no-thought is thus no-hindrance. No-thought is thus no-birth, no-thought is thus no-death.

At the time of true no-thought, no-thought itself is not. This is none other than cutting off the source of birth and death.'

When the daughter heard his talk, her eyes did not blink and she stood absolutely still. In an instant, the Venerable knew that this woman had a resolute mind. He gave her the Dharma name Changjingjin (Ever-Pure Progress), and her mother was named Zhengbianzhi (Right Knowledge). They took tonsure and practiced, and became leaders amongst nuns.[10]

Buddhism's arrival in China heralded a new manifestation of Mahāyāna Buddhism. In China, as in India at the time, Mahāyāna texts grew in importance and, alongside them, the Buddhas and bodhisattvas. One text popular in both India and China is the Lotus Sutra, a text dedicated to the bodhisattva Avalokiteśvara, which states that, in reciting his name, one is saved from many harmful dangers. The popularity of Avalokiteśvara in China diversified as 'he' became a 'she', and became Guanyin. Guanyin became one of three popular female deities in China. The other two – Queen Mother of the West and Mazu – are considered goddesses of Daoist tradition. It seems the regendering of the bodhisattva may have come about via laywomen, having a folk origin. Certainly the regendering was not a simple process, as images of Avalokiteśvara – henceforth in this chapter Guanyin – continue to demonstrate the disparity over the gender of the deity. Images exist of Guanyin that in modern parlance might be called transgendered; there are images of what essentially look like a female figure but with a wispy moustache, and many still common statues and images of Guanyin depict her as a beautiful female with a male chest. Robes are partially draped over the open chest, which is entirely devoid of female breasts.

It is typical in China that historical figures become connected to gods, and this happened with Guanyin. Guanyin is said to be a manifestation of a princess, Miaoshan. The first instance of the story of Miaoshan was a text now extant as an inscription, dated to the eleventh century. Here, I relate a version of it produced by a woman,

Guan Daosheng (1262–1319), an accomplished painter, poet, and calligrapher, 'so esteemed by male critics that they collected and preserved her works'.[11] She also produced an embroidery of Guanyin, made in part with human hair, embroidered as the hair, eyebrows, and eyelashes.[12] Guan Daosheng's summary of the Guanyin legend is also an inscription, carved into stone on the occasion of a festival in 1306.

Guanyin was the youngest daughter of King Miaozhuang, named Miaoshan. She abstained from eating meat and kept the precepts of the religion, she was intelligent and wise. As his daughters came of marriageable age, the king sought husbands for them. Miaoshan defied him, so he sent her away to a nunnery, in order to change her mind. The nuns drove her about her tasks like a slave, but she was firm in her resolve. When this failed, the king had the nunnery set alight, and five hundred nuns burned; only Guanyin survived, sitting upright, reading sutras. The flames did not harm her. The king summoned her back, his wrath grew, and he decided to have her beheaded. But the sword broke in two of its own accord, and a tiger came and carried her away on its back. The tiger set her down in the forest, she was unconscious and dreaming. She dreamt of suffering beings, dismembered, burned, pounded, ground up. She recited sutras so they would be liberated. When she awoke, venomous dragons and beasts of the forest were pursuing her, so she took refuge in a hermitage, and the old man there gave her food and took her to Xiangshan. Here she pursued religious cultivation for some years and attained religious fulfilment. One day, she had a vision of her father the king, sick and close to death. He could find no doctor so she took the form of an old monk and reported to the throne that the king could be cured only with the hands and eyes of his closest kin. The king sent for his two other daughters but they disregarded him. The king asked a monk's advice who told him to go to Xiangshan, as there was a holy elder there who works for the salvation of living beings and could help. This king sent envoys to the holy elder, who severed her hands and eyes and gave them to him. The king took them and recovered. The king was delighted and honoured the monk with high office and rich rewards. The monk declined and simply said

I Hear Her Words

the king should visit in person the next day to give thanks. The king took his carriage and when he arrived saw the holy elder without hands or eyes, her body covered in blood. He grieved and at the same time noticed how she resembled Guanyin, and so must be his third daughter, Miaoshan. He humbly besought heaven and earth to make her whole again, and soon she had hands and eyes by the thousand. She bowed to him, and they expressed delight to be father and daughter. She urged him to practise good works, and they soared aloft together. Guanyin ascended the Western paradise and entered the assembly of Buddhas. She pointed out the way to many and observed the cries of the world.[13]

There are many versions of the Miaoshan legend. Another popular text, 'The Precious Scroll of Fragrant Mountain', provides a detailed account of her story. The date of this text is not known, but it is a source of popular modern pilgrims' songs. The story of Miaoshan became widely known as a result of the chanting of and listening to recitations of this version. Pilgrimage centres have also played a large part in the popularity of Guanyin in China, up to the present day. Local women often compose their own songs about Guanyin, usually sourced in the original story but 'with some strong local coloring'. In this modern song, composed and sung by a fifty-nine-year-old woman from Jiangyin, a personal element is obvious in the envy of Guanyin for her independence and the freedoms she enjoyed from not marrying. It is typical in these types of songs for the shift of identity, evident here, between the singer and Guanyin:

> Wearing a crown of pearls and striking
> A hand-held wooden fish, I go everywhere to
>   proselytize.
> I ask buddhas of the ten directions:
> Which road leads to spiritual cultivation?
> In the west, there is no other than King Miaozhuang.
> There is a truly chaste woman in the household of King
>   Miaozhuang.
> First, she does not have to bear the ill humor of her
>   parents-in-law.

Second, she does not have to eat the food of her
    husband.
Third, she does not have to carry a child in her womb or
    on her arms.
Fourth, she does not need a maid to serve her.
Every day she enjoys peace and quiet in her fragrant
    room.
Turning over the cotton coverlet, she sleeps on the bed
    alone.
Stretching out her legs, she went into the Buddha hall.
Pulling in her feet, she withdrew into the back garden.
For the sake of cultivation, she suffered punishment
    from her parents.
But now, sitting on the lotus throne, she enjoys blessings.
Over and over again, I chant Guanyin Sūtra
On the first and fifteenth, I receive the offering of
    incense.
Adoration to the Buddha, Amitābha.[14]

Although there are numerous examples from which I can draw, many aspects of the history of Buddhism in China that highlight and illuminate women's practice, the conditions for practice were not always favourable. This can be illustrated by a phenomenon that happened in seventeenth-century literature. During this period, in China, nuns were often depicted as – contrary to the expressed objective of celibate monasticism – highly sexualized. In fictional literature of the period, some writers even went so far as to suggest that the majority of nuns were in fact prostitutes, and the majority of nunneries brothels.[15] As one example of the type of literature, in one short story a group of nuns seduce a man who is visiting their nunnery. Once he tired of orgies with the nuns, he decided he wanted to return home. The nuns got him drunk, shaved his head and dressed him as a nun. He was too embarrassed to return home until his hair had grown back, so he stayed and eventually died of exhaustion continuing to be cajoled into sex on a daily basis.[16]

         I Hear Her Words

Korea

Buddhism officially arrived in Korea in 372 CE. One of the main sources on the history of Korea mentions several women who were instrumental in the spread of Buddhism on the peninsular. Two of these were sisters – named Sa and Morye – and Sa is the first recorded Korean nun. A sixth-century queen is also recorded to have become a nun, although the royal decree allowing ordination for women was issued after this time, during the next succession to the throne. The nuns' Order in Korea were architects for the nuns' Order in Japan, as Buddhism arrived in Japan from Korea. Nuns were dispatched to Japan, and vice versa, with Japanese women going to Korea to receive novice ordination. In fact, documents record that women, rather than men, were the first Japanese to be formally ordained and become Buddhist monastics.[17]

Korean history is divided into different dynastic periods, and certain of these favoured Buddhism, while others did not. The longest ruling dynasty was the Chosŏn (1392–1910). This dynasty was anti-Buddhist, and promoted Confucianism, although there seems to have been in some cases a public adherence to Confucianism coupled with private practice of Buddhism. This is especially true for female members of the royal family and noble women, who continued the tradition of having royal nunneries built in the palace grounds. Here they could take the tonsure and lead a religious life. The dimensions of private Buddhist practices associated with such nunneries, however, reveal something akin to a union of Buddhist and Confucian beliefs. Wives and daughters pray for good rebirth for deceased family members, mirroring Confucian ancestor worship.[18]

The advent of Japanese colonialism in Korea in 1910 heralded a new era for female clergy, with the first meditation centre for nuns opening in 1916, and many others soon following. While the Japanese favoured Buddhism and created new opportunities for practice, the establishment of a dynamic nuns' order was not easy, and the inaugural nuns faced many challenges. They were tasked with rebuilding ruins to establish their centres in remote areas, and so also often needed to walk miles to meet with their teachers. The stories of these energetic nuns inspired many other women to become Buddhists, and the nuns' Order grew in strength in this period, such that in the postcolonial period nuns began to outnumber monks in Korea.[19]

During the twentieth century, a male teacher called Mangong Sŭnim had many women as students. He certified some as Sŏn (Zen) Masters. He was the teacher of the well-known Myori Pŏphui (1887–1974) and also of Mansŏng (b. 1897), both of whom were recognized as female Sŏn Masters. The essence of Sŏn, or Zen, practice is about direct experience, a vital and energetic breaking though to a profound experience of the present moment which can, with the right amount of application and practice, become a breakthrough to the experience of Awakening. A Zen teacher, or Master, is crucial for this process, to offer teaching to enable the breakthrough to happen.[20]

Mansŏng was known as a stern teacher, but well loved by her disciples. Oral accounts of her teachings still circulate, but there are no written records of them. The most popular account of her relates that, prior to becoming a master herself, she approached a male Zen Master, put her foot on his and asked, 'Whose foot is this?' Other teachings of hers include the following question and answer dialogues. Mansŏng teaches her students with incisive responses to their questions:

Q: 'How do I cultivate the way of the Buddha?'
A: 'No cultivation.'
Q: 'What about obtaining release from the cycle of birth and death?'
A: 'Who chains your birth and death?'
Q: 'How long does it take for a sentient being to become a buddha?'
A: 'There is no sentient being and no need to become a buddha.'[21]

One of the best-known Korean nuns of modern times is Kim Iryŏp. Prior to becoming a nun, Kim was part of a first generation of women intellectuals in the early 1900s, and among the first women to pursue higher education at the Ewha Womens University in 1915. She was also a feminist during this period, one which saw feminism prominent in political and public life in Korea; characterized as a focus on the 'New Woman'. This movement emphasized self-awareness, individual (social and sexual) freedom, and political rights.[22] Prior to her ordination, Kim was a prolific writer, publishing many poems and essays. She also launched a journal, entitled *New Woman*, which is credited with being the first Korean journal edited by a woman on women's issues.[23] This early poem illustrates her shift towards Buddhism as, rather than a love poem, this is a poem to the Buddha:

> Trusting your words
> My young soul struggles to trek on the road you
>   showed me
> But it's hard to tell when I'll reach where you are
> For I do not even know the way
>
> Was it 1,000 or 10,000 years ago that you called me?
> When I hear your voice inside me,
> I feel as though I'm going to see you right here.
> And I get lost in (religious) ecstasy,
> But when I return to reality, I am still where I was.[24]

After her ordination, Kim did not write again for two decades. Once she did, we can see that her interpretation of Buddhism is grounded in some of the feminist principles she cherished earlier in her life. Rather than focusing on devotion or compassionate action, Kim's teachings focus on the individual and on existential questions – what value does existence have? What is freedom and how is it truly attained? And, ultimately, how can we transform ourselves to attain nirvana? This extract from a work she published in her sixties demonstrates this focus:

> Because we are alive, we desperately claim freedom and
> peace as absolute necessities. If we are really free beings,
> how can there be any complaints or dissatisfaction?
> Freedom and peace belong to us as individuals; so
> why do we try to find them in something external to
> us? Moreover, if we are free beings, we should be free
> from the boundaries called the universe, the numbers

called time, and the limits called space. Why are we still bound by time and space and unable to free ourselves from the birth and death of this body? It is because, even though we define ourselves as human beings, we have lost the original mind of human beings; this original mind is creativity equipped with all kinds of qualities. Since we have lost our original mind, we fail to ask the fundamental questions about our existence. That is, we fail to ask why we still call this 'I' our own when we cannot take charge of our lives. Human beings primarily consist of the material mind that senses joy and sorrow. We are beings controlled by a thought that is thinking of thought. Only when we live according to the 'mind of nothingness', which is the thought before a thought arises, does life as a human being begin. Only when each of us finds the original mind of a human being, which is the 'existence of nothingness', and are capable of putting it at our own disposal, does the human being's life open up. When that happens, we become independent beings no longer susceptible to being manipulated by the environment. Once a person reaches this state, whenever, wherever, and whatever kind of life he leads, no matter the shape of his body, he finds nirvana.[25]

Taiwan

Buddhism was transmitted to the island of Taiwan much later than to other parts of East Asia. It was not taken up and practised until the 1600s, as a result of migration from China.[26] The history of Buddhism in this period on the island is not entirely clear, it seems that Chinese settlers often replicated the temples and practices they were familiar with from China. One deity that arrived there during this period was the ubiquitous Guanyin, who was to become as popular in Taiwan as she was in China.[27]

It is not until the twentieth century that we have clear and accurate records of the lives of Buddhist women and nuns in Taiwan. During the twentieth century, early on, nuns already outnumbered monks in Taiwan, and this continues to the present day.[28] In this modern period, numerous nuns have built and led their own monasteries, holding financial and management power over nuns and monks; many of these are highly educated women, actively involved in teaching, education, charity, and cultural affairs.[29] With the nuns' community being so strong, and many nuns taking leadership roles, the eight special rules, whilst still known in Taiwan, have not been adhered to. Instead there has been silent acceptance that it was not appropriate for a monk to expect a nun to bow to him. But, as noted earlier in this book, this changed during a series of events in the 1990s and 2000s and created a media storm in Taiwan, prompting a renewed debate on the relevance of the rules.[30] This is not the sole example of moral activism by nuns in Taiwan. Another prominent example is support for lesbian and gay (LGBTQ+) rights, which resulted in a nun, Zhaohui, presiding over the first Buddhist lesbian marriage ceremony in Asia in 2012.[31]

A nun who has been especially influential is shaping Buddhism in Taiwan is Zhengyan. Taiwanese Buddhism is said to have four guardians, who replicate the four guardian kings of early Buddhist cosmology. In early cosmology there are four males, but in contemporary Taiwanese Buddhism one of the four guardians is a woman, the charismatic Zhengyan. Zhengyan founded the Tzu Chi Foundation in 1966, a charity and nongovernment organization. It has become one of the largest Buddhist organizations in the Chinese-speaking world, reportedly having more than ten million followers globally. The foundation:

> has operated hundreds of global humanitarian relief
> campaigns mostly focusing on disaster relief (e.g.,
> the Indian Ocean earthquake and tsunami in 2004,
> and Hurricane Katrina in 2005). It has also expanded
> its influence through the diaspora network to
> countries like America and connects these diaspora
> communities through its television station and internet
> broadcasting.[32]

Zhengyan is a hugely popular figure, both in Taiwan and around the globe, and many followers have portraits of her around their homes, in living rooms, in wallets, or at work on counters and desks, even in the car.[33] She was nominated for the Nobel Peace Prize in 1993 and pictured on the cover of *Time* magazine in 2011 as one of the world's most influential people. She appears twice daily on her TV channel, once in the morning and once in the evening.

Zhengyan's presentation of Buddhism in relation to women and female roles has been challenged as reinforcing gender roles but also lauded as a fresh conceptualization of the bodhisattva path. It puts women and traditionally feminine roles and characteristics at the heart of what it means to be a compassionate Buddhist. Zhengyan has been equated with the bodhisattva Guanyin herself, and certainly she focuses on Guanyin in her teachings by reconstructing a bodhisattva path. Zhengyan does not teach that we should call upon Guanyin when we need help. Instead we should imitate her compassion; we should ourselves engage as much as possible in compassionate action. She says:

> We will become Guanyin's watchful eyes and useful hands, and the world will never call us Buddhists a passive group again.[34]

> Bodhisattva Guanyin's merciful eyes watch over all sentient beings. She cannot bear to see their suffering and she always gives a hand to help. We are like the eyes and hands of Bodhisattva Guanyin. Whenever we hear painful voices, we should go to help.[35]

Zhengyan encourages her followers to be more like Guanyin. In her presentation of Buddhism, she harnesses the nurturing, maternal qualities of the compassion of bodhisattvas and re-envisions them. Rather than such attributes being considered feminine and contained within mothering roles within the home, Zhengyan has made them socially important attributes that people should cultivate in order to make progress on the path. This can be best summed up by a quote from one of Zhengyan's male followers, who himself starts to value such attributes when he becomes more fully aware of their social and religious significance. He starts the account of his revelation relating how he did not, initially, value the female members of Tzu Chi:

> Before I joined Tzu Chi, I regarded them as a reuse
> of social residual value. Anyway, they were simply
> housewives. I talked to them about *Buddha dharma* and
> wondered if they knew it at all. Then once I went to visit
> the poor in a mountain area with them. When we got
> near the house, a rotten smell came out, and it almost
> drove us away. I hesitated to move forward. Yet they
> entered the house at ease; they were so brave. [One . . .]
> asked the elderly woman in bed, 'May I bathe you?' She
> lifted a corner of the quilt. It's a distressing sight. All the
> excrement has dried out already. I ran into tears. I said
> to myself, how could one 'wearing trousers' (referring to
> male) yield the palm to one 'wearing skirts' (referring to
> female)? I reluctantly helped cleansing the house. I came
> to realise that *Buddha dharma* was not just about talking,
> but for practicing. The sisters generously gave a hand
> regardless of the fusty dirt. . .[36]

This scenario evokes early Buddhist scriptures, for instance, where they recount incidents of compassionate care. The best-known of the traditional stories is that of the Buddha finding and nursing a monk who is sick with dysentery. He then implores the monastic community to ensure they care for one another when sick.[37] Compassionate care is not, however, often gendered in the way it is framed here. The compassion of the bodhisattva Guanyin is morphed into practical social care that not only elevates notions of 'female' nurturing into something socially and morally desirable, but frames it squarely as religiosity to which followers should not only subscribe, but should throw themselves into wholeheartedly, and roll up their proverbial sleeves and get their hands dirty.

Tantric Buddhism

In the tantric Buddhism of Tibet, we also find a reconfiguring of female energy, but with a very different outcome.

Tantric Buddhism can be seen both as a development from Indian Mahāyāna and the incorporation of Hindu tantra into Buddhism. Hindu tantra certainly existed prior to Buddhist tantra, and Buddhist tantra can be easily seen as an incorporation or adaption of Hindu tantra, with much of the same imagery and iconography overwritten with Buddhist meaning. This does not, of course, make Buddhist tantra any less Buddhist. Hindu tantra begins, essentially, with the Hindu god Śiva, and some forerunners. Śiva is the quintessential wild ascetic, semi-naked, dressed in rags, with matted hair and face smeared with ash. The same iconography was incorporated into Buddhism so that the peaceful deities of Mahāyāna became the wild, energetic images of Buddhist tantra. The energy of the imagery was infused with Buddhist meaning to encapsulate the very idea of tantra in Buddhism: the transformation of negative energy into energy that enables Awakening. The skull cup that might be in the hand of a Hindu tantric deity, such as the well-known female Kālī, is overwritten with Buddhist meaning to symbolize impermanence.

The core features of Buddhism remain constant within tantra, although expression of them diverges. Buddhist tantra upends many of the most common assumptions about Buddhism and Buddhist practice. It remains the case that the practitioner might still seek a solitary spot for quiet meditation practice with the goal of gaining self-mastery over the mind and attaining nirvana. But rather than this being achieved through a quiet awareness and mindfulness, the wrathful tantric deity jumps into the practitioner's mind, demanding spontaneous transformation of negative energy and experiencing of the present moment. And this wrathful deity is often female.

For all forms of tantra – Hindu, Indian Buddhist, and Tibetan – the female is important. Kālī is the best-known female figure to exemplify tantra, with her dishevelled hair, necklace of human skulls, and skirt of severed arms. Similar imagery for female deities in Buddhist tantra was adopted in India and in Tibet. And, again, with each of these forms of tantra, the idea of female energy is a key aspect of how tantra works. In Hindu tantra, female energy, or *śakti*, is half of the complete soul, which needs to be reunited for liberation to be possible. In Indian Buddhist tantra the idea of the unification of male and female energy to help the adept progress on the path remained important. In Tibetan Buddhism, female energy took on its own unique potency.

Tibetan Buddhism

The first phase of transmission of Buddhism to Tibet occurred in the seventh century, and the next in the ninth. During the first transmission, the time of the Tibetan empire, non-tantric forms of Buddhism prevailed. According to legends, during this period the king of the empire, Songtsen Gampo, had two wives, a Nepalese wife named Bhṛkuṭī and a Chinese wife, Wencheng. The three of them were instrumental in establishing Buddhism in Tibet, with the two wives becoming known in their own right, even today having contemporary political currency. For this reason, a play was composed by a well-known playwright in China, entitled *Princess Wencheng*, that continues to be performed today.[38]

Prior to the ninth century and the development of tantra, there are a few sources that tell us about other royal women. One was queen regent, and another seems to have been a nun. Evidence of this nun comes from two sources, an inscription on a bell donated to a monastery and the Tibetan chronicles. The chronicles tell of her efforts in enabling the building of monasteries, sometimes crediting her with overseeing aspects of architectural engineering, and also mention that she instructed others to practice. Her name was Changchub, which means 'supreme enlightenment'.[39]

Both in India and Tibet female figures were a core part of tantric iconography. Tārā was incorporated into the tantric pantheon in India and became hugely popular in Tibet in both her peaceful and wrathful forms. But the quintessential female figure for Tibetan Buddhist tantra is the *ḍākinī*. *Ḍākinī*s, and their male counterparts, *ḍāka*s, were originally Indian. The female *ḍākinī* in Tibet, however, took on great prominence, outstripping and outshining the *ḍāka*. The *ḍākinī* represent spontaneous, potent energy, energy the practitioner must harness in order to make progress on the Buddhist path. *Ḍākinī*, and the Tibetan synonym *khandroma*, came to mean 'sky-goer' or 'sky-dancer' and the iconography of the *ḍākinī* depicts her in the sky, which is equated with emptiness. The well-known volume on the *ḍākinī* – *Ḍākinī's Warm Breath: The Feminine Principle in Tibetan Buddhism* – was authored by Judith Simmer-Brown, a practitioner and teacher within Shambhala International, and professor at Naropa University. Simmer-Brown begins her book with an account of Padmasambhava, an important mytho-historical figure who is said to be the one who brought Buddhism to Tibet. In the account, Padmasambhava himself fails to recognize a *ḍākinī* when he meets her. This, says Simmer-Brown, is typical:

> In many sacred biographies, even the most realised
> teachers do not immediately recognise the ḍākinī,
> whose ambiguous, semiotic quality accounts for the
> richness and variety of her lore. She may appear
> in humble or ordinary form as a shopkeeper, a
> wife or sister, or a decrepit and diseased hag. She
> may appear in transitional moments in visions, her
> message undecipherable. If she reveals herself, if she
> is recognised, she has tremendous ability to point out
> obstacles, reveal new dimensions, or awaken spiritual
> potential. It is essential that the Vajrayana practitioner
> does not miss the opportunity of receiving her blessing.
> But when the time is not ripe, or when inauspicious
> circumstances are present, the ḍākinī cannot be seen,
> contacted or recognised.[40]

Simmer-Brown also notes that as Western scholars began to try to define, describe, and analyse the *ḍākinī*, they, too 'did not recognise her'.

Vajrayoginī is the best known of all *ḍākinīs*. She is most often depicted as bright red in colour, with a fierce expression, in a dancing pose, and holding various objects such as a skull cup full of blood. But this is not her only form. As the quote on Vajrayoginī that begins this chapter demonstrates, she exhibits 'tenderness and protectiveness'. Another popular form is as Vajravārāhī, a form in which she appears with a sow's head. The following is a description of how a practitioner might visualize Vajrayoginī as Vajravārāhī. In tantric practice, the adept often has a consort. Most often, as the deity is male the female is consort to them. But here, in a reversal, as Vajravārāhī is the deity, the male practitioner is her consort.[41]

> And now I will teach the supreme sādhana of [Vajra-]
> vārāhī: Through the practice of the generative stage, [the
> practitioner] should visualize, as himself, a body that is
> as bright as twelve suns, [red] like vermillion powder,
> [and red] like the *bandhūka* flower and the China rose.
> [Vajravārāhī should be visualized] with three heads and
> six arms. [She should be seen] replete with all [the bone]
> ornaments, sitting firmly in the *sattvaparyaṅka* [with a
> right foot placed on the left thigh and the left foot on the
> right thigh], with a garland of skulls as her headdress,
> her hair strewn about [her], [and] as beautiful. [She
> should be seen] with a vajra and bell [in her crossed
> arms, held behind her consort's back], pressed against
> by the [kiss of the] lower [lip] of her consort. [She is
> visualized] holding a bow and arrow, [and] is poised
> [with a bowstring] drawn back to her ear; [she is seen]
> holding a skull bowl [in one hand] and a staff [lodged in
> the crook of the same arm] [and] is intent upon drawing
> in the hook. [She is visualized] in the center of a red
> lotus, as one who grants all desires.[42]

Women in the history of Tibet have been identified as *ḍākinīs*. Yeshe Tsogyal, for example, has been identified with Vajrayoginī, and Vajrayoginī as Vajravārāhī. While no direct evidence confirms Yeshe Tsogyal's historical existence, she has remained popular amongst Tibetans. She is not only considered an early master, but is also prominent in many rituals, practices, and traditions associated with or engaged with amongst Tibetan Buddhist traditions today. She was also a key figure associated with Padmasambhava.

The first biography of Padmasambhava was one amongst many texts that were said to have been hidden by Yeshe Tsogyal. It was apparently rediscovered, in the twelfth century, in a temple and is classified as a *terma* text. *Terma* texts, that were hidden and then discovered, were common in twelfth-century Tibet.

Biographies of Padmasambhava usually convey that he subdued the demons of Tibet to propagate Buddhism. Often, he is said to subdue *ḍākinīs*, but is also taught by them. Chapter 2 of the biography concludes with the following:

> Following that, he went to the charnel ground Sosaling, situated to the South of Uddiyana. There he practiced yogi discipline and was empowered and blessed by the dakini Sustained of Peace. Later he went back to the island in the ocean where previously he had been born from a lotus flower. By practicing the dakini sign language of Secret Mantra he magnetized the four classes of dakinis dwelling on the island. All the ocean nagas and planetary spirits in the heavens promised to be his servants and were bound under oath.
>
> After that, he practiced at the charnel ground Rugged Grove in Uddiyana and had a vision of Vajra Varahi who empowered him. The four classes of dakinis and the dakas and dakinis of the three levels bestowed attainments and transmission upon him. All the dakinis blessed him and taught him the dharma.[43]

Uḍḍiyāna is a region of north India said to be the 'land of the *ḍākinīs*'. Evidence has recently come to light which offers clues on why and how this ascription came about. Between the ninth and eleventh centuries, Buddhist women from this and neighbouring regions authored a significant number of tantric texts. Ten such women have been identified so far in research that is currently in its early stages. Most of the texts these women composed have not yet been translated or studied in any depth.[44] Between them these women likely authored over thirty Buddhist texts. The women include a Brahmin, Vajravatī, who composed a text on Green Tārā, and Lakṣmī (also known as

Lakṣmīṃkarā), who authored four texts: an instruction manual, a text about Vajrayoginī, a commentary and a poem. Lakṣmīṃkarā is also said to have been an incarnation of the wrathful Red Tārā. Another of the ten women, Ḍākinī Siddharājñī, authored four contemplative and ritual texts on different deities. The most productive of all was Jñānaḍākinī Niguma, who is credited with eleven compositions. In her instruction manual, Lakṣmīṃkarā demands that women should be respected:

> One must not denigrate women,
> In whatever social class they are born,
> For they are Lady Perfection of Wisdom,
> Embodied in the phenomenal realm.[45]

As well as these female authors known in Tibet, we have evidence of esteemed female teachers. The best known of these is Machig Labdrön, a historical woman who lived between the eleventh and twelfth centuries and who, like so many Tibetan teachers, is identified as various deities including Vajravārāhī.[46] Machig was instrumental in the spread of certain types of Tibetan Buddhism, and is credited with establishing her own Chöd tradition. Chöd is a specific type of Tibetan practice; the word literally means 'cutting through' and it is about cutting through obstacles that inhibit one's progress towards Awakening. Cutting through the illusion of self, or ego, is central to the practice. In a text entitled 'Clarifying the Meaning of Chöd', composed by Machig, she begins by declaring of herself, 'Machig is the ḍākinī of timeless wisdom, the birth mother of all past, present and future Buddhas. The vajra ḍākinī of the mind family'.[47] Following this is a narrative on Machig's most recent life prior to her existence as Machig. This story, retold in more than one text, upends the episodes of sexual transformation we reviewed in chapter 3: in this narrative she is born as a male who then becomes the great Machig, illustrious teacher and founder of Chöd. In her previous life as a young man she learns from various teachers and meets with a host of *ḍākinīs* and Tārā, who instruct him. They eventually persuade him to go to journey to a specific mountain. Once he arrives, the pivotal episode is related:

Early in the morning, twilight of the 15th day, a blue-black Ḍākinī wearing bone ornaments, holding a *khaṭvāṅga* [staff] and a chopping-knife, and having a very furious appearance, spoke to him as follows: 'Yogin, make up your mind to go to Tibet. I shall kill you (now), and thereby your consciousness may quickly enter into my heart.' She raised her knife and performed the gesture of killing. His consciousness entered into the Ḍākinī. . . She pronounced a blessing so that his body would not decompose, and he, having been shown the way by the Ḍākinī, went without hindrance to [the town] and there entered the womb of the Mother.[48]

The town to which he went was the town in which Machig was then born, to the same mother. As mentioned, Chöd practice is about cutting through or the cutting off of the ego, and often this is represented as a form of killing of the self. The episode relates that Machig was, essentially, born as part of Chöd, born via Chöd practice, as s/he was ritually killed in order to be reborn. According to some Chöd texts, the act of ritual 'killing' is performed by a fierce *ḍākinī* wielding a ritual knife.[49] The fact of her having been male is relevant only as a demonstration that all women do not have to be reborn as men to make progress, and that 'the future spiritual development or even perfection of a man can be realized not *in spite of* but *by means of* his rebirth as a woman'.[50] At their core, tantric and Tibetan Buddhism are about the transformation of energy, and here we witness true transformation, a transformation with regard to the worth attributed to female energy and birth as a woman.

As well as the female authors and the esteemed and well-known teachers like Machig Labdrön, there is also a female reincarnation lineage in Tibet that continues to the present day. Although rebirth and incarnation are Indian models, this type of reincarnation, of a historical figure, is uniquely Tibetan. In this process, it is believed that the consciousness of one person is transferred to another. The Dalai Lama is the best-known example of Tibetan reincarnation, yet the female reincarnation lineage of a royal woman called Chökyi

Drönma is as old as that of the Dalai Lama. The first recognized Dalai Lama was a peer of Chökyi.

Chökyi Drönma was from southwestern Tibet and lived in the fifteenth century. At a time when women were not normally ordained, she decided to renounce her royal status to become a nun and became a famed and inspirational leader. Once fully ordained, she was given the name Dorje Phagmo, which means 'Thunderbolt Female Pig'. Although this name sounds unflattering, it is connected to her identification as Vajravārāhī.[51] Although she died young, at thirty-three, she had already made a substantial mark, including promoting opportunities for other women. At her death, her disciples began searching for a young girl who might be her reincarnation. The twelfth reincarnation is currently an important figure in modern Tibet: head of a monastery and a high government cadre in the Tibet Autonomous Region. A biography of Chökyi, that likely dates from close to her time, recounts her first attempt to take her novice vows:

> Then she announced: 'In general there is no significant difference between those who succeed in being born as male and those who fail and are born as female. However, from now on, I will focus on supporting Buddhist practices for women, the source of trust for all women.' Then she offered one silver *sho* to every male and female member of the monastic community and offered many donations to support the celebrations. Holding a banner of liberation, she took the vows as a novice. From being part of a family, she became without family. She received the name Adrol Chökyi Drönma.
>
> Everyone from Palmo Choding came to meet her and show their respect. As soon as they saw her, they immediately felt great faith. . .
>
> At one point the closest disciple of the Omniscient, called Konchog Gyaltshen, said to her, 'It is astonishing that you renounced all worldly pleasures and took the vows. Now the religion and political power of [your region] will decline.' She replied, 'I do not have lesser

aspiration now than I had before. I am not satisfied with
the enjoyments of this life; I seek the enjoyment that lasts
forever. I am not satisfied with being the queen ruling
over [my region]; I want to become a place of refuge for
all living beings.' Hearing this, Konchog Gyaltshen felt
embarrassed about what he had said.[52]

It took Chökyi Drönma many attempts to take her novice vows, as
her efforts were thwarted on several occasions by family members,
including her husband. Her biography records that guards and dogs
were put at every entrance and exit from the palace to stop her from
leaving. Her husband, when he heard she had taken her novice vows,
was furious, and immediately 'ordered officials to prepare an army
to wage war.'[53] She finally persuaded him, and was able to take full
ordination.

From the late nineteenth and into the twentieth centuries – once
again, despite the lack of full ordination for most women in Tibetan
Buddhism – we find a comparably rich tradition of life stories that
includes biographies of esteemed women. One of these is Ayu
Khandro Dorje Peldrön, who lived in the 1800s, was a teacher of
Chöd and an incarnation of Vajrayoginī. Another is the Tibetan
visionary Sera Khandro (1892–1940), a prolific author who penned
works on Buddhism as well as her own autobiography. Sera Khandro
never became a nun, but nonetheless was a famed teacher.[54] She
was betrothed to marry at young age, and aged twelve had her first
vision of Vajravārāhī. In her autobiography, she writes of this vision,
thanking the *ḍākinī* for favouring her:

'You are extremely kind to bestow empowerment and
instruction upon me. Because I am one with an inferior
female body, it is difficult to accomplish the Dharma
and [benefit] beings. However I can do this, how great!
Why do I have the karmic connection to be empowered
in these two profound Treasures?' The *ḍākinī* answered,
'Noble woman, you are not one with an inferior female
body. Before, in response to Yeshe Tsogyal's inquiry,
Guru [Padmasambhava] proclaimed: "The body of a

female *bodhisattva* is a supreme body without [karmic] remainder; It is the mother [who gives birth to] the great assembly of primordially perfected Ones Gone to Bliss. Generate the aspiration to attain a supreme body like The Great Vajra Queen with the knowledge of the expanse of emptiness. . ."'[55]

Within her autobiography, Sera Khandro talks many times about her 'inferior female body'. This may not, however, have been because she was indeed preoccupied with it. Another way to read this feature of the autobiography of an eminent Tibetan teacher is as a literary device; configured in order to make her account palatable for a broad audience.[56]

For clarity, in this chapter I have compartmentalized Buddhist traditions under particular headings. But, of course, traditions, like people, tend to cross boundaries and borders. And so, especially considering its vivid poetic and visual appeal, it is unsurprising that tantra has been practised in some East Asian countries as well as in Tibet. Again, the life story of another female figure works to exemplify this. Elder Gongga was born in Beijing at the turn of the twentieth century. She first became acquainted with Buddhism in her teenage years, then studied with several teachers and became one of several Chinese disciples to spend time in Tibet with Tibetan teachers in the 1940s. She moved to Taiwan in 1958 and one year later opened the first Taiwanese temple – the Gongga Vihāra – dedicated to the spread of Tibetan Buddhism in Taiwan. Elder Gongga had many students, both male and female, some of whom went on to be architects of other influential schools of esoteric Buddhism.[57] She died in 1997, but Elder Gongga's story does not end with her death, as posthumous events demonstrate her high status. In both East Asia and Tibet, the tradition developed of preservation of the relic-body of high-status teachers. The bodies of these teachers were mummified. This is a continuation of the relic consecration of the body of the historical Buddha and his disciples in India. Elder Gongga is one of the few female teachers whose body has been mummified.[58]

* * *

The forms of Buddhism I have surveyed in this chapter differ from each other. In East Asia forms of Mahāyāna predominate, but these vary, and include the unique form that is Zen. In Tibet tantra has predominated. The different forms include the presence of female deities as part of a range of figures to be revered. Questions are often asked – not just within Buddhist traditions but more broadly – as to whether the presence of female deities within a religious schema aids the position of women within that religion. Certainly we can say for the Mahāyāna and tantric branches of Buddhist tradition they have a fuller and richer historical past of strong female characters than is the case for Theravāda traditions. This may or may not be due to the presence of female deities, as women have also been subjected to negative treatment during the centuries of these traditions prevailing in these regions of Asia.

It is also the case that certain of these female deities have had something of a presence outside of the traditions within which they are predominant. Guanyin and Tara have enjoyed some popularity within Theravada countries, for instance. In the next chapter we read again of Buddhism crossing borders; we travel to Western shores. We meet with some of the many, many women who have helped to establish Buddhism in the West, where they are practising and sharing the teachings of the Buddha in new ways.

CHAPTER 7

UNCONVENTIONAL WOMEN AND TRUTH-TELLERS: THE WEST

A rose sits in a vase on my desk.

I gaze intently at this rose which was warmed by the impartial sun and cannot help but be deeply impressed that even in its confined state, it still works earnestly at being a rose.

There is no need to be awed by the antiquity of the many art objects left by past generations. A work of art contains within it something that cannot be lost in time; eternal life throbs within it. This is the strength of those who have a world that was built from looking deeply into their own life.

The reason our innate talents can be developed at all, however, is because we are satisfied by . . . constantly being bathed in the light of the infinite.

Poem entitled 'A Rose', Kujō Takeko[1]

I begin this chapter with a poem of Kujō Takeko, who was an influential woman in modern Japan. Along with her sister-in-law, Kazuko, she set up Buddhist Women's Associations in the early 1900s. It is one of these associations that is the first evidence we have of women practising Buddhism in the West. During the gold rush in the mid-1800s, Chinese migrant workers set up associations and established temples up and down the west coast of America. There Buddhism was practised alongside Confucianism and Daoism. The Japanese Jōdo Shinshū is the oldest institutional form of Buddhism in the USA, and it dates from this period, set up to serve Japanese migrants who arrived after the Chinese. One of Takeko's women's associations was part of the early phase of growth of this tradition in the USA.[2]

Although Buddhism's interactions with the West truly begin with Alexander the Great and other Indo-Greeks in India in the centuries immediately before and after the advent of the Common Era, what was to lead to the establishment of Buddhism in the West first began in the 1800s. There was some limited knowledge of Buddhism in the West prior to this. As an example, the first record of the word 'Buddha' in the *Oxford English Dictionary* occurs in 1681, with 'dharma' following more than a century later in 1796.[3]

The transmission of Buddhism to Western shores came about via four routes. Firstly, migrant communities setting up their own groups, and secondly, from Western travellers travelling in Asia and bringing back stories of 'exotic' lands. Colonialism was another route, and it proved especially important for transmission because it led to the transportation of Sanskrit and Pāli manuscripts to the West. The fourth route was through Asians themselves travelling to the West to teach. Sometimes they were invited by Westerners interested in studying with a particular teacher. Many women, along with Kujō Takeko, were involved in the transportation of Buddhism to the West. However, in numerous potted histories of Buddhism's long journey to Western lands, the contributions of such women are hidden from view. This despite the fact that these women – amongst the first scholars of Buddhism, the first to travel extensively in Asia and the first cluster of practitioners – engaged in such activities prior to their own countries granting equal voting rights to women.

In Europe, initial interest in Buddhism in the 1800s – particularly in France, Germany, and the United Kingdom – was academic and intellectual. Portrayals of Buddhism in this milieu centred around its ethical and rational aspects. The modern idea that Buddhism is not a religion but a philosophy or way of life began in these initial phases of Western comprehension of the tradition. Some European promoters of Buddhism presented it as the Eastern equivalent of the Protestant reformation of Catholicism. Hinduism, with its focus on ritual, was derided, while Buddhism was espoused as a reformation religion that liberated Hinduism from its overarching ritual preoccupations. This can be seen in the titles of two of the very earliest publications on women in Buddhism in the West by two of the female scholars discussed in chapter 1, Mabel Bode and Caroline Rhys Davids. They are entitled, respectively, 'Women Leaders of the Buddhist Reformation' and 'The Women Leaders of the Buddhist Reformation as Illustrated by Dhammapāla's Commentary on the *Therīgāthā*'.[4]

In Europe, the initial comprehension of Buddhism as a religious or belief system was heavily impacted by the accumulation of Buddhist manuscripts. Buddhism as it first manifested in the United Kingdom in the late 1800s was a 'text-based' phenomenon.[5] Scholars were instrumental in presenting an image of Buddhism to the Western world, and two particularly influential scholars were Thomas Rhys Davids and his aforementioned wife Caroline. They, along with others, presented Buddhism to their Western audience as a religion of reason, reconfiguring the Buddha as a Socratic figure, mirroring in both his teachings and methods the oeuvre of the Greeks.

Caroline Rhys Davids' pioneering translation of the *Therīgāthā*, the poems of the early Indian nuns, was first published in 1909. In its style and tenor the English is modelled on that of the King James Bible, featuring words such as 'thou', 'hath', 'thee', and forms of verbs such as 'givest', 'bringst', 'may'st'. As we saw in chapter 1, with the poem 'The Beggars' by Grace Constant Lounsbery, this style was typical for the time. I quote below part of Caroline Rhys Davids' translation of the *Therīgāthā* poem that begins this volume and is the inspiration for its title. In this poem, Vaḍḍha heeds his mother's words:

O splendid was the spur my mother used,
And no less merciful the chastisement
She gave me, even the rune she spoke,
Fraught with its burden of sublimest good.

I heard her words, I marked her counsel wise,
And thrilled with righteous awe as she called up
The vision of salvation to be won.
And night and day I strove unweariedly
Until her admonitions bore fruit,
And I could touch Nibbāna's utter peace.[6]

In her abovementioned article 'The Women Leaders of the Buddhist Reformation as Illustrated by Dhammapāla's Commentary on the *Therīgāthā*' and her introduction to this translation, which she entitles *Psalms of the Early Buddhists: The Sisters, The Brethren*, Caroline Rhys Davids makes comparisons. She likens the nuns of the *Therīgāthā* to medieval female saints of Christianity.

Alongside Caroline Rhys Davids and Mabel Bode, the most exceptional Pāli scholar of the early twentieth century was Isaline Blow Horner, more widely known as I.B. Horner. Many of Horner's translations remain in circulation and continue to be used today. Horner was also the author of the very first English-language book on women in Buddhism, entitled *Women Under Primitive Buddhism*. This book, published in 1930, like most of her translations, has never been out of print. Drawing on her unmatched comprehension of the Pāli sources, Horner maintained that, as the textual tradition of the canon developed, monks edited out sections on women and nuns.[7] In her preface to the book, she writes:

In spite of the difficulties presented by the revised
and incomplete character of the texts, I hope that the
following pages may justify my belief that the life of
women as nuns, as long ago as the sixth century B. C., is
worthy of more than the passing attention, which, with a
few notable exceptions, is the most that it has ever been
accorded in any treatises on Buddhism.[8]

In the USA, things evolved differently from Europe, with the Theosophical Society the most important instrument in the arrival of Buddhism to North America. This society was begun by a Russian woman, Helena Blavatsky (1831–1891), along with American Henry Steel Olcott, in New York in 1875. The society was not formed purely to promote Buddhism, but with broader aims and ambitions. Buddhism, however, became one of the religious traditions that the society drew on to formulate its outlook. Blavatsky claimed to have travelled in Tibet and to have 'received' telepathic teaching from Tibetan teachers. Her claims were challenged to the extent that her journey to Tibet itself was called into question. In subsequent years and with a reassessment of the evidence it now appears likely she did make the trip as there are no other explanations for certain of her eye-witness accounts and her extensive knowledge of Buddhism.[9] The Theosophical Society, from early on, attracted a great number of women into its fold. They were often wealthy women who were involved with women's suffrage movements at the time and who would go on to become leaders and pioneers within various spheres of life: religious, political, social. These include the lesser-known Grace Constant Lounsbery, whose contribution to the history of women in Buddhism is discussed in chapter 1. Other notable women with a connection to the early days of the Theosophical Society include Mary Foster (1844–1930), who instituted a unique brand of theosophy mixed more thoroughly with Buddhism in Hawai'i, and has been called the 'first Hawaiian Buddhist'. Better-known figures are Annie Besant (1847–1933) and Alexandra David Néel.[10]

An example of Westerners gaining knowledge of Buddhism via the travelogues of nineteenth-century adventurers can be seen in the life and works of Alexandra David Néel (1868–1969). Néel was born in France in 1868 and grew up in Belgium, two European countries that did not grant women the full right to vote until the 1940s. Néel became one of the most celebrated Western pioneers of her time, and her writings on Tibet were remarkably influential. This level of trust in her writing comes from her obvious sympathy with her subject – the Tibetan people. During this period that saw colonization of parts of Asia by (on the whole) Western powers, women like Néel stand out.

Unlike other French colonial women who saw themselves as 'civilizing agents' who sought to 'raise the native to our [level of] civilization', Néel demonstrated respect for the Tibetans.[11] Other colonial explorers and scholars of Buddhism, such as Laurence Augustine Waddell, described Tibetan Buddhism as 'deep-rooted devil worship and sorcery', 'only thinly and imperfectly varnished over with Buddhist symbolism'. But Néel's own writings on Tibetan and Mahāyāna Buddhism remained instructive in subsequent decades, influencing such writers as Alan Watts, Jack Kerouac, and Allen Ginsberg.[12]

In the nineteenth century Tibet was a country that foreigners were forbidden to enter. Néel's writing on her experience of Tibet reveals an impressive comprehension of Tibetan Buddhism, mottled with theosophical beliefs and underpinned by a lively wit. Although there were few nuns in Tibet during the period of her travels, in one of her best-known works, *Magic and Mystery in Tibet*, she writes of Tibetan nuns she meets, seeing reflected in them something of her own steely spirit:

> Numerous examples of strange contrasts are to be seen in Tibet, but what most astonished me was the tranquil courage of the womenfolk. Very few Western women would dare to live in the desert, in groups of four or five or sometimes quite alone. Few would dare under such conditions to undertake journeys that last for months or even years, through solitary mountain regions infested by wild beasts and brigands. This shows the singular character of Tibetan women. They do not ignore these real dangers and they add to them by imagining legions of evil spirits taking on thousands of strange forms, even that of a demoniacal plant which grows on the edge of precipices, seizes hold of travellers with its thorny branches and drags them into the abyss. In spite of these many reasons for staying safely in their native villages, one finds here and there in Tibet, communities of less than a dozen nuns, living in isolated convents situated at a great height, some of them blocked in by the snow for

more than half of the year. Other women live as hermits in caves, and many women pilgrims travel, alone, across the immense territory of Tibet carrying their scanty luggage on their backs.[13]

Women were central figures in the development of Buddhism in other countries as well. The first known Buddhist teacher in Australia was a woman known as Sister Dhammadinnā. Born in the USA, she lived as a nun in Sri Lanka in the 1930s and 1940s, and then was offered funds by a benefactor to visit Australia in 1951. As a result of her visit, the first Buddhist organization was established there, the Buddhist Society of New South Wales, cofounded by another woman, Marie Byles, and headed up two years later by a third, Natasha Jackson.[14] Buddhism continues to attract a variety of Western converts. With the exception of Kujō Takeko, every woman I have discussed so far in this chapter is a Westerner and my aim in this chapter is to focus on Western women involved in the transmission of Buddhism to Western shores. It should be noted, however, that migrant communities have made a major contribution to the establishment of Buddhism in the West. In Europe, migrant communities make up about two-thirds of all Buddhists. Migrant communities and convert communities tend to operate differently and often separately. While migrant communities tend to build large temples to be visited on significant calendrical occasions, convert communities opt for urban centres with a full weekly programme of opportunities and rural retreat centres for an annual or biannual visit.[15]

There are many other women who were involved in or who devoted their lives to establishing Buddhism in the West and, although space does not permit me to tell tales of all of them, the contribution of each one should not be underestimated. Some of the other women worthy of note for their efforts to establish Buddhism (especially nuns' communities) in the West are Jiyu Kennett Rōshi, an English nun who founded Shasta Abbey in California in 1970 as part of the Sōtō Zen tradition, the Vietnamese nun Dam Luu, who founded the Duc Vien Temple in San Jose, and the women behind the ever popular Sakyadhita International, such as Karma Lekshe Tsomo.[16]

Despite this impressive catalogue of female scholars, travellers, and practitioners, the issue of gender has been, and continues to be, one of the most problematic plaguing Western Buddhism, in a variety of ways, for a variety of reasons. In this chapter I concentrate on three traditions of Buddhism in the West. First, I discuss Theravāda Buddhism in the West, focusing on the ways in which Theravāda groups have handled the testing issue of lack of ordination for women. Theravāda communities can exist either as a combination of Western converts and migrant Southeast Asians, or as separate communities. Next, I focus on Tibetan Buddhism in the West, which tends to operate via an admixture of ethnic Tibetans and Westerners and within which many women have risen in the ranks. Nonetheless, these communities have seen some groups enmeshed in controversies revolving around abuses of power by senior male figures. Last, I conclude with a section on the Triratna Buddhist Community, which is in essence a convert tradition. This is a group begun in the 1960s by an Englishman known as Sangharakshita, who established the new group in an attempt to create his unique approach to Buddhism aimed at a Western audience. Problematic gender dynamics exploded within this tradition with the publication of a book in 1995 by a senior figure that attempted to categorically establish women as inferior to men.

Theravāda Buddhism

Theravāda Buddhism is practised in the West as a result of all these modes of transmission; within communities established by migrant groups, as a result of invitations to Asian teachers to come to the West and, initially, as a result of Westerners heading East. This latter group includes women like Constance Gordon Cumming. Cumming penned travelogues of her time in Sri Lanka in the late 1800s which included many observations about Buddhism.[17] The first Westerners to take ordination as Buddhist monks did so within Theravāda countries in the late 1800s to early 1900s. These were Gordon Douglas, ordained as Aśoka in Sri Lanka by Burmese monks, U Dhammaloka, an Irishman ordained in Burma, and, the better known of the three, Allan Bennett [McGregor], who was also ordained in Burma, taking the name Ananda Metteyya.[18]

Ananda Metteyya was one of the first teachers welcomed to the Buddhist Society of Great Britain and Ireland in 1908. Although he intended to stay in the United Kingdom and inaugurate the practice of Theravāda Buddhism, after only eight months he returned to Burma, having encountered problems with following a monastic lifestyle in the United Kingdom. With Thomas Rhys Davids as president, the society had been set up the previous year, with the intention of becoming a society of convert practitioners. This initial attempt was not successful. But soon after, in 1924, a second society was formed by Christmas Humphreys, The Buddhist Lodge, a branch of the Theosophy Society. This was one of the first Buddhist organizations outside Asia. It continues to operate today, running classes and other events open to the public. Although initially based on certain Theravāda principles and practices, such as reciting the five precepts in Pāli, the society soon become more eclectic, with an ambition, according to Humphreys, to promote a Buddhism specifically aimed at Westerners.

During this period, a few other Western women, as well as the aforementioned Sister Dhammadinnā, travelled to Theravāda countries in order to live and practise as nuns. These included Sister Uppalavannā (Else Buchholtz), a German former violinist, who lived as an ascetic in Sri Lanka from 1926. Also, the Englishwoman Evelyn Grant Robinson took up residence in Sri Lanka in 1935 and in 1937 recited 'the Ten Precepts and change[d] her name and identity to become Sister Vajirā, a Buddhist nun'. Another German, Hannalore Wolf, who was also given the name Sister Vajirā in 1954, travelled to Sri Lanka in 1955 where she lived as a practitioner for many years.[19]

It was not until the 1960s and 1970s, however, that the West became able to more successfully 'ingest' the 'foreign cultural body' represented by Theravāda Buddhist monasticism.[20] During this period, both in Europe and the USA, migrant communities from Theravāda countries began to set up Theravāda groups and centres, and from this point Theravāda Buddhism in the West began to flourish. These groups generally attracted a mix of Asian Buddhists and Westerner converts. Within these groups, there was a need for more Westerners to take ordination as monks to develop aspects of Theravāda on foreign soil. But the concomitant desire for women to ordain was not in evidence. Despite the overall successful cultural accommodation, this unresolved problem has remained: the continued lack of ordination for women.

In the USA, with the 'Americanization' of these Theravāda groups, however, the lack of opportunity for women to be ordained begins to change in the late 1970s and 1980s.[21] As we have seen, it is around this time that, with the efforts of both men and women, women are ordained as nuns in Theravāda traditions. The first (novice) ordinations took place in America in 1986, followed by full ordinations in India in 1996 and 1998.

The best-known Western woman who ordained as a (Theravāda) Buddhist nun in this period is Ayya Khema. She was born in Germany in 1923 into an affluent Jewish family. The family were forced to leave Germany when she was a child, and so as a child she spent time in parts of Asia. She married her first husband aged twenty-two and had two children. With a 'vague sense of incompleteness' bothering her, she decided to explore her spirituality. She first encountered Indian religion in a Hindu setting, at the Sri Aurobindo Ashram, whilst travelling in India with her second husband and son in the early 1960s. She immediately realized meditation was her path. Returning to Australia, where she lived at the time, she began practising Buddhism with various teachers. She took novice ordination in Sri Lanka in 1979. Then, coming to terms with the lack of full ordination for women in Theravāda tradition, she instead received full ordination from a Chinese tradition at a temple in Los Angeles in 1988. Her Buddhist name, Khema, is the name of one of the first female disciples of the Buddha.

Ayya Khema was responsible for founding many centres and monasteries, including several for women. Although she had many male students, she was critical of the place of women in Theravāda Buddhism, and this drove her to (reluctant) activism and lobbying on behalf of women.[22] She became an esteemed teacher, author of several books, and travelled the world giving talks on Buddhism. In her teachings she concentrated on the basics of Theravāda Buddhism, teaching on meditation, suffering, impermanence, and no-self. Her most acclaimed work is *Being Nobody, Going Nowhere*, whose title illustrates her concentration of the letting go of the self in her teachings. Ayya Khema did not focus on talking about gender in her teachings because, it appears, she considered it an irrelevant category of 'self' or 'ego' that we need to transcend. She did give a few talks on the topic, and one such talk was entitled 'The Feminine Approach to Spirituality; Loving Kindness Meditation', which she delivered in 1987. In this talk she begins by outlining both the *ultimate* insignificance of sex and gender for a Buddhist practitioner, but also the very real need to think about it during the initial stages of practice:

> it is important that we realise that even though, in the ultimate sense, in the completely ultimate sense, we are nothing but phenomena, and in another not quite so ultimate sense we are just human beings. Yet because of our either being male or female we have taken on certain characteristics and approaches in daily life, which have come about to some extent through our environment, our upbringing, but also though our way of thinking about ourselves. And naturally there is a difference between how a woman and how a man thinks about himself or herself. But this is not the ultimate reality, it is quite certain that all of us, at this point in time, are living . . . in a relative reality in which we believe in 'me'. 'This is me, this is mine'. I am a certain person, I'm a woman or a man, I'm a wife or a husband, a mother or father, I'm a daughter, a teacher or a scientist. We have all sorts of identification in which we believe, and which give us our ego support. And because we 'live there' at that point, that's where we have to start from if we want to do spiritual practice. Because we can't start at the end and walk backwards towards the beginning . . . and then, as we practice, we will lose some of these

identifications, so, at the very end we can see ourselves in an absolute – and totally removed from identification – manner.[23]

Despite influential female teachers such as Ayya Khema, and the renewed institution of ordination for nuns in South and Southeast Asia, the problem of nuns' ordination continues in contemporary Theravāda movements in the West. For example, in 2009 a British-born monk, Ajahn Brahmavamso, ordained with the Thai Forest Sangha, was involved with the ordination of four women at his monastery in Australia. These women, the Venerable Vayama, Nirodha, Seri, and Hassapañña, were ordained by the American Theravāda nun Ayya Tathālokā.[24] As a result of this event, Ajahn Brahmavamso was disengaged from his tradition. Although he is still recognized as a monk he is no longer associated with Thai Forest Sangha.[25] He continues to advocate for full restoration of nuns' ordination in Theravāda Buddhism, and remains a controversial figure for traditional Theravāda communities. In 2014, a paper he was due to deliver at the 11th United Nations Day of Vesak in Vietnam on gender equality was banned at the last minute. In 2015, along with a British-born nun, Venerable Candā, he established the Anukampa Bhikkhuni Project, which aims to establish the first Theravāda monastery for nuns in the United Kingdom. As of 2018, they had successfully raised enough funds to purchase a four-bedroom property in Oxford, which is a first step towards their goal.[26] In 2019, Ajahn Brahmavamso was a recipient of the Queen's Birthday Honours in the United Kingdom, for the empowerment of women in Buddhism.

Tibetan Buddhism

The establishment of Tibetan Buddhism in the West took a similar path. As we have seen, Tibetan Buddhism was a particular interest of the Theosophical Society. Alexandra David Néel made Tibetan Buddhism more widely known, and The Buddhist Lodge introduced some elements of Mahāyāna into its broadening remit. The very first purpose-built Buddhist monastery outside Asia was in Russia, organized and funded by Mongolian Buddhists who followed Tibetan

Buddhism. The temple and monastery were finally completed in 1915, only to be desecrated during the communist revolution in 1917. The beginnings of the setting up of other groups in the West that specifically practised Tibetan Buddhism began in the 1950s and 1960s,[27] and these groups tended to be an admixture of migrant and convert Buddhists. One of the first groups was set up in Berlin in the 1950s by followers of the German-born Anagarika Govinda, as a branch of the movement he began in Darjeeling in the 1930s. Next came Kagyu Samye Ling in Scotland in 1967, and there followed a flourish of centres throughout the 1970s and 1980s. Although women have not traditionally been allowed to take full ordination in Tibetan Buddhism, this was beginning to change in Tibet prior to the Chinese invasion in 1950. As such, it was not long before women in the West – both Asian and Western – took active roles in the establishment of Tibetan Buddhism on Western soil. The way in which Western women came to be Tibetan Buddhist nuns and teachers can be exemplified by the interconnected stories of three women from the one tradition, two English and one American: Freda Bedi (Kechog Palmö), Tenzin Palmo, and Pema Chödrön.[28]

Freda Bedi was born in England in 1911. She was one of the first women to graduate from Oxford University. There she met and married an Indian fellow student, Baba Bedi. Accompanying him on his return to India after graduation, she first worked as a teacher and then for the Indian government. In 1959 she was sent to Assam to clear a refugee camp. This camp was full of exiled Tibetans who had escaped the Chinese invasion. The lamas she met there were her first encounter with Buddhism. Inspired to work on their behalf, she began a school for young lamas, at which they could prepare themselves for a career in teaching and learn English. Some of those who were set to become the most prominent lamas in the West attended Freda Bedi's school, including Chögyam Trungpa. Bedi also began the first convent for Tibetan nuns in northeast India, which continues today. She received full ordination in Hong Kong in 1972, taking the name Kechog Palmö, just a few years before her death.[29]

Tenzin Palmo, born Diane Perry, read extensively as a child and became interested in nuns, the East, Buddhism, and finally Tibetan

Buddhism. She first attended the Buddhist Society in London in 1961 aged eighteen. Then, as a result of her love of Buddhism, she was offered a job in the university library at the School of Oriental and African Studies in London. She heard of Freda Bedi and that she had started a school for Tibetan nuns in India:

> Tenzin Palmo duly wrote to Freda Bedi explaining that she was also Kargyu and would like to offer her services in whatever way she could, although she was only a trainee librarian and didn't know really what she could do. Freda Bedi wrote back: 'Please come, come. Don't worry, just come!'[30]

Tenzin Palmo and her mother entertained many of the Tibetan lamas coming from Asia to London during this period. She met the young Chögyam Trungpa and became his disciple. She eventually travelled to India and became part of Freda Bedi's convent:

> Tenzin Palmo was given two jobs, acting as Freda Bedi's secretary and teaching the young lamas basic English. Her pupils were not ordinary lamas, however, they were the tulkus, the recognized reincarnations of previous high spiritual masters, in whose hands lay the future of Tibetan Buddhism itself.[31]

Back in the United Kingdom, Chögyam Trungpa cofounded one of the first Tibetan Buddhist monasteries there, Kagyu Samye Ling in Scotland in 1967. Following this he was invited to the USA, which was to become his home. He arrived there in 1970 and began what was to become a sizable movement, first named Vajradhatu and renamed Shambhala International when leadership passed to his son. Chögyam Trungpa was a charismatic leader and the organization grew rapidly. By the 1990s there were ninety branches of the organization he had founded, in thirty states. The organization also established The Nalanda Foundation, dedicated to the arts, and Naropa Institute, a liberal arts-modelled college focusing on teaching Buddhism.

One of Chögyam Trungpa's best known female students is Pema Chödrön. Born Deirdre Blomfield-Brown in New York in the 1930s,

Pema Chödrön became a disciple of Chögyam Trungpa in her thirties after the breakup of her second marriage. She took novice ordination in 1974 and, since full ordination was denied women in Tibetan tradition, was not sure she would receive full ordination. But she was encouraged by the head of the Tibetan lineage who had conferred novice ordination on her. He encouraged her to find someone able to perform the ordination, which took several years. Finally in Hong Kong in 1981 she became the first American woman to receive full ordination in a Tibetan Vajrayāna tradition. Following her ordination, she was instrumental alongside Chögyam Trungpa in establishing the Gampo Abbey in Nova Scotia. It was the first North American Tibetan Buddhist monastery for Western men and women, and she became its director when it opened in 1985. Pema Chödrön is known for her insightful teaching, and is the author of numerous books, but it was her 1997 volume *When Things Fall Apart* that established her as a consummate Buddhist teacher.

Following the death of Chögyam Trungpa, Shambhala International experienced a period of turmoil and discomfort such as often follows the death of a charismatic leader. During his life, Chögyam Trungpa had been known to engage in behaviour of questionable ethics. He consumed a great deal of alcohol and was known for his infidelity to his wife, having several sexual relationships with his students. Pema Chödrön comments on this in the 'Crazy Wisdom' documentary dedicated to Trungpa's life. Such things were acceptable at the time, she says. She comments, humorously, that when the head of their Tibetan lineage was due to visit the USA, Chögyam Trungpa insisted his disciples smarten up, and wear suits. She remarks, '. . . sexuality didn't shock people in those days, drinking didn't shock people, but *wear a suit*, are you kidding!'[32] Prior to his death, Chögyam Trungpa had decided upon his disciple, American-born Ösel Tendzin, as his successor. What emerged after his death was that Ösel was HIV-positive and, despite knowing this, had continued to have unsafe sex. This caused a rift in the movement, with some demanding that Ösel step down. Ösel himself died a few years later, and leadership was passed on to one of Chögyam Trungpa's sons, Sakyong Jamgon Mipham Rinpoche. In 2017 serious allegations came to light about

Shambhala International and years of sexual abuse of its members, including of children, much of which was allegedly done by the Sakyong. These allegations have surfaced via work by the Buddhist Sunshine Project, an initiative begun by Andrea Michelle Winn, herself a survivor of the abuse. The Buddhist Sunshine Project has produced three reports detailing the sexual violence, via anonymous accounts. Winn reports that the #MeToo movement heralded a new influx of contacts from survivors. Many of the survivors report numerous counts of abuses of power and coercion of women by leaders and teachers into unwanted sex acts. There are also reports of consistent neglect by others in positions of power within the organization. When the reports were first published, some of those making the allegations were threatened to stay silent or dismissed from teaching or other responsibilities they had within the organization. Just one section of one of the many stories told by a survivor demonstrates how widespread the abuse had become:

> During a program you could often tell who the Sakyong
> was going to pursue that night by who he made eye
> contact with during the teaching or feast. One night I
> received a call from his kusung at 11pm or 12pm saying
> that the Sakyong would like to see me and that I should
> come to his suite. I was thrilled and nervous. When
> I got there, he was dressed solely in a robe with no
> clothes underneath. We chatted for a while. Then he led
> me into his room and began kissing me and removing
> my clothes. I said that I couldn't have sex with him.
> He seemed stunned. He thought for a while and then
> pushed my face down towards his penis and said 'Well
> you might as well finish this.' I was so embarrassed and
> horrified I did it. He rolled over in bed and didn't say
> another word to me.[33]

Following the second Buddhist Sunshine Project report, a group of the Sakyong's personal assistants (who were known as *kusung*) published a joint document supporting the claims of the survivors. They reported having seen, been aware of, looked the other way, and been party to many such abuses. Following this, in early 2019, the Sakyong announced he would step down from his teaching and leadership roles. Later that year, he wrote to the Shambhala International Board of Directors asking to be reinstated. The Board agreed this and he regained his position in March 2020. Not all members, however, were happy about this. This was, in fact, to be the spur for Pema Chödrön to make the decision to retire. In her open letter to Shambhala International she describes how she was left 'dumbfounded' that the Sakyong had requested to return to his duties, and deeply 'distressed' by the way in which the Board appeared to support a return to 'business as usual'. She related that she found it 'discouraging that the bravery of those who had the courage to speak out does not seem to be effecting more significant change in the path forward.'[34]

Shambhala International is not the only Western Buddhist group that has been hit with allegations of sexual abuse and other abuses of power. Several Western Buddhist organizations have experienced turmoil due to similar situations, most often of a sexual nature, involving founders, prominent teachers, or senior disciples.[35] The San Francisco Zen Center also had to deal with the issue of inappropriate sexual behaviour. The issues with the abbot of the San Francisco Zen Center were different. Richard Baker was accused of sexual infidelity with female students and abuses of power involving inappropriate use of the organization's wealth and exploitation of members' labour. The current abbess of the San Francisco Zen Center, Zenkei Blanche Hartman, was interviewed in 1983 about these events. She described the moment the Board made the decision to finally take these matters seriously. At this meeting, she became aware that something had changed on the Board. In the past, the Board had failed to address the issues they were aware of with their leader's behaviour. But this time, nobody tried to make excuses for his actions. Those who were critical of him were not ignored, as had been the case in previous years. Zenkei Blanche Hartman recalled:

> I began having a sense of the commitment of the group,
> the unanimity of concern and care. It reassured me that

this time, there wasn't going to be any sweeping under the rug. We were going to face it together, and I wasn't going to have to leave (Zen Center).

She also talked about the personal impact the events had on her, as someone who had been ordained by Baker:

The meeting was devastating. A sinking feeling in my stomach, like, I knew it was coming, and here it is. My life is smashed. Our life together is smashed. Something very precious in me is destroyed. At that point, I couldn't see how we could continue. It was a moment that changed Zen Center, I believe forever.[36]

For someone with limited knowledge of Buddhism and Buddhist traditions, such revelations may sound shocking, especially as Buddhism, as a tradition, hinges on compassionate action and practice of ethics. Such abuses seem to occur as a result of several factors. Western Buddhist movements and organizations are, by definition, divorced from the social, religious, and cultural context that sets a backdrop for them in Asian countries. In countries such as Thailand and Tibet, for example, Buddhism is woven into the fabric of life; children learn Buddhist stories from their grandparents, or at school, and everything from large annual countrywide events to regional, small-scale arts festivals is often built around it. As well, government legislation mandates aspects of the religion, and there is often centralized governmental administration of monasteries and their residents. In the West, Buddhist organizations are comparatively isolated and, as they grew rapidly in the 1960s, 1970s, and 1980s, the founders, leaders, and their small groups of senior close-knit disciples found themselves with ever-increasing amounts of power within movements that rely on top-down structures. The sociologist Max Weber has defined this phenomenon as 'charismatic authority'. As he points out, it is not necessary for the leader of the group to be oozing charisma. It only requires that the group seeking to be led invest the leader with such characteristics.[37] Central to Weber's theory is that the charismatic leader must benefit the well-being of those seeking to be led. As meditation creates mental calm and positivity, this factor is ever-present in these new Buddhist movements. Within organizations built around charismatic leadership, abuse of new-found power easily rears its head.[38]

Modern Western Buddhism

As well as forms of Western Buddhism that replicate teachings, practices, and traditions from one particular country or another, there are other manifestations of Buddhism in the West. There exist some nonsectarian groups, such as the Network of Engaged Buddhists, whose membership is comprised of Buddhists of many creeds, and who come together to lobby on important issues. Similarly, the Angulimala Prison Chaplaincy Service in the United Kingdom, begun by a Thai monk, Ajahn Khemadhammo, is open to anyone from any Buddhist tradition who has a sound knowledge of Buddhism including of Buddhist traditions other than their own.[39] Last, there also exist movements set up by Western teachers that were created with a purely Western audience in mind. The Triratna Buddhist Community (Triratna) is one of those.

The organization now known as the Triratna Buddhist Community was started in 1967 by Dennis Lingwood, an Englishman who had spent over twenty years in Asia. He took ordination in India in 1949 and 1950, at which he was given the Buddhist name Sangharakshita. He was invited to return to the United Kingdom by the English Sangha Trust in 1963, where he became a teacher until he was asked to leave three years later. This prompted him to begin his own Buddhist group, drawing inspiration from a range of traditions that reflected his own Buddhist training in South and Central Asia. His aim was to create a new form of Buddhism that incorporated a range of teachings and was suitable for a Western audience. The community was initially known as the Western Buddhist Order (for those ordained) and the Friends of the Western Buddhist Order (FWBO) more broadly. The movement was initially very successful and grew rapidly during the 1970s, 1980s, 1990s, and early 2000s. By the early 1990s there were twenty centres in cities around the United Kingdom, as well as satellite groups in smaller towns and cities and retreat centres in rural locations.[40] The movement has always, since inception, publicly advocated equal ordination for men and women. Historically, however, there were invariably more male than female ordained members, combined, in the earlier years, with a male-centred environment.[41]

The theory of charismatic authority also easily maps onto the dynamics of Triratna. Weber notes that once the power of the charismatic authority begins to diminish, a new set of problems arise. Sangharakshita initially stepped down from some of his leadership roles in the movement in 1995, then more fully in 2000. Between 1995 and 2000 and soon afterwards, voices of dissent arose. The first instance was with regard to Sangharakshita's views on women. This was sparked by the publication of a book in 1995 by Subhuti, one of Sangharakshita's chief disciples. Entitled *Women, Men and Angels: An Inquiry Concerning the Relative Spiritual Aptitudes of Men and Women*, the book is essentially a commentary, by Subhuti, on Sangharakshita's view of women. This view is encapsulated in the title of the book, which is taken from a saying of Sangharakshita: 'Angels are to men as men are to women – because they are more human and, therefore, more divine.'[42] The central aim of the book is to establish that women have less 'spiritual aptitude' than men, that women are less able to make progress on the Buddhist path than men. A subsidiary aim is to challenge the idea of history as a history of female oppression. After acknowledging that men and women have the same potential for Awakening, Subhuti writes:

> But men and women in general have different *aptitudes* for spiritual life, indeed women generally have less spiritual aptitude than men – or, to put it positively, men generally have more spiritual aptitude than women. So what is aptitude in this regard? It is the ability to actualise that capacity for Enlightenment, which is the potential of all beings. Men generally are better able to actualise that potential than women. It should be well noted that this does not say that women do not have the aptitude to actualise their potential – that would be tantamount to

saying they do not have the potential. It simply says that
men generally are better able to actualise their potential
for Enlightenment than women.[43]

Subhuti's book gained traction within the organization for some
years following publication, and it became important for women in
the ordination training process. But acceptance of the arguments
within the pages of the book was never complete. It gained notoriety
early on, and was not always for sale in Triratna bookstores. Anita
Doyle, who wrote a review of the book for the Buddhist magazine
Tricycle in 1996, claims that she found the copy she purchased 'not
on display but in a closed cupboard'.[44]

The context out of which Subhuti's book arose is unusual. In its
character, however, the parameters of his (and Sangharakshita's)
negative conceptualization of women is not dissimilar to that iterated
and reiterated, both in Buddhist texts and elsewhere, down the centuries.
What is surprising about this situation, though, is that these views were
held, and the book published, in the 1990s. Such views are much more
easily explained away with regards to, say, for instance, our unnamed
twelfth-century Tibetan Buddhist commentator, whom we met with
in chapter 2. For those raised within ancient and medieval society in
which traditional views about women are largely hegemonic, for a belief
to be embraced that women are less able than men in some way or
another is much less of a surprise. For such a view to be not only held
but to form the centre of a published work from a modern Buddhist
movement, whose apparent aim is to make Buddhism palatable for
a Western audience, is less easy to explain. In the United Kingdom,
in the twentieth century, in a society radically reformed by second-
wave feminism, within which manifold advances have been made
to enable fairer treatment of women, the appearance of a work such
as this is odd. The response to the book, however, in such a context,
is not. Second-wave feminism made its presence felt in the response
elicited by *Women, Men and Angels*. As a result of its publication some
left the organization, citing this book as the reason. Amongst those
who stayed, displeasure about the book and the views it espoused
grew. This level of discontent reached a zenith such that, only a few

years following publication, the book was recalled by the publishers – Windhorse Publications – and all copies pulped.[45] Hence, although the negative view of women held by Subhuti and others is not dissimilar to those found within the history of Buddhism, the response to the propounding of the views was. Unlike the negative statements about women that I reviewed in chapter 2, Subhuti's book and the idea that women have less aptitude than men did not become a standardized part of the Triratna exposition of Buddhism, due to the efforts of those disavowed by it and their supporters. Unlike the negative statements made about women in Buddhism in the history of the religion that have shaped gender dynamics, in this case the negativity was quashed after just few years and did not become a foundation around which to build tradition within Triratna. On more than one occasion Subhuti has apologized for the book and its contents, most recently in 2017 in an interview with a senior female Order member, Maitreyi. That continued apology remains necessary demonstrates the persistent tensions caused by the publication of the book within the movement. In the interview Subhuti states that it is now his view that 'comparison of two classes of individuals, or beings, is useless'.[46]

Aside from *Women, Men and Angels*, members of Triratna are keen to make known that, within the organization, men and women have the same ordination process, and women ordain other women. As well, the organization has a significant following in India, where a branch of the movement has been flourishing since the 1960s. The focus in this arm of the movement is on the Indian reformer Bhimrao Ramji Ambedkar, to the extent that this Indian branch of Tiratna is known as 'Ambedkarite Buddhism'. Ambedkar was a contemporary of Gandhi, and involved in writing the constitution of India during regaining of independence in 1947. Ambedkar was always, throughout his life, concerned with the plight of those in the lower strata of Indian society, hailing himself from a poor, low caste family, who are these days known as *dalits*. Having spent much of his life fighting to improve conditions for these in the lower strata, Ambedkar finally came to the realization that the only way to end social discrimination was to reject Hinduism, as the Hindu caste system was the root of the problem. Ambedkar studied several other religions and finally decided to convert to Buddhism, which he did in 1956, just a few weeks before his death. Many thousands of *dalits* converted alongside him, and thus began the Ambedkarite Buddhism movement in India.

Unlike Subhuti and Sangharakshita, Ambedkar always advocated for women. And his view was that the Buddha had done the same. In a paper published in 1950, he writes:

> By admitting women . . . the Buddha . . . gave them the right to knowledge and the right to realize their spiritual potentialities along with men. . .
>
> This freedom which the Buddha gave to the women of India is in fact of far greater importance and outweighs whatever stigma which is said to be involved in the subordination of the *Bhikkhunis* to the *Bhikkhu Sangha*. This was not an empty freedom.
>
> In allowing women to become *Bhikkhunis* the Buddha not only opened for them the way to liberty, he also allowed them to acquire dignity, independent of sex . . . in allowing women to become *Bhikkhunis* he opened them the way to equality with men.[47]

Ambedkar is eulogized and honoured in *dalit* literature and in women's songs, which lionize him as the 'body and soul of the Dalits', and celebrate that he is 'in every Buddhist . . . in every vein and limb'.[48] In many regions of India, Dalit literature, especially poetry, has been used as an instrument to voice the oppression of lower status groups – not only by *dalit* Buddhists, but amongst other *dalit* groups as well. Such literature is not generally well known or available in English. Within this genre, since at least the 1970s, the poems of women have begun to become popular. Below is a poem to the Buddha's wife, Yasodharā, by Hira Bansode, a well-known Dalit poet and a Buddhist. In this poem, Bansode, with mixed emotions, questions the place of Yasodharā both within Buddhist tradition and the life story of the Buddha. She wonders if Yasodharā felt a 'raging storm' in her heart for being abandoned by the Buddha, and is herself maddened by the way Yasodharā is so often sidelined in accounts of Buddhism at the time of the Buddha. Ultimately, Bansode is calmed – and we the reader can temper ourselves too – because we can still see and find a place for Yasodharā, a memory:

> O Yashodhara!
> You are like a dream of sharp pain,
> life-long sorrow.
> I don't have the audacity to look at you.
> We were brightened by Buddha's light,
> but you absorbed the dark
> until your life was mottled blue and dark,
> a fragmented life, burned out,
>
> O Yashodhara!
> The tender sky comes to you for refuge
> seeing your shining but fruitless life
> and the pained stars shed tears
> My heart breaks,
> seeing your matchless beauty,
> separated from your love,
> dimming like twilight.
> Listening to your silent sighs,
> I feel the promise of heavenly happiness is hollow.
>
> Tell me one thing, Yashodhara, how did you
> contain the raging storm in your small hands?
> Just the idea of your life shakes the earth
> and sends the creaming waves
> dashing against the shore.
> You would have remembered
> while your life slipped by
> the last kiss of Siddharth's final farewell,
> those tender lips.
> But weren't you aware, dear,
> of the heart-melting fire
> and the fearful awakening power
> of that kiss?

Lightning fell, and you didn't know it.
He was moving towards a great splendor,
far from the place you lay. . .

He went, he conquered, he shone.
While you listened to the songs of his triumph
your womanliness must have wept.
You who lost husband and son
must have felt uprooted
like the tender banana plant
But history doesn't talk about
the great story of your sacrifice.
If Siddharth had gone through
the charade of *samadhi*
a great epic would have been written about you!
You would have become famous in purana and
     palm-leaf
like Sita and Savitri
O Yashodhara!

I am ashamed of the injustice.
You are not to be found in a single Buddhist Vihara.
Were you really of no account?
But wait – don't suffer so.
I have seen your beautiful face.
You are between the closed eyelids of Siddharth.
Yashu, just you.[49]

The work of Triratna in India has resulted in the lives of many low status Indian women being improved. This combined with other positive elements. Within Triratna women are ordained with an equal status to men. Women ordain other women. The senior team that took over leadership from Sangharakshita is comprised of men and women. The current Chair of that team is a woman. All these factors combine within a complexly gendered history; a history of negativity towards women combines with affirmative action projects and a current air of equality that reflects modern liberal gender politics. As such, Triratna appears as a microcosm of the history of the Buddhist tradition, within which women excel in practice and become esteemed leaders but within which certain individuals seek to disenable women.

* * *

Both historically and today, despite countless hurdles, innumerable women have found ways – inventive, creative, innovative – to continue to practise Buddhism, to teach, and to attain high levels of religious experience. I began this chapter with stories of Western women who became esteemed scholars of Buddhism, adventurously travelled to forbidden lands, and – with insight ahead of their time – brought back tales of Asian religion. Remembering the negative statements about women in chapter 2, both with regard to the beginning of Buddhism in the West and its continuation, the idea that women are morally weak, emotionally undeveloped, weak in wisdom, or intellectually atrophied can be emphatically and categorically thrown out.

In the more recent examples, Pema Chödrön and Zenkei Blanche Hartman stand out as exemplars of ethics. They were both prepared to do the right thing morally, in the end, despite the personal hardship it might cause them. We could read these as modern examples of women standing up and saying no to bad treatment of other women. But the picture is more complicated than that. The Board that the Zenkei was part of, that initially brushed things under the carpet, then made the decision to face the truth, was comprised of men and women, as was the Shambhala International Board of Directors that Pema Chödrön challenged. With regard to ordination of women in Theravāda traditions, we see men alongside women willing to make a stand, at some personal cost, to demand women be treated fairly. In the Triratna community, women and men agitated against Subhuti's book and were responsible for its recall and removal.

Hence, as Ayya Khema declared in her 1987 talk, 'The Feminine Approach to Spirituality', there comes a point when dwelling on gender no longer needs to be the primary concern. Once men and women come together and stand up, say no in one voice to continued poor treatment of women, and are successful in their efforts, things can change. Attitudes can change, as can behaviour. Organizations can develop new structures and allow new opportunities. At that point Buddhist communities can again turn their attention back to their central concerns – to observing ethics, studying doctrine, practising the Buddha's path, and prioritizing the realization that, in the 'ultimate sense we are just human beings'.[50]

REACHING ACROSS
THE DIVIDE

The separation between you and world ceases to be very far and maybe ceases to exist at all. And therefore when something's hot, it really is hot, and it burns you up. Fire just burns you up, and wind blows you into a million pieces, and water drowns you, and earth buries you. And you're just not there anymore. At the same time, the fire warms you, like it never warmed you before. And the wind in the trees is like hearing the sound of eternity. And the earth is your witness, and water is always moving and fluid and endless. And you are inseparable from all things.

Pema Chödrön[1]

Prior to the cover image for this book being decided, when looking for an image for the cover I came across one that resonated with me. It is a photograph of the interior of a temple in Thailand. The temple walls are embossed with a mottled gold and red design, the room is well lit, with pink flowers hugging the walls and creating a veneer across the front of the shrine. The shrine is on the back wall of the temple. It is imposing, beautiful, brightly illuminated. Aloft the tall structure is a golden Buddha, looking down over the inhabitants. The practitioners seated in the room are several monks and one *mae chi*. In Thai tradition, as we have learned in this book, monks are considered senior to female renunciates. They are also revered by the laity. As such, a raised platform is often set up so that monks, when they sit, are seated higher than others. In any hall, temple, shrine room, if one seeks to install a raised platform for the monks to sit on, it needs to be placed in a position so that it does not restrict the movement of people around the venue. In this photograph, the platform, therefore, is situated to one side. This has enabled the *mae chi* to take centre stage. In this beautiful, imposing room, the *mae chi* is the focal point. She sits on the floor, not on the raised platform, but she can and does sit facing the Buddha image. The configuration has enabled her, more so than the monks, to sit square-faced in front of the Buddha, fully inhabiting the available space. The monks are sidelined, and the photograph even captured one looking sideways on, perhaps envious of the *mae chi*. This photograph encapsulates the primary content of the book. Over the centuries within which Buddhism has existed, in the many regions around the world within which Buddhism has been practised, the space inhabited by women has been vast. Any allowances granted women, however circumscribed by societal strictures, have enabled countless women to excel as esteemed teachers, devoted disciples, and inspired leaders. The central aim of this book has been to demonstrate that.

In Part I of the book, Asking Questions About Buddhism, chapters on ethics, texts, and Buddhist doctrine highlight much debated issues and themes. When paying attention to these, I also attempt to make clear that whilst many of these are considered key obstacles they are not always primary concerns in the lives of modern Buddhist women.

These women, instead, just get on with it. Get on with the job of practising, get on with teaching, fundraising, researching, lobbying. The question 'Does Buddhism support gender equality?' needs to be asked with such women in mind. We need to be sure, in answering, that we have included within our definition of Buddhism all of the many women whose lives have been told in this book, who have shaped Buddhist tradition, and continue to do so today. We need to ensure that we acknowledge that Buddhist goals are not the same as feminist calls for social justice, although some similarity with regard to the principle of non-harm can be adduced. When we study Buddhist texts, we need to ensure we study a balanced range, that we give due attention to the lives and teachings of women down the centuries, as well as acknowledging the misogyny we find in other texts. When reflecting on the misogyny, we need to be aware that men do not come off well in such discourses either. Acknowledging the many contributions of women to Buddhism, it should be clear why women have prevailed, despite negativity. No Buddhist doctrine nor ethical formations support the idea that women are inferior to men. The real aim is letting go of preoccupations with gender. Whether one is a man or a woman is, ultimately, as inconsequential as whether you hold a container of clean or dirty water in your hand.

In Part II, Voices Through the Centuries, I have attempted to produce an expansive survey. Mapping and charting practices of Buddhist women though the history of the tradition, I focus on lives lived. In so doing, as in the backdrop for Part I, I attempt to demonstrate that women are very much part of both Buddhism's past and what makes Buddhism what it is today. Across continents and different time periods the same struggles reverberate. Women in the history of Buddhism have continually laboured to be recognized and have their contributions acknowledged. From ancient India to the modern United Kingdom, women have been told they are not good enough. But this has not stopped them; many have triumphed regardless. And whilst the well-worn disparagement comes as no surprise to many, I hope the stories of resilience do. Taking even just one life of these many potent stories of women challenges the disparagement of women we find in Buddhist texts and Buddhist

I Hear Her Words

tradition. The stories together build a compelling narrative that demonstrates that the best rebuttal to charges of inferiority is real life.

I was pleased to be asked to write this book, and have enjoyed completing it. My part, however, in this is the easy part. In the creation of this short introductory work I am profiting from much fine scholarship that has been carried out over the last few decades. The painstaking and often demanding work that has been undertaken by an army of scholars has made this book possible. Textual scholars and linguistics experts have unearthed rare manuscripts, created editions, pored over translations. Archaeologists have tolerated intense heat, tropical insects, jungle, and aggravating dust to discover rare finds. Anthropologists have overcome cultural and language barriers, stomached the inadequacies of budget hotels, and skilfully negotiated with officialdom to accomplish invaluable fieldwork.

In the last few years, I have been asked to review articles for publication by a variety of publishers. On a few occasions, although the topic was gender, I found that the work of female scholars was largely sidelined and thus missing from the bibliographies, such that my reviews were largely lists of secondary sources the authors needed to take account of. I remembered this when I was close to finishing this book, and checked my draft bibliography to discover that over 70% of it was the work of women scholars. I hope this book will thereby demonstrate that, for a new generation of scholars, there is certainly no need to sideline or ignore the scholarship of women. On the contrary, it should garner equal respect. That said, not all of the scholarship I relied on to complete this book is the work of women, so I want to acknowledge the work of male scholars too. Many individuals continue to view sexism and gender politics as a battle between men and women. I do not. In my view, sexism is an attitude, one that can be held by a man or by a woman.[2] Women can be sexist just as men can be, either towards men as a group or towards other women. I hope this book can be seen as a collaborative project to the extent it draws on scholarship of all genders to become what it is.

Over the centuries, as well, many men have helped – and continue to help – to improve the circumstances for women within Buddhism. Traditionally, Ānanda is positioned as an advocate of women, although the validity of this can be called into question. Nonetheless, countless male reciters – who were part of the oral transmission via which Buddhism was initially transmitted, prior to the writing down of the texts – recited stories of female disciples and poems by early Buddhist nuns, such that we continue to have access to these today. Early Indian inscriptions have women recording themselves as direct disciples of male teachers. King Devanampiyatissa in Sri Lanka inaugurated the Order of nuns on the island. In the medieval period, Nichiren worked to enable women, as did the twelfth-century Tibetan teacher, Phadampa. In the modern period, Ambedkar and Ajahn Brahm have helped the cause.

Although men have helped, and a harmonious society with standards of mutual care will always be the most productive, in this book women have taken centre stage. While women in Buddhism have been held back by the eight special rules, by lack of opportunities for full ordination on a par with men, by the idea that women need to be reborn as men to make progress, or that women cannot become Buddhas, these have not immobilized women. Far from it. Instead, women have continued to leave their mark, and my hope is that this book in some way commemorates that. They have overcome hurdles to receive ordination. They have transcended family and societal pressures, created narratives that subvert such views as women must always be born as men to succeed, all but evanesced the eight special rules, recast Buddhism to revere women as Buddhas, or have reimagined the bodhisattva path.

In chapter 3 I discussed dependent arising, no-self, and emptiness. When researching this I was struck by a phrase used by one scholar. He comments that the teachings are there to enable the practitioner to rid themselves of a 'profound existential alienation', and be able to experience interconnectedness.[3] I have experienced this type of alienation both by being positioned as inferior, due to my gender, and as superior, due to being white. When travelling with a guide in Thailand, boarding a river boat I stood close to three monks. The guide immediately moved in between me and them and pushed me aside. I was too close, he said. It was not appropriate. Conversely, when living in India, two of my students would often accompany me when I went to the market, the superstore or the bank. On each occasion, without even a look passing between them, they would stroll up to the front of the queue (rightly) assuming we would get served ahead of everyone else because I was white. They were dumbfounded when I told them, after this happened a few times, that it made me uncomfortable. They had not previously, knowingly, had an experience of a person not taking advantage of social privilege. Both were experiences of alienation, though in one case I was cast as inferior, in the other superior.

It is a rare person, I am sure, who has not, at times, considered themselves superior to others. Hierarchy exists within all aspects of human social life, often for good reason. Hierarchies enable university professors to teach their students. They enable bank managers to organize their staff. They enable fathers to protect their children. But many hierarchies are unnecessary. Considering oneself superior or inferior is often unproductive, harmful, and born from feelings of fear, hatred, sadness, or even happiness. In my view, any type of reaching across a divide and engaging with the 'other' – those different to yourself – can be a moral exercise, whether that is men reaching out to women, black to white, heterosexual to homosexual, conservative to liberal. With the many challenges we face in the modern world, such as environmental disasters, deadly viruses, and dangerous political figures, coming together and realizing our shared humanity is just as important now as it has always been. If and when men and women can work together and create community, good can come out of that. When we experience hope and love that is moving, fluid, endless, and a morality that envisages us as inseparable from all things, we go some way towards achieving what the Buddha ordained.

* * *

I began this volume relating the soft ambition of Haiku Master Chiyo-ni, and I conclude with a dedicatory poem to her, written by one of her disciples. Of her ordination, Chiyo-ni writes that she is undertaking to become a Buddhist nun because she hopes, as a consequence, to find peace. Many women, I am sure, make the decision to become Buddhists for the same reason. Many do not expect they will become inspirational leaders, innovative lobbyists or esteemed teachers. Most will not expect their stories to be told, centuries later, to inspire others. And whilst many may not set out to change the world, some, it seems, cannot help themselves!

head shaven
for some reason[4]

NOTES

OPENING EPIGRAPH

1 Translated by Hallisey 2015: 109.

INTRODUCTION

1 Translated by Donegan and Ishibashi 1998: 43.
2 For more on Chiyo-ni, see chapter 4.
3 The historical Buddha has a variety of names. He is known as
Sākyamuni, meaning 'the 'sage of Sākyas', the Sākyas being the Indian
clan to which he belonged. He is known by his birth name Siddhattha
Gotama, Gotama being the family name, and Siddhattha his personal
name. He had many other epithets besides these. His wife, too, is
known by several names. Yasodharā is the most popular of her names,
followed probably by Rahulamātā, meaning 'mother of Rahula'. It was
typical in the context for persons to be given names relating to their
kin relationships, 'mother of . . .', 'son of . . .'. In this book, I usually
standardize spelling to Pāli, except on a few occasions when the
Sanskrit spelling is necessary to make a point.
4 Walters 2013: 172.
5 Translated by Walters 2019: 136. For these quotes from the *Apadāna*,
I have used a new online, open access source, created by Jonathan
Walters, which is a new and the first full English translation of this
Pāli text (www.apadanatranslation.org). On this website, you can read
forty (auto)biographies of early Buddhist nuns. Also see chapter 7 for a
modern poem on Yasodharā.
6 Translated by Walters 2019: 138, 142.
7 Walters 1995: 116–17.
8 Translated by Walters 2019: 54–5.
9 See chapter 5 for more on Mahāyāna Buddhism and its characteristics
and distinguishing features.

10 Zhang 1983, and on Gaṅgottarā see chapter 3.
11 Translated by Grant 2003: 4.
12 I have paraphrased the rules, particularly the first one. Although this first one has come to be known as a rule that nuns, however senior, must bow to monks, however junior, bowing is not mentioned in all versions of the rule. Instead the rule prescribes that a nun must rise from her seat and pay proper respect and homage to the monk, which, essentially, would involve a bow. For a discussion of the eight rules see Anālayo 2016: 91–116.
13 Chung 1999.
14 Cheng 2007: 89.
15 Lu 2016.
16 Cheng 2007: 85–90.
17 Egge 2013.
18 Anālayo 2014.
19 I use this as an example whilst acknowledging that both texts and inscriptions characterize queens as seeking rebirth as men.
20 Cheng 2007: 62.
21 Cheng 2007: 64.
22 MN III. 65. Translated by Ñāṇamoli and Bodhi 1995: 929. All references in this book to texts in Pāli are to Pali Text Society editions.
23 Anālayo 2009: 166.
24 Translated by Willis 1985: 69.
25 Dhammadinna 2015 and 2017.
26 Cheng 2007: 78.
27 Tr. Bodhi 2000: 1724. This passage appears more than once in the canon. *Nibbāna* is the Pāli spelling of nirvana, and *dhamma* the Pāli spelling of dharma.
28 Collins and McDaniel 2010: 1389–90.
29 See Martin 2005. Writing about women in the history of Tibetan Buddhism, he comments, 'If there was – and I believe this was so – a reluctance in those and later times to recognise, and therefore record for posterity, the accomplishments of women, it becomes justifiable and even necessary to magnify what evidence we do have' (p.50).
30 Translated by Donegan and Ishibashi 1998: 223. Chiyo-ni was ordained at age fifty, this poem was written when she was sixty-six years old.

CHAPTER 1

1 Lounsbery 1963: 33.
2 Lounsbery 1935.
3 Lounsbery 1911: 8–9.
4 From the poem entitled 'Work', Lounsbery 1911: 24.
5 Jayawardena 1995: ix–x.
6 I have written this list repeating the phrase 'abstention from'. However, this is not exactly the way it is written in Sanskrit and Pāli texts.

7 Groner 2018: 34 and 35.
8 I am leaving aside the question of transsexuality/transgender in this example.
9 Early Hindu texts present a viewpoint that women have two inherent natures, one wild and the other domestic and, if the wild is not reined in, it is not possible to keep them domestic.
10 *Manusmṛti* 9.2–4 translated by Doniger 1991: 197.
11 Brown 2001: 28–9.
12 Rhys Davids Family, Cambridge University Oriental Library Archive Collection (CUOLAC), RD T/21/4/1 letter dated 9 May 1894.
13 CUOLAC, RD T/21/4/1 letter dated 28 Feb. 1894.
14 Foley 1893: 348.
15 Interview with Uma Chakravarti (Gender Studies Group, Delhi University 2011: 2).
16 Chakravarti 2014: 61
17 Roy 2010: 2.
18 Kwok 2002: 23.
19 Gross 1993: 3.
20 Kawahashi 1994: 448.
21 Gross 1993: 25.
22 Kwok 2002: 28
23 Hu 2019.
24 Hu 2019: 204.
25 Salgado 2007: 50. My square bracket parenthesis added.
26 Cheng 2007: 89.

CHAPTER 2

1 *Candrottarādārikāvyākaraṇa*. Translated in Braarvig and Harrison 2002: 62.
2 On this issue see Sponberg 1992. Sponberg describes this as 'a move from psychological astuteness to psychopathological misogyny' (p.20).
3 *Saṃyutta-nikāya* I 128 (translated in Bodhi 2000: 221–2). The aggregates, what makes up a person, and form mind and body, are discussed in chapter 3.
4 *Saṃyutta-nikāya* I 131 (translated in Bodhi 2000: 224).
5 *Aṅguttara-nikāya* IV 57–8 (translated in Bodhi 2012: 1039–40).
6 Translated by Goodman 2016: 235. My addition in parenthesis.
7 *Aṅguttara-nikāya* I.1-10 (translated in Bodhi 2012: 89–90).
8 *Aṅguttara-nikāya* III.68 (translated in Bodhi 2012: 683). As in the first instance, the text first talks about the form of a woman, then the sound, smell, taste, and touch.
9 *Dīgha-nikāya* II 141 (translated in Walshe 1987: 264).
10 The chapter title is *strīvighāta*.
11 *Theragāthā*, verse 157 (translated in Norman 1969: 22).
12 *Saundarananda* 8.31–4 translated by Covill 2007: 161

13 *Saundarananda*. 8.37 translated by Covill 2007: 163.

14 *Saundarananda* 8.15–21.

15 I analyse this passage more comprehensively in Collett 2013.

16 Another whose story is told in the *Mahāratnakūṭa* is the eight-year-old girl Sumati, in a text bearing her name, the *Sumatidārikāparipṛcchā*, who proves herself very capable, especially given her age (Paul 1985: 199–211).

17 The story is also popularly depicted on artwork on Buddhist monuments.

18 Sponberg 1992: 20–1.

19 Translated by Paul 1985: 41–2.

20 Translated by Paul 1985: 29.

21 Mrozik 2007: 91.

22 According to Buddhist notions of rebirth, one can, after death, be reborn into various other realms, including hells.

23 Mrozik 2007: 75–6.

24 Translated by Goodman 2016: 75–6. The text this extract comes from is extreme. The consequences of other breaches of the precepts are equally injurious. A Pāli commentary on the *Dhammapada* describes what happens to a man who rapes a Buddhist nun, and whilst it does not go into this same type of detail, the briefer comments are of the same order – the earth bursts open, swallows him whole, and he is reborn into a terrible hell-world (*Dhammapada* commentary II 48–52).

25 Translated by Goodman 2016: 84, *Udayanavatsarājaparipṛcchā*.

26 Translated by Goodman 2016: 85.

27 Translated by Goodman 2016: 85.

28 Mrozik 2007.

29 Martin 2005: 50.

30 In his Introduction Martin notes that 'the sum total of biographical information available for women leaders of the eleventh and twelfth centuries is about one to two per cent, as compared to ninety-nine to ninety-eight per cent for men' (2005: 51). As noted in the Introduction (p.17), this is part of his argument that what we do have on women should be 'magnified' to reflect the way that the history of women's lives is less likely to be preserved.

31 Martin 2005: 75.

32 Martin 2005: 77–8. The quotation marks represent the item the section is a comment on.

33 Martin 2005: 78.

CHAPTER 3

1 Translated by Grant 2003: 43.

2 *Majjhima-nikāya* II 32 (translated in Ñāṇamoli and Bodhi 1995: 655–6).

3 Kulananda 1994: 69–70.

4 Collett Cox (1993) has authored a paper that assesses the development of these two different formulations of dependent arising. To attempt to understand why there are two different formulations – one general and one that focuses on the person – she assesses early Abhidharmic evidence. Her conclusions are that the two strands developed separately.

5 *Udāna* 1.i (translated in Woodward 1987: 1).

6 *Saṃyutta-nikāya* I 136 (translated by Bodhi 2000: 233).

7 Translated by Roebuck 2010: 17.

8 In some cases we do not know who the authors were of Buddhist texts and, in other cases, such as with the canon(s), we understand these to have developed over time and therefore to be the cumulative word of many authors, composers, collators, editors, and redactors. This is something that makes assessment of negative statements about women difficult to measure in some cases. That is, it is difficult to know whether they were generally held and advocated views or the work of one author or redactor. I.B. Horner, as a result of her extensive – perhaps we could say unparalleled – comprehension of the Pāli canon and commentaries, understood the negative statements and passages about women to have been made by monk editors (Horner 1930/1990: xx).

9 There is a question relating to the doctrine of dependent arising as to whether it is advocating that human beings have free will or whether it is a form of determinism. For discussion of this see Repetti 2019.

10 *Anātman* is *ātman* with the negative prefix -an, meaning 'not', similar to the prefix -a in *avidyā*.

11 The text is the *Milindapañha*.

12 Zhang 1983: 37–9. I have changed two of the words in Zhang's translation to accord with how I write about the aggregates above. Zheng has 'conceptions' for 'perception' and 'impulses' for 'volition'.

13 *Aṣṭasāhasrikāprajñāpārmitāsūtra*, translated by Conze 1973: 20–1.

14 *Mūlamadhyamikakārikā*, translated by Garfield 1995: 45.

15 Goodman 2009: 299–300.

16 Goodman 2009: 303–4.

17 Translated by Conze 1973: 44.

18 *Pramāṇavārttikakārikā*, translated by Eltschinger 2010: 35.

19 Translated by Crosby and Skilton 1995: 70, 72.

20 Mrozik 2007.

21 Translated by Crosby and Skilton 1995: 130–1.

22 Translated by Thurman 1976.

23 Schuster 1981: 54–5.

24 Paul 1985: 175. Other scholars who have published on the topic include Rita Gross (1993), who devotes several pages to it in her book, Lucinda Joy Peach, who published an excellent article on it in 2002, and Serinity Young, who discusses it in depth in her book (2004).

25 For a discussion of gender as the primary category and sex the secondary in pre-Enlightenment Europe, see Laqueur 1990.
26 Paul 1985: 194.
27 Osto 2007.
28 For a reconfiguration of the idea of sex change in a ninth-century text from Japan, see Blair 2016.
29 Developing feelings of compassion is the right response to words and actions that do not break the law. Verbal or physical abuse of any sort warrants more definite action. For examples of moral and compassionate action in the face of abuses of power and sexual abuse, see chapter 7.

CHAPTER 4

1 Translated by Adamek 2009: 17.
2 See Blackstone 2000: 13–36 on the question of whether the nuns are the authors of the poems.
3 In recent years, a new translation of the *Therīgāthā* has been published by Charles Hallisey (2015), in which he aims to reproduce the poems as poetry. Also, a full English translation of the canonical biographies of the nuns, by Jonathan Walters (2019), is now available online at http://apadanatranslation.org/.
4 This is the same disciple we met with in chapter 3. Śāriputra is the Sanskrit spelling, Sāriputta the Pāli.
5 In this volume, in recounting these biographies, I have noted some of the most significant differences between different versions of the biographies, but I have not noted variations with regards details. For fully annotated versions of the biographies, with all changes noted, see Collett 2016. For the versions that appear here, I have amalgamated features of different accounts with regard to details, scenes, and episodes. The only differences I have noted are with regard to the story arc, and then only on issues I want to draw out. With regard to choosing which details to add in or leave out, I have made choices in relation to what might be of most interest to the reader; that is, for instance, adding in as much detail as there is, even if this only appears in one version.
6 Translated by Hallisey 2015: 13.
7 Anālayo 2011: 17.
8 Her answer is in accord with the twelve links of dependent arising as discussed in chapter 3.
9 In this discourse, Dhammadinnā specifies the eightfold path, which comes, in the Pali canon, to represent the path generally.
10 See Collett 2011 for more on the seven sisters.
11 *Majjhima-nikāya* commentary II 357.
12 *Majjhima-nikāya* commentary II 357.
13 *Therīgāthā* commentary 18.

14 *Therīgāthā* 107–11 (translated in Hallisey 2015: 65).
15 Sattuka means 'enemy'. He is considered an enemy of the king because his actions create disharmony in the otherwise smooth running of the king's sovereignty.
16 Translated by Walters 2019. These final two verses are not unique to Bhaddā, and appear in many of the (auto)biographies that make up the *Apadāna*.
17 *Therīgāthā* verses 112–16 (translated in Hallisey 2015: 67).
18 *Apadāna* 558 Em.
19 *Aṅguttara-nikāya* commentary I 357.
20 *Dhammapada* commentary II 261.
21 *Aṅguttara-nikāya* commentary I 357 and *Therīgāthā* commentary 106.
22 In some of the accounts, the desire to see her parents arises only at the time she is pregnant with her second child.
23 Translated by Walters 2019.
24 *Aṅguttara-nikāya* commentary I 359.
25 *Apadāna* 560.
26 *Apadāna* 560.
27 See Adamek 2009 and Georgieva 2000.
28 Adamek 2016.
29 Translated by Tsai 1994: 15.
30 Translated by Overmyer 1991: 105.
31 Translated by Tsai 1994: 18. This sounds very similar to the arguments made for not reviving the Theravāda Order of nuns.
32 Tsai 1994: 18. I have changed all Chinese transliteration in the quotations from Tsai to Pinyin.
33 Tsai 1994: 19 and 117, n11. In the tradition of Confucius, the focus is on morality and filial piety but both are very androcentric; the moral person is usually called 'The Gentleman', and the most important filial relationships are those between father and son.
34 Translated by Tsai 1994: 19.
35 These aspects of Chinese Confucian society are brought to life in the 1998 animated Disney movie *Mulan*, particularly with the character of her companion, Mushu, whom she first meets when she is performing ancestor worship.
36 Translated by Tsai 1994: 20.
37 See the Introduction. The idea here is similar to that of Hindu/Brahmanic tradition, that a woman should be under the guardianship of men.
38 Translated by Tsai 1994: 20.
39 Translated by Tsai 1994: 21.
40 Daoism, like Buddhism, is a system that concentrates on inner cultivation and believes that, through the practice of inner contemplation, one is able to see and live in accord with The Way (*dao*).
41 Translated by Tsai 1994: 29.
42 Translated by Tsai 1994: 29.

43 For more on Guanyin, see chapter 6.
44 The extensive and important work of Beata Grant has brought the biographies of these nuns to life. See, for instance, Grant 1996 and 2009.
45 Grant 2009: 39.
46 Translated by Grant 2009: 46.
47 Grant 2009: 49.
48 Translated by Grant 2009: 51. A *mahākalpa* is a very long period of time.
49 Translated by Grant 2009: 59.
50 Translated by Grant 1996: 63.
51 Translated by Grant 1996: 64.
52 Kurihara and Imai 2003: 94–6.
53 Deal 1999: 176–84.
54 Ueda 2003: 38.
55 Translated by Donegan and Ishibashi 1998: 25.
56 Donegan 2008: 97.
57 Translated by Donegan and Ishibashi 1998: 118.
58 Donegan and Ishibashi 1998: 44.
59 Translated by Donegan and Ishibashi 1998: 46.
60 Translated by Donegan and Ishibashi 1998: 47.
61 The biographies could more accurately be called hagiographies.
62 See chapter 5 for more on *mae chi*s and Buddhism in Thailand.
63 See Seeger 2018.
64 Seeger 2018: 85–6 (Pāli removed). In Luang Pu Man's words we find two aspects of Buddhist belief already discussed in this volume. Earlier in this chapter, we saw the Indian nuns Dhammadinnā, Bhaddā Kuṇḍalakesā, and Pātācārā; all lived previous lives in which they practised, which, as here, impacted upon their ability to practise in their life with the historical Buddha, Gotama. Luang Pu Man's mention of the impermanence of all conditioned things illustrates one way in which modern Thai Buddhists relate to the teaching of dependent arising, as discussed in chapter 3.
65 Seeger 2018: 89. See, for instance, Sumedhā's vitriol on the body as an object of desire in the *Therīgāthā*, in which she, in response to her father encouraging her to enjoy the pleasures of the married life he is arranging for her, tells him: 'Why should I cling, like a worm, to a body that will turn into a corpse, a sack always oozing, frightening, stinking foul and putrid, filled with foul things' (verse 469 translated by Hallisey 2015: 219).
66 Seeger 2018: 90.

CHAPTER 5

1 Inscription translated by Jacobsen 2013: 80. Jacobsen also notes of the queen mother, 'These pious acts included using her influence to convince her son the king to restore Angkor Wat' (2013: 80).

2 The idea of an unbroken lineage is important in most Buddhist traditions. It is, however, more of an ideal than a verifiable reality. The notion is that each ordination lineage should be traceable back to the Buddha, such that every new monk or nun is ordained by another, who was ordained by another, . . . back to the Buddha's own ordinations of his immediate disciples. For many traditions, ordinations are only valid if they are conducted within the strictures of such a schema.

3 Salgado in Tsomo 2000: 33.

4 Bartholomeusz 1994: 18 and 209 n6.

5 Bartholomeusz 1994: 18.

6 As well as these listed and named nuns, the *Dīpavaṃsa* also mentions that these were not the only nuns, there were others.

7 *Epigraphia Zelyanica* vol. 1 1912: 228.

8 Obeyesekere 2013.

9 Bartholomeusz 1994: 21.

10 Currently, *sil-mātās* have the option to adhere to either eight or ten precepts. See the discussion of Buddhist precepts in chapter 1.

11 The nunnery is named the Madivala Upāsikārāmaya.

12 Bartholomeusz 1994: 145. Although the two formulations of the recitation of the three refuges look almost the same, the pronunciation of the final letter, which is the only difference, has a dramatic impact on how each sounds (Bartholomeusz 1994: 247 n58).

13 *Bana* in this context means a type of Buddhist teaching.

14 Lehrer 2019: 104.

15 Weddikkara 2002: 80.

16 'The sixteen women interviewed can in no way be considered representative of the Sinhala Buddhist population as a whole. All, except one, classify themselves as middle class; all, except two, have received higher education and have had a professional life; and all, except one, now live in urban areas. . . Seven of the women are married, one is unmarried, three are divorced or separated, four are widows, while one, the nun, left her husband upon renouncing late in life. At the time of the interviews, the youngest woman was 38, the oldest 80' (Snel 2001: 13).

17 Snel 2001: 32.

18 Snel 2001: 33–4.

19 Snel 2001: 66. This is only an excerpt from Mrs Violet's answer to the question, her full answer is longer.

20 Ko 1892: 49. I have updated some orthography.

21 Moore 2004. Moore notes that the archaeological remains from Sri Ksetra show a mix of Theravāda, Mahāyāna, and Hindu practices and beliefs.

22 See, for example, Aung-Thwin 2005.

23 Moore 2004: 16.

24 The chronicles dated to later periods do relate the apparent history of this period.

25 Luce 1969: Vol. 1, 306. Luce notes the label inscriptions, but unfortunately the images are no longer discernible. I would like to thank Claudine Bautze-Picron for kindly supplying me with a photograph of this part of the temple wall.

26 From India, there is an image that may be of Uppalavaṇṇā, but this is not confirmed.

27 Thompson 2016: 3.

28 English translation by Ashley Thompson, with the help of Sally Goldman; Thompson 2008: 112–14 ([the Buddha] added). Original text and French translation in Cœdès 1942: 161–79, K. 485.

29 Cœdès 1942: 161–79.

30 Thompson 2016, esp. Introduction and ch. 4.

31 Jacobsen 2008: 79.

32 Pou 1975: 283–353.

33 Guthrie 2004: 144–5; Jacobsen 2013: 82ff. The words *nāṅ jī* appear in the inscriptions, which may be a reference to some type of female asceticism in Cambodia. The words *pos* and/or *pvas* could mean 'entering into the religious life'.

34 Kent 2005: 203–4.

35 Kent 2005.

36 Ezer 2005.

37 Huot 2015: 17. 'Donchee' is another way to write *ṭūn jī*.

38 Ikeya 2005: 55.

39 Tin 1935: 151.

40 Shorto 1958: 363–4.

41 Shorto 1958: 363–4. In relation to those 'men and women' who corrupt the gift, it is hoped they will be reborn into 'wretched states'.

42 Harriden 2012: 54–8.

43 Translated by Tun 1983: 120–1. I have changed a few pieces of the formatting and corrected two typographical errors from the original.

44 Tun 1983: 123. The royal orders also tell us other things about laywomen from the 1600s onwards, such as other female donors having monasteries built (Tun 1985a: 46), and the queens and other women being instructed to conduct lay devotional rituals every day to aid the king who was away at war (Tun 1985b: 73).

45 Daw San was her pen name, she was born Ma San Youn (Ikeya 2013: 27).

46 Ikeya 2013: 27.

47 Ikeya 2013: 28–32.

48 Kawanami 2013: 160–8

49 Kawanami 2013: 185–7.

50 Kawanami 2013: 29–50.

51 Kawanami 2015: 295.

52 Kawanami 2015: 307.

53 Rigby 2017.
54 It was always assumed, however, that women were following Buddhism, albeit with lay status, as exemplified in inscriptions (Bradley 1909).
55 See Tathālokā Therī, in her aptly entitled article 'Glimmers of a Thai Bhikkhuni Sangha History' (2015). Tathālokā is herself a nun in the Theravāda tradition, having received full ordination in 1997. She founded the first Theravāda retreat centre for female monastics in California in 2005.
56 Seeger 2006: 159–60 and Kabilsingh 1991: 45–8.
57 BBC Heart and Soul 2019.
58 Kabilsingh 1991: 31–2. She continues, 'The concept that women are unclean stems from the physical fact of menstruation and ancient taboos against blood that are found in various cultures around the world.'
59 Lindberg Falk 2007: 7–8.
60 Lindberg Falk 2000: 61–72.
61 Collins and McDaniel 2010: 1390.
62 Collins and McDaniel 2010: 1397 and 1398.

CHAPTER 6

1 Translated by Shaw 1994: 42.
2 Tibet is not currently an independent country. The region is under the rule of the People's Republic of China, as it has been since the 1950s, and is known as the Tibet Autonomous Region or the Xizang Autonomous Region.
3 Fister 2018.
4 Jesuit missionaries in China were the first to award her this appellation (Yü 2001: 223).
5 See Muldoon-Hules (2017) on the narratives of women in this text; the *Avadānaśataka*.
6 Conze 1954: 196–202. The text is called the *Āryatārābhaṭṭārikānāmāṣṭottaraśatakastotra*.
7 A modern prayer flag from Tibet describes her as such, 'Standing amid a blazing circle, like the aeon-ending fire; surrounded by joy, right leg stretched out, left drawn in. . .' (Lopez 1997: 551).
8 Translated by Templeman 1981: 2.
9 Adamek 2009: 9.
10 Translated by Adamek 2007: 232 (Chinese characters removed.) My descriptions of the text follow Adamek's observations (2007: 229–37). For more on potential female authorship see also Adamek 2016.
11 Purtle 1999: 126.
12 Li 2012: 138 and 155 fig. 1.
13 Dudbridge 2004: 41–6. Dudbridge also relates the longer account that Guan Daosheng's summary is taken from. Guan Daosheng's

inscription is telegraphic at times, so in my paraphrasing I have added one or two details from the longer account. Much of my summary is taken verbatim from Dudbridge's translation of the inscription, and in that sense it is a direct quote.

14 Yü 1995: 180.
15 Grant 2009: 1–6. In this literary genre, monks were also often cast badly.
16 Goldman 2001: 72.
17 Cho 2009 and 2012.
18 The Chosŏn dynasty also appears decidedly misogynist, with the annals recording some unspeakably violent punishments meted out to women who were unfaithful (Bruno 2007). Nonetheless, throughout the Chosŏn the nuns' Order did survive, despite the efforts of the authorities, such as an order in 1413 that all virgin nuns should be married 'in order to correct human morality' (Jorgensen 2011: 121).
19 Cho 2009.
20 Laywoman Nakayama Mumoya relates how her female Zen teacher used to abruptly dismiss all her attempts to answer the puzzle (known as a *koan*) set by her teacher, 'Don't spout logic! It's just your ego!' or 'That's emotion!' or 'That's theory!' (King 1995: 519).
21 Schireson 2009: 133–4.
22 Nelson 2016: 1049, and expanded version.
23 Park, in Iryŏp and Park 2014.
24 Translated by Oh 2003: 183 (Kim's *Miraese* 1.22).
25 Iryŏp and Park 2014: 33–4 (Korean removed).
26 Taiwan is part of the Republic of China, and has not been an independent country for most of its history.
27 Jones 1999: 4–9.
28 Cheng estimates that 70–75% of monastics in Taiwan are nuns (Cheng 2007: 39).
29 Lu 2016.
30 Cheng 2007: 85–90.
31 Lee and Han 2016.
32 Lee and Han 2016: 60.
33 Huang 2009: 15–16.
34 Reed 2003: 198 citing Ching 1995, 66.
35 Lu 2016: 362.
36 Lu 2016: 363.
37 For references see Salguero 2015: 40 and n12.
38 Warner 2011: 242.
39 Uebach 2005: 42. The annals report that she 'had the walls of the temples made of burnt brick, got the junctions filled up with molten lead, and had a roof made of copper set up'.
40 Simmer-Brown 2001: 4.
41 English 2002: 60.
42 Translated by English 2002: 60. Sanskrit removed.

43 Tsogyal 1993: 40. Translated by Erik Pema Kunsang.
44 Kragh 2017. Kragh has reconstructed some of the names of the women into Sanskrit that are only preserved in Tibetan. Of the texts, some are extant in Sanskrit, others only in Tibetan, and others in both languages.
45 Translated by Shaw 1994: 39. 'Lady Perfection of Wisdom' is a reference to Prajñāpāramitā.
46 Herrmann Pfandt 2000.
47 Translated by Harding 2013. Harding spells her name Machik, which is a variation that I have amended here for the sake of consistency.
48 Translated by Herrmann Pfandt 2000: 20, with two simplifications added in parenthesis.
49 Herrmann Pfandt 2000: 21.
50 Herrmann Pfandt 2000: 25.
51 Diemberger 2007: 1.
52 Translated by Diemberger 2007: 174 (internal referencing removed).
53 Translated by Diemberger 2007: 175.
54 Jacoby 2014.
55 Translated by Jacoby 2009: 128. 'Mtsho rgyal' in Jacoby's translation has been changed to 'Yeshe Tsogyal' and Tibetan and Sanskrit references removed.
56 Jacoby 2009.
57 Bahir 2018.
58 Travagnin 2016 and, for more on mummification in East Asian Buddhism, see Gildow and Bingenheimer 2002.

CHAPTER 7

1 Takeko 1985: 43.
2 Hughes Seager 2002: 107–8.
3 Bluck 2006: 4.
4 Caroline Rhys Davids' article was published prior to her marriage under her maiden name of Caroline Foley (1893). Bode's paper appeared in the same year, 1893.
5 Almond 1988.
6 Rhys Davids 1909: 104–5. In the Introduction, she provides justification as to why she has changed the order in her work, situating the verses of the nuns first (pp.xiv–xv).
7 Horner 1930/1990: xx.
8 Horner 1930/1990: xxii.
9 Goodrick-Clarke 2004: 5.
10 On Mary Foster see Masters and Tsomo 2000: 235–48.
11 Ha 1999: 114–15.
12 Waddell 1895: xi. Also see Thévoz 2016: 157 and 150.
13 Néel 1931: 43.
14 Adam 2000: 138–9.

15 Baumann 2002. Tsomo reports that, as of 2001, there were several hundred Chinese Buddhist nuns in the USA, along with several hundred Vietnamese and around sixty Korean nuns (Tsomo 2002: 256). The number of Western convert nuns, she notes, is too difficult to map.

16 On Dam Luu see Duc 2000: 104–22 and Do and Khúc 2009: 124–30. As a glimpse into her life: 'In 1976, Dam Luu was pressured to make false accusations against a monastic friend, and when she refused she was threatened and harassed by the government. After four failed attempts to leave Vietnam, she finally managed to escape in a small fishing boat in 1978. . . Dam Luu arrived in the United States as a refugee in 1980 when she was forty-eight years old. She had less than twenty dollars to start her new life. Thanh Cat, a Vietnamese Buddhist monk in East Palo Alto, California, sponsored her resettlement in the United States, and she was later reassigned to San Jose where she eventually founded Chua Viet Nam' (Du and Khúc 2009: 131, and see Duc 2000: 107).

17 Harris 2006: 110–17.

18 See, most recently, Turner, Cox, and Bocking 2020: 136.

19 For Robinson see Bartholomeusz 1994: 169 and for Wolf see Helmuth 1997.

20 Bell 2000: 12.

21 Numrich 1999: 59ff.

22 Boucher 1989.

23 Transcription of talk, audio available online (Khema n.d.). The second ellipsis is in place of a repeat of the words 'in a relative reality'. Compare this also to what Ayya Khema says on the nature of the self generally: 'We are constantly trying to reaffirm self. Which already shows that this "self" is a very fragile and rather wispy sort of affair, because if it weren't why would we constantly have to reaffirm it? Why are we constantly afraid of the "self" being threatened of its being insecure, of its not getting what it needs for survival? If it were such a solid entity as we believe it to be, we would not feel threatened so often. We affirm "self" again and again through identification. We identify with a certain name, an age, a sex, an ability, an occupation. "I am a lawyer, I am a doctor. I am an accountant, I am a student." And we identify with the people we are attached to. "I am a husband, I am a wife, I am a mother, I am a daughter, I am a son." Now, in the manner of speech, we have to use "self" in that way – but it isn't only in speech. We really think that that "self" is who we are. We really believe it. There is no doubt in our mind that that "self" is who we are. When any of these factors is threatened, if being a wife is threatened, if being a mother is threatened, if being a lawyer is threatened, if being a teacher is threatened – or if we lose the people who enable us to retain that "self" – what a tragedy!' (Khema 1983). See chapter 3 for more on the Buddhist doctrine of no-self.

24 Starkey 2020: 1; Kittelstrom 2009.

25 Tomalin 2014: 114–15.

26 Anukampa Bhikkhuni Project n.d. This is a private dwelling, not a public centre.

27 The Chinese invasion of Tibet in 1959, which resulted in a mass exile from the country, forced many Tibetan teachers to look for a new home.

28 As well as these three, there are many other notable women in modern Tibetan traditions in the West, including, to name but two, Lobsang Chodron (Ann McNeil), ordained in 1970, and Thubtun Chodren, currently the Abbotess of Sravasti Abbey, a Tibetan monastery for Western monks and nuns in Washington state.

29 For the life of Freda Bedi, see Mackenzie 2017.

30 Mackenzie 1998: 27. Kargyu is the tradition of Tibetan Buddhism to which these women belonged.

31 Mackenzie 1998: 37.

32 In the documentary, Chögyam Trungpa's widow, Diane Mukpo, talks openly about his infidelity, and in her book also about other extramarital affairs, her own included (Mukpo and Gimian 2008).

33 Buddhist Sunshine Project 2, final report 2018: 17.

34 Chödrön 2020.

35 See Bell 2002: 238. In her chapter Bell reviews both Shambhala International and the San Francisco Zen Center, although noting these are not the only cases. Bell's chapter was composed years prior to these newer allegations emerging.

36 Butler 1983.

37 Weber 1968: 1111–57 (first published in 1922 in German). I take my lead here from Sandra Bell, who understands the recent history of these groups to be examples of Weber's charismatic authority. See Bell 1998 and 2002.

38 This is not the only reason abuse happens, it can be endemic in an institution as well, for instance. I cite this as a possible explanation for these modern examples, as I expect readers of this book with little knowledge of Buddhism will be wondering why there are so many examples of this in modern, Western Buddhist movements. Sexual abuse also happens within Buddhist institutions in Asia, and information about this, and the extent of it, is just beginning to surface.

39 According to the Buddhist Prison Chaplain job description, a prospective chaplain 'Must be a committed Buddhist living by a moral standard of at least that of the Five Precepts and must be a regular meditator. Must have a competent understanding of Buddhist Teaching and Practice. Must have knowledge of Buddhist schools other than the one to which he or she belongs and be willing to help and encourage interest in and practice of those schools when required' (Angulimala n.d.).

40 Bluck 2006: 153–5.

41 According to Starkey, citing Vajragupta, there were for many years many more male order members than female, but in recent years this

has begun to change, and 'In spring 2018, there were 450 female Order members in the UK (compared with 583 men) and worldwide, there were 860 [female] *dharmacharinis* and 1,317 [male] *dharmacharis.*' (2020: 46). This number will include Order members who are classed as 'inactive', meaning they are no longer associated with the Order and movement, but have not formally resigned.

42 Sangharakshita 1995.

43 Subhuti 1995: 25.

44 Doyle 1996.

45 The recall of the volume and subsequent pulping occurred around 1998 or 1999, according to Priyananda, Director of Windhorse Publications 2010–20 (personal communication 17 February 2020).

46 Buddhist Centre (2017). The second major change to happen following Sangharakshita's retirement was renewed and more extensive allegations of sexual abuse, coercion, and sexual exploitation by Sangharakshita and some of his leading disciples; allegations of abuse of men by men. Several newspaper articles have been published on this topic, the most recent in 2019 (Doward 2019).

47 Ambedkar 1979: 120–1.

48 Junghare 1988: 117. Also, a key feature of Triratna in India is work that has been undertaken to support equal treatment of women and girls, and enable them to improve their lives. The Karuna Trust, a branch of Triratna that has operated in India for forty years, initiates and runs numerous projects that aim to empower women and girls. Such projects include, for instance, The Green Tara Foundation, which currently supports a thousand girls from Pune slums to stay in school, The Maitri Network, which works to raise awareness of the continued discrimination faced by Dalit and Adivasi women, and The Nagpur Girls Hostel, which enables girls and young women from the region to access secondary and further education (Karuna Trust n.d.).

49 Dangle 2010.

50 Starkey (2020) finds, in her new book on women in British Buddhism, that this is often the case. The women are less concerned with gender than might be imagined to be the case.

EPILOGUE

1 Boucher 1993: 93.

2 Or by any who do not prefer this binary terminology.

3 Garfield 2010: 341.

4 Translated by Donegan and Ishibashi 1998: 253.

REFERENCES

Adam, Enid. 2000. 'Women in Buddhism in Australia', *Journal of Global Buddhism* 1: 138–43.

Adamek, Wendi Leigh. 2007. *The Mystique of Transmission: On an Early Chan History and Its Context*. New York: Columbia University Press.

Adamek, Wendi Leigh. 2009. 'A Niche of Their Own: The Power of Convention in Two Inscriptions for Medieval Chinese Buddhist Nuns', *History of Religions* 49/1: 1–26.

Adamek, Wendi Leigh. 2016. 'Revisiting Questions about Female Disciples in the *Lidai fabao ji* (Record of the Dharma-Treasure through the Generations)', *Pacific World: Journal of the Institute of Buddhist Studies* 18: 57–65.

Almond, Philip C. 1988. *The British Discovery of Buddhism*. Cambridge: Cambridge University Press.

Ambedkar, Bhimrao Ramji. 1979. 'The Rise and Fall of Hindu Women. Who is Responsible for it?', in *Dr. Babasaheb Ambedkar: Writings and Speeches*, Vol. 17, Part Two, Hari Narake, Dr M.L. Kasare, N.G. Kamble and Ashok Godghate (eds), 109–29. New Delhi: Ministry of Justice and Empowerment.

Anālayo, Bhikkhu. 2009. 'The Bahudhātuka-sutta and its Parallels on Women's Inabilities', *Journal of Buddhist Ethics* 16: 136–90.

Anālayo, Bhikkhu. 2011. '*Chos sbyin gyi mdo* – Bhikṣuṇī Dharmadinnā Proves Her Wisdom', *Zhonghua foxue xuebao* 24: 3–33.

Anālayo, Bhikkhu. 2014. 'Karma and Female Rebirth', *Journal of Buddhist Ethics* 21: 107–50.

Anālayo, Bhikkhu. 2016. *The Foundation History of the Nuns' Order*. Bochum: Numata Center for Buddhist Studies.

Angulimala. n.d. The Buddhist Prison Chaplaincy Service, available at https://angulimala.org.uk/buddhist-prison-chaplain-job-description/, accessed on 18 November 2020.

Anukampa Bhikkhuni Project. n.d. Home Page, available at https://anukampaproject.org/bhikkhuniresidence/, accessed on 18 November 2020.

Aung-Thwin, Michael A. 2005. *The Mist of Rāmañña: The Legend That Was Lower Burma*. Honolulu: University of Hawai'i Press.

Bahir, Cody R. 2018. 'Reformulating the Appropriated and Relinking the Chain Challenges of Lineage and Legitimacy in Zhenyan Revivalism', in *The Hybridity of Buddhism: Contemporary Encounters between Tibetan and Chinese Traditions in Taiwan and the Mainland*, Fabienne Jagou (ed.), 91–108. Études thématiques 29. Paris: École française d'Extrême-Orient.

Bartholomeusz, Tessa J. 1994. *Women under the Bō Tree: Buddhist Nuns in Sri Lanka*. Cambridge: Cambridge University Press.

Baumann, Martin. 2002. 'Buddhism in Europe: Past, Present, Prospects', in *Westward Dharma: Buddhism Beyond Asia*, Charles S. Prebish and Martin Baumann (eds), 85–105. Berkeley and Los Angeles: University of California Press.

BBC Heart and Soul. 2019. '100 Women: Venerable Dhammananda', available at https://www.bbc.co.uk/programmes/w3ct0046, accessed on 18 November 2020.

Bell, Sandra. 1998. '"Crazy Wisdom," Charisma, and the Transmission of Buddhism in the United States', *Nova Religio* 2/1: 55–75.

Bell, Sandra. 2000. 'Being Creative with Tradition: Rooting Theravāda Buddhism in Britain', *Journal of Global Buddhism* 1: 1–23.

Bell, Sandra. 2002. 'Scandals in Emerging Western Buddhism', in *Westward Dharma: Buddhism Beyond Asia*, Charles S. Prebish and Martin Baumann (eds), 230–44. Berkeley and Los Angeles: University of California Press.

Blackstone, Kathryn R. 2000. *Women in the Footsteps of the Buddha: Struggle for Liberation on the Therīgāthā*. Delhi: Motilal Banarsiddass.

Blair, Heather. 2016. 'Mother of the Buddhas: The *Sutra on Transforming Women into Buddhas* (*Bussetsu Tenyo Jōbutsa Kyō*)', *Momumenta Nipponica* 71/2: 263–93.

Bluck, Robert. 2006. *British Buddhism: Teachings, Practice and Development*. London and New York: Routledge.

Bode, Mabel. 1893. 'Women Leaders of the Buddhist Reformation', *Journal of the Royal Asiatic Society* 25/3: 517–66.

Bodhi, Bhikkhu (tr.). 2000. *The Connected Discourses of the Buddha: A Translation of the Saṃyutta Nikāya*. Boston: Wisdom Publications.

Bodhi, Bhikkhu (tr.). 2012. *The Numerical Discourses of the Buddha: A Translation of the Aṅguttara Nikāya*. Boston: Wisdom Publications.

Boucher, Sandra. 1989. 'Foreword', in Ayya Khema, *Be an Island: The Buddhist Practice of Inner Peace*. Boston: Wisdom Publications.

Boucher, Sandy. 1993. *Turning the Wheel: American Women Creating the New Buddhism*. Boston: Beacon Press.

Braarvig, Jens and Paul Harrison. 2002. 'Candrottarādārikāvyākaraṇa', in *Buddhist Manuscripts*, Vol. II, Jens Braarvig (ed.), 51–68. Oslo: Hermes Publishing.

Bradley, Cornelius Beach. 1909. 'The Oldest Known Writing in Siamese: The Inscription of Phra Ram Khamhaeng of Sukhothai, 1293 A.D.', *Journal of Siam Society* 6/1: 1–68.

Brown, Sid. 2001. *The Journey of One Buddhist Nun: Even Against the Wind*. Albany: State University of New York Press.

Bruno, Antonetta Lucia. 2007. 'Images of Women in the Literature of the Chosŏn Period: Passion and Eroticism in the Conflict between Official and Unofficial Discourse in Korea', *Rivista degli studi orientali* 78/4: 157–76.

Buddhist Centre. 2017. 'Maitreyi Interviews Subhuti on "Women, Men And Angels"', available at https://thebuddhistcentre.com/adhisthana-kula/maitreyi-interviews-subhuti-women-men-and-angels, accessed on 19 November 2020.

Buddhist Sunshine Project 2. 2018. Available at https://andreamwinn.com/offerings/bps-welcome-page/, accessed on 27 November 2020.

Butler, Katy. 1983. 'Events Are the Teacher: Working through the Crisis at the San Francisco Zen Center', *Coevolution Quarterly* Winter 1983, available at http://www.katybutler.com/publications/wer/index_files/wer_eventsteacher.htm, accessed on 18 November 2020.

Chakravarti, Uma. 1981. 'The Rise of Buddhism as Experienced by Women', *Manushi* 1: 6–10.

Chakravarti, Uma. 2014. 'Oppositional Imaginations: Multiple Lineages of Feminist Scholarship', in *A Journey into Women's Studies: Crossing Interdisciplinary Boundaries*, Rekha Pande (ed.), 60–74. London: Palgrave Macmillan.

Chakravarti, Uma and Kumkum Roy. 1988. 'Breaking out on Invisibility: Rewriting the History of Women in Ancient India', in *Retrieving Women's History: Changing Perspectives of the Role of Women in Politics and Society*, S. Jay Kleinberg (ed.), 319–37. Berg: UNESCO.

Cheng, Wei-Yi. 2007. *Buddhist Nuns in Taiwan and Sri Lanka: A Critique of the Feminist Perspective*. London and New York: Routledge.

Ching, Yu-ing. 1995. *Master of Love and Mercy: Chen Yen*. Grass Valley, CA: Blue Dolphin.

Cho, Eun-Su. 2009. 'Reinventing Female Identity: A Brief History of Korean Buddhist Nuns', *Seoul Journal of Korean Studies* 22/1: 29–53.

Cho, Eun-Su (ed.). 2012. *Korean Buddhist Nuns and Laywomen: Hidden Histories, Enduring Vitality*. Albany: State University of New York Press.

Chödrön, Pema. 2020. 'Letter from Ani Pema Chödrön', *Shambhala Times*, available at https://shambhalatimes.org/2020/01/16/letter-from-ani-pema-chodron/, accessed on 18 November 2020.

Chung, In Young. 1999. 'A Buddhist View of Women: A Comparative Study of the Rules for *Bhikṣunīs* and *Bhikṣus* Based on the Chinese *Prātimokṣa*', *Journal of Buddhist Ethics* 6: 29–105.

Cœdès, G. 1942. *Inscriptions du Cambodge*, vol. II. Hanoi: EFEO.

Collett, Alice. 2011. 'The Female Past in Early Indian Buddhism: The Shared Narrative of the Seven Sisters in the Therī-Apadāna', *Religions of South Asia* 5/1: 209–26.

Collett, Alice. 2013. 'Beware the Crocodile: Male and Female Nature in Aśvaghoṣa's *Saundarananda*', *Religions of South Asia* 7: 60–74.

Collett, Alice. 2016. *Lives of Early Buddhist Nuns: Biographies as History*. New Delhi: Oxford University Press.

Collins, Steven and Justin McDaniel. 2010. 'Buddhist "Nuns" (*mae chi*) and the Teaching of Pali in Contemporary Thailand', *Modern South Asia* 44/6: 1373–408.

Conze, Edward (ed.). 1954. *Buddhist Texts through the Ages*. Oxford: Bruno Cassirer.

Conze, Edward (tr.). 1973. *The Perfection of Wisdom in Eight Thousand Lines and Its Verse Summary*. Bolinas, CA: Four Seasons Foundation.

Covill, Linda (tr.). 2007. *Handsome Nanda, by Ashvaghosha*. Oxford: New York University Press and JJC Foundation.

Cox, Collett. 1993. 'Dependent Origination: Its Elaboration in Early Sarvastivadin Abhidharma Texts', in *Researches in Indian and Buddhist Philosophy: Essays in Honour of Professor Alex Wayman*, Ram Karan Sharma (ed.), 119–42. Delhi: Motilal Banarsidass Publishers.

Crosby, Kate and Andrew Skilton (trs.). 1995. *Śāntideva, the Bodhicaryāvatāra*. Oxford: Oxford University Press.

Dangle, Arjun (ed.) 2010. *Poisoned Bread: Marathi Dalit Literature*, Jayant Karve and Philip Engblom (trs.). Hyderabad: Orient Blackswan.

Deal, William E. 1999: 'Women in Japanese Buddhism: Tales of Birth in the Pure Land', in *Religions of Japan in Practice*, George Tanabe (ed.), 176–84. Princeton: Princeton University Press.

Dhammadinna, Bhikkhuni. 2015. 'Predictions of Women to Buddhahood in Middle-Period Literature', *Journal of Buddhist Ethics* 22: 505–32.

Dhammadinna, Bhikkhuni. 2017. 'Karma Here and Now in a Mūlasarvāstivāda *Avadāna*: How the Bodhisattva Changed Sex and Was Born as a Female 500 Times', *ARIRIABSU* XXI: 63–94.

Diemberger, Hildegard. 2007. *When a Woman Becomes a Religious Dynasty: The Samding Dorje Phagmo of Tibet*. New York: Columbia University Press.

Do, Hien Duc and Mimi Khúc. 2009. 'Immigrant Religious Adaptation: Vietnamese American Buddhists at Chua Viet Nam', in *Religion at the Corner of Bliss and Nirvana*, Lois Ann Lorentzen, Joaquin Jay Gonzalez III, Kevin M. Chun, and Hien Duc Do (eds.), 124–30. Durham, NC and London: Duke University Press.

Donegan, Patricia. 2008. *Haiku Mind: 108 Poems to Cultivate Awareness and Open Your Heart*. Boston, MA: Shambhala Publications.

Donegan, Patricia and Yoshie Ishibashi. 1998. *Chiyo-ni: Woman Haiku Master*. Tokyo, Boston, Singapore: Tuttle Publishing.

Doniger, Wendy with Brian K. Smith (trs.). 1991. *The Laws of Manu*. London: Penguin.

Doward, Jamie. 2019. 'Buddhist, Teacher, Predator: Dark Secrets of the Triratna Guru', *The Observer*, 21 July.

Doyle, Anita. 1996. 'Review of Women, Men and Angels by Subhuti (Alex Kennedy)', *Tricycle: The Buddhist Review* Summer, available at https://tricycle.org/magazine/women-men-and-angels/, accessed on 27 November 2020.

Duc, Thich Minh. 2000. 'Dam Luu: An Eminent Vietnamese Buddhist Nun', in *Innovative Buddhist Women: Swimming against the Stream*, Karma Lekshe Tsomo (ed.), 104–122. Cornwall: Curzon.

Dudbridge, Glen. 2004. *The Legend of Miaoshan*. Revised edition. New York: Oxford University Press.

Egge, James R. 2013. *Religious Giving and the Invention of Karma in Theravada Buddhism*. Oxford and New York: Routledge.

Eltschinger, Vincent. 2010. 'Ignorance, Epistemology and Soteriology, Part II', *Journal of the International Association of Buddhist Studies* 33/1–2: 27–74.

English, Elizabeth. 2002. *Vajrayoginī: Her Visualization, Rituals, and Forms*. Sommerville, MA: Wisdom Publications.

Ezer, Ozlem. 2005. 'Peace Between Banyan and Kapok Trees: Untangling Cambodia through Thavory Huot's Life Story', Women Peacemakers Program, Joan B. Kroc Institute for Peace and Justice, University of San Diego, 1–49, available at https://www.sandiego.edu/peace/documents/ipj/Thavory-Huot-Cambodia.pdf, accessed on 27 November 2020.

Fister, Patricia. 2018. 'Commemorating Life and Death: The Memorial Culture Surrounding the Rinzai Zen Nun Mugai Nyodai', in *Women, Rites, and Ritual Objects in Premodern Japan*, Karen M. Gerhart (ed.), 269–303. Leiden: Brill.

Foley, Caroline Augusta. 1893. 'The Women Leaders of the Buddhist Reformation as Illustrated by Dhammapāla's Commentary on the *Therīgāthā*', *Transactions of the Ninth International Congress of Orientalists* 1: 340–60.

Garfield, Jay L. 1995. *The Fundamental Wisdom of the Middle Way: Nāgārjuna's Mūlamadhymakakārikā*. Oxford, New York: Oxford University Press.

Garfield, Jay L. 2010. 'What Is It Like to Be a Bodhisattva? Moral Phenomenology in Śāntideva's *Bodhicaryāvatāra*', *Journal of the International Association of Buddhist Studies* 33/1–2: 333–57.

Gender Studies Group, Delhi University. 2011. 'Interview with Uma Chakravarti', *Gender Studies Journal* 1/3: 2–5.

Georgieva, Valentina. 2000. *Buddhist Nuns in China: From the Six Dynasties to the Tang*. PhD diss., Leiden University.

Gildow, Douglas and Marcus Bingenheimer. 2002. 'Buddhist Mummification in Taiwan: Two Case Studies', *Asia Major* 15/2: 87–127.

Goldman, Andrea S. 2001. 'The Nun Who Wouldn't Be: Representations of Desire in Two Performance Genres of "Si Fan"', *Late Imperial China* 22/1: 71–138.

Goodman, Charles (tr.). 2009. 'Vasubandhu's *Abhidharmakośa*: A Critique of the Soul', in *Buddhist Philosophy: Essential Readings*, William Edelglass and Jay Garfield (eds), 297–309. New York: Oxford University Press.

Goodman, Charles (tr.). 2016. *The Training Anthology of Śāntideva: A Translation of the Śikṣā-samuccaya*. New York: Oxford University Press.

Goodrick-Clarke, Nicholas. 2004. 'Introduction', in *Helena Blavatsky*, Nicholas Goodrick-Clarke (ed.), 1–22. Berkeley, CA: North Atlantic Books.

Grant, Beata. 1996. 'Female Holder of the Lineage: Linji Chan Master Zhiyuan Xinggang (1597–1643)', *Late Imperial China* 17/2: 51–76.

Grant, Beata. 2003. *Daughters of Emptiness: Poems of Chinese Buddhist Nuns*. Somerville, MA: Wisdom Publications.

Grant, Beata. 2009. *Eminent Nuns: Women Chan Masters of Seventeenth Century China*. Honolulu: University of Hawai'i Press.

Groner, Paul. 2018. 'The Bodhisattva Precepts', in *The Oxford Handbook of Buddhist Ethics*, Daniel Cozort and James Mark Shields (eds), 29–50. Oxford: Oxford University Press.

Gross, Rita M. 1993. *Buddhism After Patriarchy: A Feminist History, Analysis, and Reconstruction of Buddhism*. Albany: State University of New York Press.

Guthrie, Elizabeth. 2004. 'Khmer Buddhism, Female Asceticism, and Salvation', in *History, Buddhism and New Religious Movements in Cambodia*, John Amos Marston and Elizabeth Guthrie (eds), 133–49. Honolulu: University of Hawai'i Press.

Ha, Marie Paule. 1999. 'Engendering French Colonial History: The Case of Indochina', *Historical Reflections / Réflections Historiques* 25/1: 95–125.

Hallisey, Charles. 2015. *Therigatha: Poems of the First Buddhist Women*. Cambridge, MA: Harvard University Press.

Harding, Sarah (tr.). 2013. *Machik's Complete Explanation: Clarifying the Meaning of Chöd*. Expanded edition. Vol. 11. Boston: Shambhala Publications.

Harriden, Jessica. 2012. *The Authority of Influence: Women and Power in Burmese History*. Copenhagen: NIAS Press.

Harris, Elizabeth. 2006. *Theravada Buddhism and the British Encounter: Religious, Missionary and Colonial Experience in Nineteenth Century Sri Lanka*. London: Routledge.

Helmuth, Hecker. 1997. 'Biography of Hannalore Wolf (Sister Vajirā)', Path Press (tr.) 2008, available at https://pathpress.wordpress.com/biographical/%20biography-of-hannelore-wolf-sister-vajira/, accessed on 19 November 2020.

Herrmann Pfandt, Adelheid. 2000. 'On a Previous Birth Story of Ma gcig Lab sgron ma', *The Tibet Journal* 23/3: 19–31.

Horner, I.B. 1930/1990. *Women under Primitive Buddhism*. Delhi: Motilal Banarsidass.

Hu, Hsiao-Lan. 2019. 'The White Feminism in Rita Gross's Critique of Gender Identities and Reconstruction of Buddhism', in *Buddhism and Whiteness*, George Yancy and Emily MacRae (eds), 293–308. London: Lexington Books.

Huang, C. Julia. 2009. *Charisma and Compassion: Cheng Yen and the Buddhist Tzu Chi Movement*. Cambridge, MA: Harvard University Press.

Hughes Seager, Richard. 2002. 'American Buddhism in the Making', in *Westward Dharma: Buddhism Beyond Asia*, Charles S. Prebish and

Martin Baumann (eds), 106–19. Berkeley and Los Angeles: University of California Press.

Huot, Thavory. 2015. 'A Golden Ship', *Sakyadhita Newsletter* Winter: 17.

Ikeya, Chie. 2005. 'The "Traditional" High Status of Women in Burma: A Historical Reconsideration', *Journal of Burma Studies* 10/1: 51–81.

Ikeya, Chie. 2013. 'The Life and Writings of a Patriotic Feminist: Independent Daw San of Burma', in *Women in Southeast Asian Nationalist Movements*, Susan Blackburn and Helen Ting (eds), 23–47. Singapore: NUS Press.

Iryŏp, Kim and Jin Young Park (tr.). 2014. *Reflections of a Zen Buddhist Nun: Essays by Zen Master Kim Iryŏp*. Honolulu: University of Hawai'i Press.

Jacobsen, Trude. 2008. *Lost Goddesses: The Denial of Female Power in Cambodian History*. Copenhagen: NIAS Press.

Jacobsen, Trude. 2013. 'In Search of the Khmer Bhikkhunī: Reading Between the Lines in Late Classical and Early Middle Cambodia (13th–18th Centuries)', *Journal of the Oxford Centre for Buddhist Studies* 4: 75–87.

Jacoby, Sarah H. 2009. '"This Inferior Female Body": Reflections of Life as a Tibetan Visionary through the Autobiographical Eyes of Se ra mkha' 'gro (Bde ba'I rdo rje, 1892–1940)', *Journal of the International Association of Buddhist Studies* 32/1–2: 115–50.

Jacoby, Sarah. 2014. *Love and Liberation: Autobiographical Writings of the Tibetan Buddhist Visionary Sera Khandro*. New York: Columbia University Press.

Jayawardena, Kumari. 1995. *The White Woman's Other Burden: Western Women and South Asia During British Rule*. London and New York: Routledge.

Jones, Charles B. 1999. *Buddhism in Taiwan: Religion and the State, 1660–1990*. Honolulu: University of Hawai'i Press.

Jorgensen, John. 2011. 'Marginalised and Silenced: Buddhist Nuns of the Chosŏn Period', in *Korean Buddhist Nuns and Laywomen: Hidden Histories, Enduring Vitality*, Eun-su Cho (ed.), 119–46. Albany: State University of New York Press.

Junghare, Indira Y. 1988. 'Dr. Ambedkar: The Hero of the Mahars, Ex-Untouchables of India', *Asian Folklore Studies* 47/1: 93–121.

Kabilsingh, Chatsumarn. 1991. *Thai Women in Buddhism*. Berkeley, CA: Parallax Press.

Karuna Trust. n.d. 'Our Projects', available at https://www.karuna.org/our-projects, accessed on 19 November 2020.

Kawahashi, Noriko. 1994. 'Review of *Buddhism After Patriarchy: A Feminist History, Analysis, and Reconstruction of Buddhism* by Rita Gross', *Japanese Journal of Religion* 21/4: 445–9.

Kawanami, Hiroko. 2013. *Renunciation and Empowerment of Buddhist Nuns in Myanmar-Burma: Building a Community of Female Faithful*. Leiden: Brill.

Kawanami, Hiroko. 2015. 'Is there a Future for Buddhist Nuns in Myanmar?', in *Metamorphosis: Studies in Social and Political Change in Myanmar*, Renaud Egreteau and François Robinne (eds), 291–319. Singapore: NUS Press.

Kent, Alexandra. 2005. 'Sheltered by *dhamma*: Reflecting on Gender, Security and Religion in Cambodia', *Journal of Southeast Asian Studies* 42/4: 193–209.

Khema, Ayya. n.d. 'Dharma Talks', Dharma Seed, available at https://dharmaseed.org/teacher/334/talk/7952/, accessed on 19 November 2020.

Khema, Ayya. 1983. *Meditating on No-Self*. Bodhi Leaves No. B 95. Kandy: Buddhist Publication Society.

King, Sallie. 1995. 'Awakening Stories of Zen Women', in *Buddhism in Practice*, Donald S. Lopez Jr. (ed.), 513–24. Princeton: Princeton University Press.

Kittelstrom, David. 2009. 'History in the Making?' [guest post], *Go Beyond Words, The Wisdom Publications Blog*, 3 November, available at https://gobeyondwords.wordpress.com/2009/11/03/history-in-the-making/, accessed on 19 November 2020.

Ko, Taw Sein. 1892. *The Kalyāṇī Inscriptions erected by King Dhammaceti at Pegu in 1476 AD: Text and Translation*. Rangoon: Government Printing Office.

Kragh, Ulrich Timme. 2017. 'Determining the Corpus of South Asia Female-Authored Buddhist Texts of the Ninth to the Eleventh Centuries', in *From Local to Global, Papers in Asian History and Culture, Prof. A.K. Narain Commemoration Volume*, Vol. III, Kamal Sheel, Charles Willeman, and Keneth Zysk (eds), 627–44. Delhi: Buddhist World Press.

Kulananda. 1994. 'Conditionality and the Two Truths', *Western Buddhist Review* 1.

Kurihara, Toshie and Mariko Imai. 2003: 'A History of Women in Japanese Buddhism: Nichiren's Perspectives on the Enlightenment of Women', *Journal of Oriental Studies* 13: 94–118.

Kwok, Pui-lan. 2002. Introduction, in *Postcolonialism, Feminism and Religious Discourse*, Laura E. Donaldson and Pui-lan Kwok (eds), 14–38. New York: Routledge.

Laqueur, Thomas Walter. 1992. *Making Sex: Body and Gender from the Greeks to Freud*. Cambridge, MA and London: Harvard University Press.

Lee, Chengpang and Ling Han. 2016. 'Mothers and Moral Activists: Two Models of Women's Social Engagement on Contemporary Taiwanese Buddhism', *Nova Religio: The Journal of Alternative and Emergent Religions* 19/3: 54–77.

Lehrer, Tyler A. 2019. 'Mobilizing Gendered Piety in Sri Lanka's Contemporary Bhikkhunī Ordination Dispute', *Buddhist Studies Review* 36/1: 99–121.

Li, Yuhang. 2012. 'Embroidering Guanyin: Constructions of the Divine Through Hair', *East Asian Science, Technology, and Medicine* 36: 131–166.

Lindberg Falk, Monica. 2000. 'Thammacarini Witthaya: The First School for Girls in Thailand', in *Innovative Buddhist Women: Swimming against the Stream*, Karma Lekshe Tsomo (ed.), 61–71. Richmond: Curzon.

Lindberg Falk, Monica. 2007. *Making Fields of Merit: Buddhist Female Ascetics and Gendered Orders in Thailand.* Copenhagen: NIAS Press.

Lopez Jr, Donald S. 1997. 'A Prayer Flag for Tārā', in *Religions of Tibet in Practice*, Donald S. Lopez Jr. (ed.), 410–14. Princeton: Princeton University Press.

Lounsbery, Grace Constant. 1911. *Poems of Revolt and Satan Unbound.* New York: Moffat, Yard and Company.

Lounsbery, Grace Constant. 1935. *Buddhist Meditation in the Southern Schools: Theory and Practice for Westerners.* London: Kegan Paul, Trubner and Co.

Lounsbery, Grace Constant. 1963. 'The Importance of Paña Sīla', in *The Five Precepts: Collected Essays*, Paul Dahlke, Bhikkhu Sīlācāra, L.R. Oates, and G. Constant Lounsbery, *The Wheel* No. 55. Kandy: Buddhist Publication Society.

Lu, Hwei-Syin. 2016. '"The Bodhisattva's Path" as Gender-Neutral Practices: A Case Study of the Buddhist Tzu Chi Community in Taiwan', in *Bloomsbury Research Handbook of Chinese Philosophy and Gender*, Ann A. Pang-White (ed.), 357–76. New York: Bloomsbury Publishing.

Luce, G.H. 1969. *Old Burma–Early Pagan.* New York: J. J. Augustin.

Mackenzie, Vicki. 1998. *A Cave in the Snow.* New York and London: Bloomsbury Publishing.

Mackenzie, Vicki. 2017. *The Revolutionary Life of Freda Bedi: British Feminist, India Nationalist, Buddhist Nun.* Boulder: Shambhala Publications.

Martin, Dan. 2005. 'The Woman Illusion? Research into the Lives of Spiritually Accomplished Women Leaders of the 11th and 12th Centuries', in *Women in Tibetan Buddhism: Past and Present*, Janet Gyatso and Hanna Havnevik (eds), 49–82. London: Hurst.

Masters, Patricia and Karma Leksho Tsomo. 2000. 'Mary Foster: "The First Hawaiian Buddhist"', in *Innovative Buddhist Women: Swimming against the Stream*, Karma Lekshe Tsomo (ed.), 235–48. Richmond: Curzon.

Moore, Elizabeth. 2004. 'Interpreting Pyu Material Culture: Royal Chronologies and Finger-Marked Bricks', *Myanmar Historical Research Journal* 13: 1–57.

Mrozik, Susanne. 2007. *Virtuous Bodies: The Physical Dimensions of Morality in Buddhist Ethics.* New York: Oxford University Press.

Mukpo, Diana J. and Carolyn Rose Gimian. 2008. *Dragon Thunder: My Life with Chogyam Trungpa.* Boston, MA: Shambhala Publications.

Muldoon-Hules, Karen. 2017. *Brides of the Buddha: Nuns' Stories from the Avadānaśataka.* Lanham, MD: Lexington Books.

Ñāṇamoli and Bhikkhu Bodhi (trs.) 1995. *The Middle Length Discourses of the Buddha: A New Translation of the Majjhima Nikāya.* Boston: Wisdom Publications.

Néel, Alexandra David. 1931. *Magic and Mystery in Tibet*. London: Penguin Books.

Nelson, Eric S. 2016. 'Review of Iryŏp, Kim, and Jin Young Park (tr.), 2014, *Reflections of a Zen Buddhist Nun: Essays by Zen Master Kim Iryŏp* (revised and extended)', *Philosophy East and West* 66/3: 1049–51.

Norman, K.R. (tr.). 1969. *Elder's Verses*. Vol. 1. London: Pali Text Society.

Numrich, Paul David. 1999. *Old Wisdom in the New World: Americanization in Two Immigrant Theravada Buddhist Temples*. Knoxville: University of Tennessee Press.

Obeyesekere, Ranjini. 2013. '*Dhammapada-aṭṭhakathā / Saddharmaratnāvaliya*: Women in Medieval South Asian Buddhist Societies', in *Women in Early Indian Buddhism: Comparative Textual Studies*, Alice Collett (ed.), 221–46. New York: Oxford University Press.

Oh, Bonnie B.C. 2003. 'Kim Iryŏp's Conflicting Worlds', in *Creative Women in Korea: The Fifteenth through the Twentieth Centuries*, Young Key and Kim Ranaud (eds), 174–91. New York: East Gate, M. E. Sharpe.

Osto, Douglas. 2007. *Power, Wealth and Women in Indian Mahāyāna Buddhism: The Gaṇḍavyūha-sūtra*. London: Routledge.

Overmyer, Daniel L. 1991. 'Women in Chinese Religions: Submission, Struggle, Transcendence', in *From Benares to Beijing: Essays on Buddhism and Chinese Religion*, Koichi Shinohara and Gregory Schopen (eds), 91–120. Oakville, Ontario: Mosaic Press.

Paul, Diana Y. 1985. *Women in Buddhism: Images of the Feminine in the Mahāyāna Tradition*. 2nd edition. Berkeley: University of California Press.

Peach, Lucinda Joy. 2002. 'Social Responsibility, Sex Change, and Salvation: Gender Justice in the Lotus Sūtra', *Philosophy East and West* 51/2: 50–74.

Pou, Saveros. 1975. 'Inscriptions modernes d'Angkor 34 et 38', *Bulletin de l'École française d'Extrême-Orient* LXII: 283–353.

Purtle, Jennifer. 1999. 'Guan Daosheng (1262–1319)', in *Women Writers of Traditional China: An Anthology of Poetry and Criticism*, Kang-i Sun Chang, Haun Saussy, and Charles Yim-tze Kwong (eds), 126–30. Stanford University Press.

Reed, Barbara E. 2003. 'Guanyin Narratives, Wartime and Postwar', in *Religion in Modern Taiwan: Tradition and Innovation in a Changing Society*, Philip Clart and Charles Brewer Jones (eds), 186–203. Honolulu: University of Hawai'i Press.

Repetti, Rick. 2019. *Buddhism, Meditation, and Free Will: A Theory of Mental Freedom*. Oxford and New York: Routledge,

Rhys Davids, Caroline. 1900. *A Buddhist Manual of Psychological Ethics: Translation of the First Book in the Abhidhamma Piṭaka, entitled Dhammasaṅgaṇī*. London: Pali Text Society.

Rhys Davids, Caroline (tr.). 1909. *Psalms of the Early Buddhists*. Oxford: Pali Text Society.

Rigby, Jennifer. 2017. 'Meet Burma's Feminist Buddhist Nun: How Ketu Mala is Working to Change Opinions about Gender in a Highly

Traditional Buddhist Country', *Tricycle*, 8 January, available at
https://tricycle.org/trikedaily/meet-burmas-feminist-nun/, accessed
on 19 November 2020.

Roebuck, Valerie (tr.). 2010. *The Dhammapada*. London: Penguin.

Roy, Kumkum. 2010. *The Power of Gender and The Gender of Power:
Explorations of Early Indian History*. New Delhi: Oxford University
Press.

Salgado, Nirmala S. 2007. *Buddhist Nuns and Gendered Practice: In Search
of the Female Renunciant*. New York: Oxford University Press.

Salguero, C. Pierce. 2015. 'Reexamining the Categories and Canons of
Chinese Buddhist Healing', *Journal of Chinese Buddhist Studies* 28:
35–66.

Sangharakshita. 1995. *Peace is a Fire*. Cambridge: Windhorse
Publications.

Schireson, Grace. 2009. *Zen Women: Beyond Tea Ladies, Iron Maidens, and
Macho Masters*. Boston: Wisdom Publications.

Schuster, Nancy. 1981. 'Changing the Female Body: Wise Women and
the *Bodhisattva* Career in some *Mahāratnakūṭasūtras*', *Journal of the
International Association of Buddhist Studies* 4/1: 24–69.

Seeger, Martin. 2006. 'The *Bhikkhunī*-Ordination Controversy in
Thailand', *Journal of the International Association for Buddhist Studies*
29/1: 155–84.

Seeger, Martin. 2018. *Gender and the Path to Awakening: Hidden Histories of
Nuns in Modern Thai Buddhism*. Chiang Mai: Silkworm Books.

Shaw, Miranda. 1994. *Passionate Enlightenment: Women in Tantric
Buddhism*. Princeton: Princeton University Press.

Shorto, H.L. 1958. 'The Kyaikmaraw Inscriptions', *Bulletin of the School of
Oriental and African Studies* 21/1–3: 361–7.

Simmer-Brown, Judith. 2001. *Dakini's Warm Breath: The Feminine Principle
in Tibetan Buddhism*. Boston: Shambhala Publications.

Snel, Helle. 2001. *Buddhist Women Meditators of Sri Lanka*. Kandy:
Buddhist Publication Society.

Sponberg, Alan. 1992. 'Attitudes toward Women and the Feminine in
Early Buddhism', in *Buddhism, Sexuality, and Gender*, José Ignacio
Cabezón (ed.), 3–36. Albany: State University of New York.

Starkey, Caroline. 2020. *Women in British Buddhism: Commitment,
Connection, Community*. London and New York: Routledge.

Subhuti. 1995. *Women, Men and Angels: An Inquiry Concerning the
Relative Spiritual Aptitudes of Men and Women*. Cambridge: Windhorse
Publications.

Takeko, Kujō. 1985. *Muyuge: Flower without Sorrow*. Tokyo: Nembutsu
Press.

Tathālokā, Therī. 2015. 'Glimmers of a Thai Bhikkhuni Sangha', *Gautami
Samayika* 5/5, Srabon 1422: 111–22.

Templeman, David (tr.). 1981. *The Origin of the Tārā Mantra* by Jo Nang
Tāranātha. Dharamsala: Library of Tibetan Works and Archives.

Thévoz, Samuel. 2016. '"On the Threshold of the Land of Marvels":
Alexandra David Neel in Sikkham and the Making of Global
Buddhism', *Transcultural Studies* 1: 149–86.

Thompson, Ashley. 2008. 'Performative Realities: Nobody's Possession',
in *At the Edge of the Forest: Essays on Cambodia, History, and Narrative
in Honour of David Chandler*, Ann Ruth Hansen and Judy Ledgerwood
(eds), 93–120. Ithaca, NY: Cornell Southeast Asian Programme
Publications.

Thompson, Ashley. 2016. *Engendering the Buddhist State: Territory,
Sovereignty and Sexual Difference in the Inventions of Angkor*. London
and New York: Routledge.

Thurman, Robert A.F. (tr.). 1976. *The Holy Teaching of Vimalakīrti: A
Mahāyāna Scripture*. Philadelphia: Pennsylvania State University.

Tin, Pe Maung. 1935. 'Women in the Inscriptions of Pagan', *Journal of the
Burma Research Society* 25/3: 149–59.

Tomalin, Emma. 2014. 'Gender, Buddhism and Bhikkhuni Ordination:
Transnational Strategies for the Feminist Transformation of Religion
in the 21st Century', in *Religion, Gender, and the Public Sphere*, Niamh
Reilly and Stacey Scriver (eds), 108–18. New York: Routledge.

Travagnin, Stefania. 2016. 'Elder Gongga (1903–1997) between China,
Tibet and Taiwan: Assessing Life, Mission and Mummification of a
Buddhist Woman', *Journal of the Irish Society for the Academic Study of
Religions* 3: 250–72.

Tsai, Kathryn Ann (tr.). 1994. *Lives of the Nuns: Biographies of Chinese
Buddhist Nuns from the Fourth to Sixth Centuries. A Translation of the
Pi-ch'iu-ni chuan, compiled by Shih Pao-ch'ang*. Honolulu: University of
Hawai'i Press.

Tsogyal, Yeshe. 1993. *The Lotus Born: The Life Story of Padmasambhava*.
Translated by Erik Pema Kunsang. Boston: Shambhala Publications.

Tsomo, Karma Lekshe (ed.). 2000. *Innovative Buddhist Women: Swimming
against the Stream*. Richmond: Curzon.

Tsomo, Karma Lekshe. 2002. 'Buddhist Nuns: Changes and Challenges',
in *Westward Dharma: Buddhism Beyond Asia*, Charles S. Prebish and
Martin Baumann (eds), 255–74. Berkeley and Los Angeles: University
of California Press.

Tun, Than (ed. and tr.). 1983. *The Royal Orders of Burma, A.D. 1598–1885.
Part One, A.D. 1598–1648*. Kyoto: Center for Southeast Asian Studies,
Kyoto University.

Tun, Than (ed. and tr.). 1985a. *The Royal Orders of Burma, A.D. 1598–1885.
Part Two, A.D. 1649–1750*. Kyoto: Center for Southeast Asian Studies,
Kyoto University.

Tun, Than (ed. and tr.). 1985b. *The Royal Orders of Burma, A.D. 1598–1885.
Part Three, A.D. 1751–1781*. Kyoto: Center for Southeast Asian Studies,
Kyoto University.

Turner, Alicia, Laurence Cox, and Brian Bocking. 2020. *The Irish Buddhist:
The Forgotten Monk Who Faced Down the British Empire*. New York:
Oxford University Press.

Uebach, Helga. 2005. 'Ladies of the Tibetan Empire (Seventh to Ninth Centuries CE)', in *Women in Tibet*, Janet Gyatso and Hanna Havnevik (eds), 29–48. London: Hurst.

Ueda, Makoto (ed.). 2003. *Far Beyond the Field: Haiku by Japanese Women*. New York: Columbia University Press.

Waddell, Laurence Augustine. 1895. *The Buddhism of Tibet, or Lamaism: With Its Mystic Cults, Symbolism and Mythology, and Its Relation to Indian Buddhism*. London: W. H. Allen.

Walshe, Maurice (tr.). 1987. *The Long Discourses of the Buddha: A Translation of the Dīgha Nikāya*. Boston: Wisdom Publications.

Walters, Jonathan S. 1995. 'Gotamī's Story: Introduction and Translation', in *Buddhism in Practice*, Donald S. Lopez, Jr (ed.), 113–38. Princeton: Princeton University Press.

Walters, Jonathan S. 2013. 'Wives of the Saints: Marriage and Kamma in the Path to Arahantship', in *Women in Early Indian Buddhism: Comparative Textual Studies*, Alice Collett (ed.), 160–91. Oxford and New York: Oxford University Press.

Walters, Jonathan, S. 2019: *The Legends of the Buddhist Saints: Apadānapāli*, available at http://apadanatranslation.org/, accessed on 19 November 2020.

Warner, Cameron David. 2011. 'A Miscarriage of History: Wencheng Gongzhu and Sino-Tibetan Historiography', *Inner Asia* 13: 239–64.

Weber, Max. 1968. *Economy and Society: An Outline of Interpretive Sociology*. New York: Bedminster Press.

Weddikkara, Lalani. 2002. *The Role of Buddhism in the Changing Life of Rural Women in Sri Lanka since Independence*. MA diss., Edith Cowan University, available at https://ro.ecu.edu.au/theses/746, accessed on 19 November 2020.

Willis, Janice D. 1985. 'Nuns and Benefactresses: The Role of Women in the Development of Buddhism', in *Women, Religion, and Social Change*, Yvonne Yazbeck Haddad and Ellison Banks Findly (eds), 59–85. Albany: State University of New York Press.

Woodward, F.L. 1987. *Udāna: Verses of Uplift. Minor Anthologies, Part II*. London: Pali Text Society.

Young, Serenity. 2004. *Courtesans and Tantric Consorts: Sexualities in Buddhist Narrative, Iconography, and Ritual*. London: Routledge.

Yü, Chün-fang. 1995. 'Chinese Women's Pilgrims' Songs Glorifying Guanyin', in *Buddhism in Practice*, Donald S. Lopez Jr. (ed.), 176–82. Princeton: Princeton University Press.

Yü, Chün-fang. 2001. *Kuan-yin: The Chinese Transformation of Avalokiteśvara*. New York: Columbia University Press.

Zhang, Zhenji (ed.). 1983. *A Treasury of Mahāyāna Sūtras: Selections from the Mahāratnakūṭa Sūtra*. University Park, PA and London: Pennsylvania State Press.

INDEX

Introductory Note

References such as '178–9' indicate (not necessarily continuous) discussion of a topic across a range of pages. Wherever possible in the case of topics with many references, these have either been divided into sub-topics or only the most significant discussions of the topic are listed. Because the entire work is about 'women' and 'Buddhism', the use of these terms (and certain others which occur constantly throughout the book) as an entry point has been minimized. Information will be found under the corresponding detailed topics.

WINDHORSE PUBLICATIONS

Windhorse Publications is a Buddhist charitable company based in the United Kingdom. We place great emphasis on producing books of high quality that are accessible and relevant to those interested in Buddhism at whatever level. We are the main publisher of the works of Sangharakshita, the founder of the Triratna Buddhist Order and Community. Our books draw on the whole range of the Buddhist tradition, including translations of traditional texts, commentaries, books that make links with contemporary culture and ways of life, biographies of Buddhists, and works on meditation.

As a not-for-profit enterprise, we ensure that all surplus income is invested in new books and improved production methods, to better communicate Buddhism in the 21st century. We welcome donations to help us continue our work – to find out more, go to windhorsepublications.com.

The Windhorse is a mythical animal that flies over the earth carrying on its back three precious jewels, bringing these invaluable gifts to all humanity: the Buddha (the 'awakened one'), his teaching, and the community of all his followers.

Windhorse Publications
38 Newmarket Road
Cambridge CB5 8DT
info@windhorsepublications.com

Consortium Book Sales & Distribution
210 American Drive
Jackson TN 38301
USA

Windhorse Books
PO Box 574
Newtown NSW 2042
Australia

THE TRIRATNA BUDDHIST COMMUNITY

Windhorse Publications is a part of the Triratna Buddhist Community, an international movement with centres in Europe, India, North and South America and Australasia. At these centres, members of the Triratna Buddhist Order offer classes in meditation and Buddhism. Activities of the Triratna Community also include retreat centres, residential spiritual communities, ethical Right Livelihood businesses, and the Karuna Trust, a United Kingdom fundraising charity that supports social welfare projects in the slums and villages of India. Through these and other activities, Triratna is developing a unique approach to Buddhism, not simply as a philosophy and a set of techniques, but as a creatively directed way of life for all people living in the conditions of the modern world.

If you would like more information about Triratna please visit thebuddhistcentre.com or write to:

London Buddhist Centre
51 Roman Road
London E2 0HU
United Kingdom

Aryaloka
14 Heartwood Circle
Newmarket NH 03857
USA

Sydney Buddhist Centre
24 Enmore Road
Sydney NSW 2042
Australia